the READING coach

A HOW-TO MANUAL FOR SUCCESS

Jan Hasbrouck, Ph.D.

Carolyn Denton, Ph.D.

SOPRIS WEST™ EDUCATIONAL SERVICES
A CAMBIUM LEARNING COMPANY

BOSTON, MA • LONGMONT, CO

ISBN 1-59318-407-7

Printed in the United States of America

Published and Distributed by

Sopris West™
EDUCATIONAL SERVICES

A Cambium Learning Company

4093 Specialty Place • Longmont, Colorado 80504
(303) 651-2829 • www.sopriswest.com

111991/129162/4-06

To my students and workshop participants across the years who taught me what I know about coaching and consultation—through your questions, your curiosity, and your passion to collaborate skillfully with your colleagues to help students become the best they can be.

JEH

To my daughters, Christy Vaca and Laura Denton.

CAD

ACKNOWLEDGMENTS

We owe a lot to Candance Kiene for her outstanding edits of the initial drafts of our chapters. She helped make our ideas flow and found ways to make our two voices sound like one. Thank you, Candance!

ABOUT THE AUTHORS

Jan Hasbrouck, Ph.D., is an educational consultant, trainer, and researcher who recently served as the executive director of the Washington State Reading Initiative. Dr. Hasbrouck worked in schools as a reading specialist for 15 years before becoming a professor at the University of Oregon and later at Texas A&M University. Dr. Hasbrouck consults with schools, districts, and state agencies, helping teachers and administrators design and implement effective instructional programs for students who struggle with reading. Her research in areas of fluency, coaching and consultation, and second language learners has been published in numerous professional journals and books.

Carolyn Denton, Ph.D., is on the faculty of the Department of Special Education of the University of Texas at Austin and serves on the board of directors of the Vaughn Gross Center for Reading and Language Arts at the University of Texas. Dr. Denton is a former classroom and reading intervention teacher with nearly 20 years of experience teaching in public schools. Before joining the faculty of the University of Texas at Austin, she was a member of a research team at the Center for Academic and Reading Skills at the University of Texas Health Science Center at Houston, studying the effects of reading intervention on students' reading and on their brain functioning. Currently, she is a co-principal investigator on a large federally funded research project to study effective reading intervention practices in multiple schools, including the role of the reading coach, and a study of intervention for struggling middle school readers. She is the author of a first grade reading intervention program and has also authored and co-authored several journal articles and book chapters on reading disability, reading intervention, and schoolwide models for preventing reading difficulties. Dr. Denton provides workshops and consultation for school districts and state agencies throughout the United States.

CONTENTS

1

OVERVIEW OF COACHING: WHAT? WHY? GOALS?

What Is a "Reading Coach"?

Classroom teachers and reading specialists are being asked to provide support and guidance to their colleagues through a process called "coaching." Coaching has become a popular model in schools (Poglinco & Bach, 2004) and is seen as the current hot trend in professional development ("Coaches," 2004). It is seen as a way to help teachers strengthen their instructional skills and knowledge as well as their students' reading skills. However, the role of "reading coach" is often not clearly defined.

A search on the Internet for a definition of reading coach results in descriptions of several models. One model uses the term to describe the role of adult volunteers and teachers who provide 1:1 reading assistance to children who are learning to read (Clark, 2004; "Coaches," 2004). Students who help other students with reading, usually in 1:1 tutoring situations, are also being called reading coaches. These models of coaching are different from the one you will learn about in this book.

In our model, we define a reading coach as an *experienced teacher who has a strong knowledge base in reading and experience providing effective reading instruction to students, especially struggling readers*. In addition, a reading coach has been *trained to work effectively with peer colleagues* to help them improve their students' reading outcomes and *receives support* in the school for providing coaching to other teachers, instructional assistants, parents, or administrators, as needed.

A key way to support coaches is to give them enough time during a school day to provide coaching services. These services may include a variety of activities, such as observing lessons, providing feedback for instructional improvement, developing intervention plans for struggling readers, helping to identify and address schoolwide concerns related to reading, facilitating collaboration among teaching teams, and providing training for staff development. Unfortunately, few teachers who are given the role of reading coach receive sufficient support or training to perform it adequately (Hall, O'Neill, Hasbrouck, & Parker, 2003; Poglinco & Bach, 2004). Many teachers are expected to learn how to coach their colleagues while they are performing this new and unfamiliar role. We know that just because someone is an excellent reading teacher is no guarantee of their success in working with their colleagues (Poglinco & Bach, 2004). This challenging situation is complicated by the fact that very few administrators understand the demands of the new role on their staff members (Hall et al., 2003; Poglinco & Bach, 2004).

Why Is the Role of Reading Coach Becoming So Popular?

In 1999, the federal government passed the Reading Excellence Act (REA). REA granted funds to states to help impoverished schools (1) teach every child to read by the end of the 3rd grade; (2) improve reading instruction through the use of findings from scientifically based reading research; and (3) provide early intervention to children experiencing reading difficulties and prevent inappropriate referrals to special education. REA funds could be used to help provide professional development and tutoring to children. A number of the schools participating in the REA project decided to use some of their funds to provide reading coaches in their buildings. The idea was for the coaches to help provide instruction directly to students *and* to work with other teachers to improve the reading instruction in their classrooms.

In January 2002, the U.S. Congress enacted the No Child Left Behind (NCLB) Act, with goals that are similar to the earlier REA. The Reading First Initiative under NCLB included funds to help teachers strengthen their current skills and gain new ones in effective reading instructional techniques, and it suggested that reading coaches were a viable way to provide professional development to teachers at the classroom level. What was missing in some of these plans was guidance about *how* teachers were going to become coaches and specific information about what exactly a reading coach is supposed to do. We have written this book to help you address those concerns and other issues that reading coaches encounter as they begin their new role in a school, including:

- How to introduce the new role of coach into a school;

- How to provide advice to peer colleagues with out insulting or annoying them;

- How to work with teachers who are *resistant* to your help;

- How to work with the principal; and

- How to address schoolwide issues such as curriculum, assessments, scheduling, and interfacing among Title I, special education, and the general classroom.

What Does a Reading Coach Do?

The current knowledge base on coaching is sparse. Researchers are just beginning to look at the role of reading coach, and some are conducting surveys to determine what the coaches are being asked to do (Dole, 2004; Morrow, 2003; Poglinco & Bach, 2004). From these studies, we know that at times a reading coach may be called upon to handle any of the following tasks:

- *Observe* reading lessons and provide feedback to teachers.

- *Model* effective teaching techniques and strategies.

- *Advise and support* teachers to improve reading lessons (materials, planning, instruction, assessments).

- Participate in *team teaching*.

- *Facilitate collaboration* within grade level or vertical teams of teachers.

- Conduct *workshops* to help introduce teachers to new strategies.

- Help new teachers *organize and manage* their reading programs.

Reading coaches need information and a variety of skills to complete these important tasks successfully.

What Is "Coaching"?

We have been working for nearly 20 years teaching educators and other school-based professionals in universities, in workshops at conferences, and in state, district, and school in-service presentations on how to work effectively with one's professional colleagues to improve the academic and behavioral outcomes of students. The participants in these trainings have included reading specialists, school psychologists, special education teachers, adaptive physical education teachers, physical and occupational therapists, speech-language pathologists, assessment specialists, and even school principals. We found it was beneficial to take a broad view of the role of coach and to provide training for these folks from widely varied professional backgrounds using a well-studied model of school service delivery called "consultation" (Kampwirth, 1999; Sugai & Tindal, 1993). We have developed a model of coaching that we based on the research on classroom consultation. We call our model Student-Focused Coaching (SFC), which is defined as: as *a cooperative, ideally collaborative relationship, with parties mutually engaged in efforts to provide better services for students.* There are a lot of words in this definition! Let's break it down a bit more.

Some key words in the definition are *better services for students*. Coaching can sometimes seem quite complex and even intimidating. Coaching can feel awkward and uncomfortable when, for example, you are working with a highly experienced teacher, perhaps one who has many years more experience than you. You may find yourself working with colleagues who have a very different philosophy about teaching than you do or a negative attitude about some of their students or the families of those students. It helps to keep in mind that the processes that are part of coaching are not about you and not about the teacher. Coaching is, bottom line, *about the students*. Keeping students' needs at the heart of coaching can help us in the inevitable moments of discomfort to refocus on what we should be doing. The purpose of coaching is to provide better services for students. For a reading coach, this means helping students become better readers!

Another key word in our definition is *relationship*. Coaching cannot occur outside of a professional relationship. When you work with other teachers as a coach, you may have the opportunity to work with someone who is, or who may become, a personal friend. More often you may be working with a peer colleague (or parent or administrator) who you barely know. At times—we hope they are rare—you may even find yourself working with a person with whom you have a tense, uncomfortable relationship. If this happens, remember: Coaching is *about the students*, not about making friends or having a good time talking to a fellow teacher! Those involved in coaching may need to find a way to get past their own personal discomfort and resolve to work together despite differences.

Coaching is based upon a relationship that is, at a minimum, *cooperative*. This is a key point: *You cannot provide coaching services to someone who does not want to cooperate with you*. Coaching is simply not possible in those situations. If working with a coach is not voluntary, the process becomes something more like supervision rather than coaching. Ideally, through effective coaching, you can help change a minimally cooperative relationship to one that is at some point fully collaborative, where you and your colleague are equally involved, equally trusting, equally respectful of each other's skills and knowledge, and equally committed to helping students. In Chapter 3, we will talk more about how to start and maintain cooperative and collaborative professional relationships.

The final key words in our definition of Student-Focused Coaching are *mutually engaged in efforts* to help students. Coaches undertake three kinds of efforts:

1. As *Facilitator*, a coach helps effective, skillful teachers continue to succeed and leads a school toward a commitment to the success of all students.

2. As *Collaborative Problem Solver*, a coach employs a systematic, structured process to work with teachers to address problems in the classroom that may be keeping students from making adequate gains.

3. As *Teacher/Learner*, a coach shares effective, proven strategies with groups of teachers to provide professional development.

What Are the Goals for a Reading Coach?

We hope this book will help you become a skillful, confident, and effective reading coach who can build professional relationships with colleagues and work with them to help students become successful readers. As you engage in these challenging and important efforts, we encourage you to stay focused on the following four broad goals:

GOAL #1: *To improve students' reading skills and competence*. Coaching is an important way to help students. Coaching must focus on students' needs and how the teachers, parents, and everyone in the system can help each student become the best possible reader, thinker, and learner.

GOAL #2: *To solve referred problems*. If you are a coach, teachers, parents, and administrators will seek you out to help solve various problems and concerns related to reading. Helping to solve the problems is a worthy goal, but a skillful coach always puts Goal #2 into context, with the primary focus on Goal #1. It is always about the *students* first.

GOAL #3: *To learn from each other*. One of the primary reasons coaching works is that it provides opportunities to share knowledge and expertise and to learn from each other. The best reading coaches do not see coaching as simply an opportunity to spread their wisdom and experience to other teachers who are less informed or less skilled. Instead, these coaches are sincerely interested in helping *every* student become a confident and skillful reader and, in the process of working with peer colleagues to achieve this, to add to their own "bag of tricks," or repertoire of professional tools. The best coaches see a personal learning opportunity in every coaching encounter.

GOAL #4: *To prevent future problems*. A reading coach can do far more than simply help a teacher improve a single student's learning. A coach can help build teachers' understanding, knowledge, skills, competence, and confidence in their reading instruction so they will be better prepared to handle concerns in the future. At the school level, a coach can also help identify and address broader concerns in a way that prevents problems from starting in the first place.

What Is the Purpose of the Book?

We wrote this book for reading coaches with two purposes in mind. Our first purpose is to help define the role of reading coach for the coaches themselves, for the peer colleagues with whom they will be working, and for the administrators who will supervise, support, and evaluate the coaches. Our second purpose is to identify and provide support to develop the skills and competencies required to become an effective reading coach.

In Chapter 2, we present an overview of the background knowledge a reading coach needs.

By Chapter 3, we are ready to help you get started as a coach! Here we describe the three interrelated functions for a school-based reading coach: Facilitator, Collaborative Problem Solver, and Teacher/Learner. Chapter 3 also includes a guide to introducing the role of coach into a school, along with a discussion of issues related to ethics and confidentiality and a guide for building a caseload. The coach as Facilitator is introduced here.

Chapter 4 helps you begin to form your own personal "coaching toolbox" by discussing some of the nuts and bolts of coaching: skillful communication and time management strategies.

Chapter 5 details how coaches can use a systematic problem-solving model to work with teachers to address students' complex reading challenges in the role of Collaborative Problem Solver.

By Chapter 6, we are ready to start gathering information to officially begin helping teachers to help their students. We discuss using assessment data for decision making, conducting classroom observations, and interviewing teachers and parents.

In Chapter 7, ideas are presented for designing, evaluating, and supporting effective instruction and interventions to help students become skillful readers.

Chapter 8 describes how a coach serves as a Teacher/Learner through designing and providing useful, effective, and sustained professional development.

Chapter 9 explores the role of the coach as a Facilitator of schoolwide collaboration. This chapter focuses on the skills a reading coach will need to tackle the broader issues that may face a school, and how to help teachers and leaders work together to plan ways to improve students' reading skills.

We conclude with Chapter 10, which we hope will be helpful for administrators and supervisors who will work with reading coaches. We have also provided a list of resources that reading coaches will find useful in their work.

Coaching in the Real World

We want to assure you that we work in the real world and understand that you do, too. Schools are complex and challenging environments. Students who come to school with little preparation for learning to read, negative experiences with reading or even no experiences with reading, or poor attitudes about the act of reading and their own abilities to become readers are serious challenges that face us every day. These realities are sometimes made worse by inadequate instructional materials, lack of support from high-quality professional development efforts, philosophical conflicts about how students should be taught to read, and more.

We want to begin our book by acknowledging these realities with a reminder from Roger Kroth that it goes without saying that in schools we will *never have enough money, enough time,* or *enough trained personnel* to do the hard work we have undertaken (Kroth & Edge, 1997). We simply cannot use any of these as excuses or we will become too discouraged to keep on trying to meet the needs of all our students. We accept these realities and proceed with our challenging work in spite of them. We adhere to a no-excuses model for our work. We cannot give up. Our job is too critically important: *We must teach all of our students to read!*

2

FOUNDATIONAL KNOWLEDGE FOR THE READING COACH

In Chapter 1, we said that a reading coach is an *experienced teacher* who has strong *knowledge* in reading and is especially experienced in *providing effective reading instruction* to struggling readers. In this chapter, we give you an overview of the foundational knowledge you need to be a successful reading coach. We make suggestions you can use in your reading program based on characteristics of successful reading programs and on our experiences in real schools where all, or nearly all, students learn to read. This information is meant to provide an overview of research-based reading instruction. It is important that each reading coach participate in professional development to provide him or her with a firm grounding in reading instruction that has been supported by scientific research. There are several avenues available to the coach for this kind of professional development. One is training in *Language Essentials for Teachers of Reading and Spelling* (*LETRS*) (Moats, 2004).

In the past 30 years there have been dramatic increases in what we know and understand about the main components of reading instruction. Our knowledge is based on converging evidence over time, which is an important component of any science and includes some truly exciting findings in several disciplines, such as brain imaging, genetics, cognitive development, and instruction (Denton, Vaughn, & Fletcher, 2003). We have learned a lot about how children learn to read and why it is so difficult for some of our students.

Key Research on Reading Instruction

We think reading coaches should consider themselves professional educators. Professionals, by implication, are well trained and highly qualified in their areas of specialization, whether they are lawyers, doctors, or educators. You can assume that professionals in any field keep up with the most current definitions of best practice and feel a responsibility to engage in practice that has evidence to support its effectiveness, or, at a minimum, is likely to be

effective in certain situations. In various professions, this kind of evidence is obtained from research studies.

As professional educators, we face a particular challenge in using research to inform our practice. We are well aware that the phrase "the research says" has been used to "prove" nearly every possible intriguing new idea about how to teach any possible topic, skill, or strategy. In education, the term *research* has become generic, referring to a variety of activities other than systematic investigation to establish facts (Ellis, 2001).

Unlike some other professions, education has no gatekeeper to steer its professionals toward the most reliable research findings. For our medical colleagues, the Food and Drug Administration (FDA) makes sure that new medicines are subjected to rigorous review before physicians can prescribe them. Educators have no counterpart to the FDA (Ellis, 2001). One way we can guard against adopting questionable or unproven practices, or recommending them, is to avoid relying on results from single studies. We serve our students and colleagues best if we rely instead on a *convergence* of evidence that forges common ground among theories or evidence derived from experimentation or observation. (If you would like more information about how to judge the quality or usefulness of professional research data, we highly recommend a very readable book to help get you started: Arthur K. Ellis's *Research on Educational Innovations*, published by Eye on Education.)

Much of the current understanding of reading instruction has been described in two important documents every reading coach should be familiar with: (1) the report of a committee of experts for the National Institutes of Health (Snow, Burns, & Griffin, 1998) entitled *Preventing Reading Difficulties in Young Children*; and (2) a report by the National Reading Panel (NRP) (2000), a group that systematically and meticulously searched for quality research on reading instruction and summarized its findings in a document that is readily available on the Internet at www.nationalreadingpanel.org.

Among the many topics dealt with in these two consensus documents, the most important for reading coaches are, perhaps, the ones that identify the potential stumbling blocks to becoming a successful reader, identify the principles of effective instruction for struggling readers, and describe successful reading programs. Two of the most important conclusions of the documents are that:

- High-quality instruction provided in the early years of school can *prevent* reading difficulties for many children; and

- Most older, struggling readers *can learn to read*, although it often becomes more difficult as students fall progressively further behind their classmates.

These are truly exciting and empowering findings for anyone who cares about teaching students to read!

What Does Quality Reading Instruction Look Like?

For many years there has been an argument among educators about how reading should be taught, especially in the primary grades. In the meantime, good teachers struggled to meet the needs of the incredibly diverse students sitting in every classroom. A single 3rd grade classroom may have students whose instructional reading levels range from 1st to 6th grades! So what's a teacher to do?

The consensus of research is that the most effective reading teachers in the primary grades do not place themselves in the "phonics camp" or the "whole language camp." What these teachers do is (1) provide explicit phonemic awareness and alphabetic decoding instruction to students who need it; (2) emphasize reading for meaning; and (3) provide many opportunities for students to read and write in meaningful ways (Pressley, Rankin, & Yokoi, 1996; Snow et al., 1998). The best teachers know that it is up to them to find out what their students know and do not know, what students can and cannot do, and what students are confused about, and then to *teach* those concepts and skills. And these teachers also know that it is not enough for students to learn skills. They must know how to *apply* the skills to understand what they are reading—the ultimate goal of reading! They know that the way to motivate children to read is to provide for their success by teaching them what they need to learn *and* to provide a print-rich environment with lots of engaging opportunities to read and write.

So, then, teachers should find out what their students need to know and teach it. Sounds easy, but we know it isn't. Luckily, research can guide us to approaches and programs that have worked with many students. Research conducted in real schools with real students has repeatedly pointed to some key characteristics of effective reading instruction. This kind of instruction is particularly critical for struggling readers, but it is beneficial for all students. We will describe the key components in the next section, but first we want to talk about two topics for which research has not provided hard and fast answers.

First, we have no proof that there is one "best" program or set of materials for teaching reading. Several researchers have identified highly successful schools that use different programs and approaches (Denton, Foorman, & Mathes, 2003; Lein, Johnson, & Ragland, 1997; Parker, O'Neill, Hall, & Hasbrouck, 2004). For example, in a study of schools that serve challenging populations of students and yet achieve outstanding results in reading, Denton, Foorman, et al. (2003) described five successful programs. Teachers in one school delivered instruction to small groups of students who read leveled books. A second school used a schoolwide prescriptive program; a third school used a structured, direct-instruction, phonics-based program. A fourth school used a program that provided a framework for delivering systematic instruction but allowed teachers to be flexible in planning lessons within the framework. And in the fifth school, teachers were trained in both guided reading and an explicit phonics program. In some of these schools, students read decodable text, but in others they read books that were leveled for difficulty but not phonetically decodable.

Parker and colleagues (2004), in their study of 68 successful schools that enrolled challenging populations, made a similar observation. They found no evidence for superiority of a single reading program, but they did find that teachers in these schools had a detailed understanding of the adopted reading materials, valued the materials, and used them extensively. Although the successful schools studied by Denton, Foorman, et al. (2003) and Parker et al. (2004) had different approaches to reading instruction, they *did* have some important things in common, including a focus on established standards or goals for all students and an emphasis on using assessment data to develop lessons to *teach each individual student* to read successfully. We will discuss the characteristics of successful schools in more detail later in this chapter.

The second topic we want to talk about is that, although we know that some instructional programs and approaches have been effective in teaching nearly all students to read, we cannot know exactly what will be successful with that individual struggling reader who is sitting in front of you. In other words, although research can give you insight into the critical elements of effective reading instruction, we suggest that the expert reading teacher, and the reading coach, must have a deep "bag of tricks"—different ways of teaching the same content and skills—in order to meet the assessed and targeted needs of each struggling reader. Teachers who stick to only one approach, method, or published program may be missing out on other ways of teaching that would be effective for particular students.

In their study of highly challenged yet highly successful reading schools, Denton, Foorman, et al. (2003) described one school in which classroom and reading intervention teachers had extensive training in diverse programs, including highly explicit phonics programs that include reading decodable text, guided reading, and a program that focuses on developing phonemic awareness

in students with severe difficulties in this area through intense focused lessons. Adler & Fisher (2001) made a similar observation in their case study of a successful high-poverty school. In this school, teachers had access to several reading programs (such as direct instruction of phonics, phonemic awareness programs, and guided reading and writing) and were not confined to an attitude that "one size fits all." Teachers in these schools had many tools to draw from to meet the needs of each student and found ways to use them successfully to teach their students to read.

That is not to say that anything goes when it comes to reading instruction! Clearly, there are some elements of quality instruction that are central to *nearly all* instructional programs that have produced strong results for children. As we noted previously, the best teachers of reading *provide explicit instruction in the key areas of reading*, along with *ample opportunities to apply these skills through many opportunities to read and write connected text*. There are no "magic materials." But there are powerful instructional strategies that can make a profound difference for our students when used by skilled, caring, and well-supported teachers.

What Are the Key Components of Reading?

A summary of research has shown that students need instruction and practice in skills related to:

- *Phonemic awareness.* An auditory skill that involves the ability to notice, identify, and manipulate the sounds in spoken words.

- *Phonics and decoding skills.* Understanding that the sounds in spoken words are represented in print by letters and combinations of letters, and the ability to apply the knowledge of the English "code" to read unknown words.

- *Oral reading fluency.* The ability to read text accurately, quickly, and with good expression.

- *Vocabulary.* Knowledge of word meanings.

- *Reading comprehension.* The complex and multifaceted ability to make meaning of written text.

Instruction in *phonemic awareness and phonics* has been shown to be beneficial only in kindergarten and grades one and two, *except for older struggling readers* who have not yet mastered these skills. *Oral reading fluency* should be emphasized as soon as a student can read at least 60 words, and instruction designed to support the development of fluent reading should continue at least through the 4th grade. Any student who struggles with fluency (performing below the 50th percentile in reading fluency) should continue to receive fluency instruction even after the 4th grade. (We provide a table of oral reading fluency norms for Grades 1–8 in the Appendix.) *Vocabulary and reading comprehension* instruction should be included in reading and language arts from pre-kindergarten (by reading to students and talking about what is read) through high school.

The content of reading instruction in the primary grades is particularly important. Effective instruction for beginning readers must be designed to promote accurate and quick word recognition skills, fluent reading of connected text, and strategies for enhancing the deep processing of text. At this stage, explicit instruction in phonics and decoding is critical. Beyond knowledge of letters, sounds, and words, children must be able to read connected text smoothly and accurately. Readers must recognize words fluently in order to comprehend text, but fluency alone is not sufficient for achieving deeper levels of understanding. Skillful comprehenders are strategic; they normally follow a plan when approaching text. Children who do not develop effective comprehension strategies independently must be taught to use them.

Explicit, Targeted, and Intensive Reading Instruction

Research has consistently shown that effective reading instruction for students who struggle is *explicit, targeted, and intensive*. It is important that the reading coach understand these terms.

EXPLICIT INSTRUCTION

We sometimes refer to *explicit* instruction as "telling it like it is." Students who struggle with reading may be confused easily (Clay, 1987). They need to be directly or explicitly taught the knowledge and skills needed for successful reading. They also need to be taught—explicitly—

how these concepts and skills come together in efficient reading (see Foorman & Torgesen, 2001).

When a teacher provides explicit instruction, students do not have to guess or infer what they should learn. The teacher models, demonstrates, or clearly explains the concept or skill and guides the students as they practice it. For example, a teacher who is explicitly teaching the sound of the letter combination *ai* might point to these two letters written on a card and say, "The sound of these letters is usually /ā/ (the long a sound). When you see *ai* together in a word you will usually say /ā/. What sound do these letters usually make? Let's read some words that have *ai* in them."

A teacher who does *not* provide explicit instruction might show the students a sentence in a book that includes a word with the *ai* pattern. For example, a page in a book may have a picture of ducks on a wet street with rain coming down and the words: *Then it started to rain.* The teacher might ask students to look at the word *rain*, think about what would make sense in the sentence, and try to read the word. Then the teacher might point out that the *ai* in the word *rain* makes the long *a* sound. Research has consistently shown that this nonexplicit approach is *not* as effective for struggling readers. Students who have difficulties learning to read, as well as most other students, learn best when provided with explicit instruction that tells it like it is.

Some characteristics of explicit instruction are that the teacher:

- Plans lessons that are purposeful and focused on objectives
- Models skills and strategies
- Explains concepts clearly
- Re-teaches and clarifies instruction as needed
- Provides guided practice in skills and strategies (supporting students as they practice new or difficult skills)
- Provides students with prompts and scaffolding to enable them to be successful
- Provides specific corrective feedback related to reading skills and strategies
- Provides specific praise related to reading skills and strategies that students use correctly

- Provides opportunities for students to apply skills and strategies independently, monitors students to be sure they are successful, and provides support when needed

- Achieves a high rate of successful and accurate student responses

Older students who are unable to read at basic levels need explicit instruction in decoding just as much as students in the primary grades do (Dickson & Bryant, 2002). Teachers can provide the instruction in a way that is respectful of older students' levels of intellectual development (Curtis & Longo, 1999). For example, struggling readers in high school may enroll in a course in which they learn concepts such as the different types of syllables, the nature of the schwa sound, and Latin and Greek derivations of English words. They can learn to apply skills based on these concepts to reading and understanding words.

TARGETED INSTRUCTION

Providing targeted instruction means teaching what students need to learn. Teachers who provide targeted instruction continually monitor their students' progress in the key dimensions of reading and provide extra instruction and practice when students need it. The importance of providing many opportunities to practice, including cumulative practice of what has already been learned, cannot be overestimated.

Assessment is the essence of targeted instruction. Teaching struggling readers effectively means continuously monitoring and assessing their strengths and needs. In many of the schools where most students learn to read successfully, groups of teachers and administrators or literacy coordinators meet regularly to review the results of ongoing assessment. This helps the educators see whether each student is making progress and enables them to design instruction to meet the students' needs.

Another facet of targeted instruction is that the teacher provides text at an appropriate level of difficulty to each student. Always keep the three levels of text difficulty in mind—*independent*, *instructional*, and *frustration*. You can determine a student's reading levels by administering an informal reading inventory (IRI). You can use the IRI to determine the level of text the student should read during reading instruction and the level the student can read independently (the appropriate level for homework assignments). You can also determine the level that is too difficult for the student (frustration level). Many students who are consistently asked to read frustration-level text develop habits like guessing or skipping words, or waiting for the teacher or other students to tell them difficult words. They may also have behavior problems as a result of repeated failure and frustration.

For any text, you can use a general rule that we call the "one-to-ten rule." If a student makes more than one error for every ten words read, the text is too hard. This is the standard of 90% accuracy. If the student reads 20 words and makes more than two errors; 30 words and makes more than three errors; and so on; the student's accuracy level is below 90%, an indication that the text is on the frustration level for that student. Students are more likely to make progress in reading if they are given text that sets them up for success—text on their instructional levels—rather than text that presents continual frustration. *Success is a strong motivator.*

INTENSIVE INSTRUCTION

Finally, in schools with effective reading programs, students who do not make progress, even in classrooms with quality core reading programs, receive supplemental intensive instruction. By intensive, we mean instruction that is offered to small groups of students for an extended period each day and that students are actively engaged in learning, practicing, and applying essential reading skills for a large part of each lesson. There is research that indicates that most struggling readers in the primary grades who do not make adequate progress with regular classroom reading instruction learn well when they receive supplemental instruction in groups of three to four students (see Mathes & Denton, 2002; Torgesen, 2000).

The Importance of Practice

Now that you know that instruction for struggling readers should be *explicit*, *targeted*, and *intensive*, don't forget that students need *many* opportunities to practice and apply what they are taught. Struggling learners need lots of practice to really *learn* new content and skills.

Think about the level of learning that we want students to achieve. Do we want them to merely be introduced to skills such as letter-sound associations, blending sounds into words, or applying comprehension strategies to understand what they read? Being introduced to key reading content and skills is not enough. Students need to incorporate new learning into their everyday routines. Ineffective habits such as impulsively guessing at words must be replaced with effective strategies such as sounding out unfamiliar words and monitoring whether what is being read makes sense. The goal of reading instruction is for students to apply what they learn as they read and write text *automatically, independently, and consistently* in the classroom, at home, and elsewhere. In other words, applying effective skills and strategies effectively has to become a habit. This takes lots and lots of repeated practice. Some sources recommend that lessons designed to teach key reading skills be composed of only 20% new material and 80% practice of previously learned skills.

Students need three kinds of practice. They need to:

1. *Practice new skills just after they are introduced.* For example, when students are taught that the letter combination *oa* usually has the long *o* sound, they need to practice identifying the sound of *oa*, along with other letter sounds they have learned. They need to practice reading words with the *oa* pattern, such as *boat.* Then they can practice reading oa words mixed in with words that contain other letter patterns they have learned: *boat, float, tree, eat, goal, team, sweep, croak.*

2. *Cumulatively practice skills learned in the past as they learn new ones.* Have students practice new learning *integrated* with what they have learned in the past. If struggling learners are not provided with cumulative practice, they tend to forget things they have learned in the past as new items of knowledge or new skills are introduced.

3. *Practice applying skills in reading and writing with feedback.* As students read orally or write independently, observe them carefully, provide feedback if they make errors, and remind them to apply what they have been taught.

The Role of Feedback

Research in effective instruction for struggling readers has resulted in other guiding principles. One of these is the power of feedback given to students as they learn.

There are three important kinds of feedback: *specific praise, scaffolding, and corrective feedback.*

SPECIFIC PRAISE

Research has demonstrated that positive feedback (such as specific praise) is more effective in promoting change and growth in a student than criticism. Effective reading teachers consistently offer praise when their students apply the strategies and skills they have been taught.

There are two very important considerations in offering praise. First, it has to be *authentic.* Teachers should never say that a student did something well if that is not the case. This kind of "fake praise" does more harm than good. Students see through it and get the message that the teacher could not think of something in the student's performance that was truly worth praising and had to make something up. Second, the praise must be *specific.* Simply saying "good job" repeatedly begins to sound empty and does little to promote student growth. Some examples of specific praise include:

- "You figured out that word all by yourself. That's what good readers do."

- "When you got to that hard word I saw you trying to sound it out. You nearly had it. It's so important to keep trying even if you sometimes don't quite get it. Let's go back and take a look at that word."

- "You made a mistake on that word, but you went back and fixed it. Nice job."

SCAFFOLDING

Scaffolding is defined by Graves and Braaten (1996) as "providing a support to help learners bridge the gap between what they know and can do and what they need to accomplish in order to succeed in a particular learning task" (p. 169). In other words, instructional scaffolding enables a student to be successful with support from the teacher at a task that he or she could not successfully accomplish independently.

To provide effective scaffolding, you must be able to determine a learner's abilities and needs. Effective scaffolding is a particular kind of "helping" that is specifically tailored to support the developing skills of an individual student. A very important feature of scaffolding is that it is temporary. As students get more proficient at a task, they need less and less support. Typically, the level of skills or text difficulty is gradually raised so that students can continue to make progress. They are once again scaffolded at a more difficult level. Table 2.1 describes some types of instructional scaffolding.

CORRECTIVE FEEDBACK

Students need information about their errors. If they don't realize they made an error, they are likely to repeat it, and when students practice their mistakes, the mistakes become habits. When a student makes an error, effective teachers provide corrective feedback and scaffolding. This kind of feedback is powerful. To a large extent, what a teacher says or does when the student makes an error determines what the student will do in the future and, ultimately, whether the student will learn to read successfully.

Keep two important things in mind when giving corrective feedback. First, always provide this kind of feedback in a *neutral* tone, with the attitude of simply providing information. Never be deriding or punitive. Second, try not to give corrective feedback too quickly when students make errors as they read or write. One of the goals of effective reading instruction is to help students develop the ability to monitor their own reading

and writing and correct their own errors. At times, wait a few seconds before giving the feedback to see whether the student will notice the error on his or her own. Some examples of corrective feedback are:

- "You almost had this word. This word is *training*."
- "You made a mistake in this part. Can you find it?"
- "The word you wrote is *has*. Can you write *was*?"
- "That's not quite right. Let's take another look."

The Role of Assessment

Four types of reading assessments are used in effective reading programs: *screening*, *diagnosis*, *progress monitoring*, and *outcome* assessments (Kame'enui, 2002). Each has a key role in supporting the success of all students in the school.

SCREENING

The first category of assessments involves the use of brief *screening* measures. Screening measures are normally administered at the beginning of a school year to identify students who have reading difficulties and may need supplemental intervention. New students are screened as they enter school throughout the year.

Table 2.1 **Types of Instructional Scaffolding**

Type	Examples
Planning for success	• Choosing text at the student's instructional level. • Teaching a limited amount of content or skills at one time.
Modeling	• Providing a clear and simple demonstration of what students should do to perform a task such as sounding out words.
Prompting	• Providing reminders to implement effective strategies to read and spell words: *Sound it out; say the word slowly as you write it.*
Supplying partial information	• Providing the sound of a letter within a word so that a student can sound out the word successfully. • Providing a partial answer to a comprehension question to help a student recall information.
Breaking tasks into smaller steps	• Prompting students as they apply a comprehension strategy one step at a time.
Linking to something the student knows	• If a student forgets the sound of /ou/ while trying to read the word *pound*, remind the student of the word *out*, which has the same pattern.

Screening assessments are short and quick to administer. They focus on reading skills that research says are important for reading development. By comparing scores from screening measures to benchmark scores, you can determine whether a student is probably on track to learn to read successfully or may need specialized intervention in order to become a skillful reader.

It is especially important for schools to give screening assessments to beginning readers in kindergarten and 1st grade. This will identify students early who may become struggling readers, and intervention can be provided before their difficulties become increasingly challenging. Researchers have found that children's letter knowledge and phonological awareness are good predictors of future reading progress (see Scarborough, 1998). We included some examples of early reading screening instruments in the "Resources for the Reading Coach" at the end of this book.

For students who are beyond the initial stages of reading instruction, brief assessments of oral reading fluency are surprisingly effective tools for quickly screening for reading difficulties. Besides being a key reading skill in itself, fluency is based on efficient word recognition and the processing of unknown words (decoding and sight word recognition) and is strongly related to reading comprehension (Fuchs, Fuchs, Hosp, & Jenkins, 2001; National Reading Panel, 2000). The fact that oral reading fluency can be assessed with high reliability through timed, one-minute readings (Deno, Mirkin, & Chiang, 1992) makes it feasible to consider screening all students in a school for reading difficulties (Shinn, 1998). Scores obtained from these brief but powerful assessments can then be compared with benchmark standards such as those developed by Hasbrouck and Tindal (1992) to find out whether a student needs further diagnostic assessments. We include a table of oral reading fluency benchmarks in the Appendix.

It is important to further evaluate students who are identified as being at risk for reading difficulties, or those who are found to have reading problems after brief screening measures, to verify the conclusion and to learn more about the nature of their difficulties. No screening measure is 100% accurate. Sometimes students' reading difficulties are missed (and become apparent later to their teachers). More often, students who are actually doing "just fine" perform poorly on a screening assessment for one reason or another. If students who do poorly on a brief screen later receive more in-depth assessment, those who do not really need additional instructional reading support can be identified. Keep in mind that the initial screening is just that—the initial, or first, step.

DIAGNOSIS

Diagnostic measures function mainly to identify student strengths and weaknesses and then to guide instructional decisions. Diagnostic assessments must focus on the five key components of reading identified in the NRP report (2000): *phonemic awareness*, *phonics and decoding skills*, *fluency*, *vocabulary*, and *comprehension*, as appropriate for students at each grade level. Researchers have repeatedly demonstrated that teachers who assess student performance directly and use that information to plan instruction have better educational outcomes (Ysseldyke, 2001). Quite simply, teachers who know what their students know and don't know, and what their students can and cannot do, know what to teach! Effective teachers of struggling readers provide "targeted" instruction that is designed specifically to build on their students' strengths and target their areas of need. We have included a list of some simple informal diagnostic measures in the section Resources for the Reading Coach.

PROGRESS MONITORING

It is especially powerful to assess student growth in key reading skills at regular intervals over an extended period of time (Fuchs & Fuchs, 1986; Hasbrouck, Ihnot, Parker, & Woldbeck, 1999). This type of assessment is called *progress monitoring*, and using it provides teachers with concrete evidence of student growth. When students do not make adequate progress, teachers can examine their own teaching and make changes or adjustments that may support their students in making more accelerated progress (Fuchs, Fuchs, & Stecker, 1989; Shinn, 1998).

Teachers of beginning readers can monitor student progress in skills such as reading high-frequency words and knowing the sounds of letters and combinations of letters. You can monitor progress in reading connected text by assessing a student's ability to read accurately and fluently. For students who are beyond the earliest stages of reading acquisition, brief assessments (one to two minutes) of oral reading fluency have been shown to be sensitive and reliable measures for monitoring growth in decoding and fluency (Baker & Good, 1995; Deno et al., 1992), and they appear to be strongly correlated with comprehension (Fuchs et al., 2001). The validity of these brief oral reading fluency assessments has been demonstrated for both monolingual English readers (Deno et al., 1992) and bilingual students learning to read in English (Baker & Good, 1995). If you assess a student's oral reading fluency regularly (for example, every two weeks on the same day of the week), you can plot the scores on a line graph, providing a clear picture of the student's progress. You can check the graphs to determine whether students are making enough progress or whether a change in instructional methods or materials is needed. The graphs are useful when discussing a student's progress with parents and others who work with the student (Shinn, 1989, 1998).

Other reading skills can be monitored in a similar way. Good and Kaminski (2003) developed the *Dynamic Indicators of Basic Early Literacy Skills* (DIBELS), a complete system of progress monitoring that assesses phonemic awareness, phonemic decoding, oral fluency, and oral retell skills. DIBELS phonemic awareness and decoding progress-monitoring materials are available for kindergarten and Grade 1; oral reading fluency monitoring materials are available through Grade 6 and also in Spanish for kindergarten through Grade 3. Progress-monitoring materials have also been developed for computer administration. (For more information, see the Resources for the Reading Coach section.)

Finally, teachers can develop their own progress-monitoring tools by selecting equally difficult items from the curriculum they teach and administering them on a regular schedule to measure student growth. We list books that provide more information about this approach in our Resources section.

EVALUATING OUTCOMES

The final type of assessment that is essential for an effective reading program is *outcome* measures. They identify students who meet established educational goals and standards at the end of the school year (such as reading at grade level or meeting Individualized Education Program, or IEP, goals) and those who do not. You need to know whether or not your students can meet benchmarks established for grade-level readers. Students who can meet the standards independently are much more likely to thrive

without further reading intervention (Vaughn & Linan-Thompson, 2003). Assessment of outcomes may also be used to evaluate the effectiveness of educational programs for groups of students.

Why Do Some Readers Struggle?

In spite of all we have learned about reading instruction and intervention, we are all too aware that there are still significant numbers of students who do not learn to read satisfactorily. A nationwide assessment of reading conducted as part of the National Assessment of Educational Progress (National Center for Educational Statistics, 2003), commonly known as the "Nation's Report Card," has consistently shown that almost 40% of the students in Grade 4 do not read at a "basic" level. Among students who are members of ethnic and linguistic minority groups, the percentage is closer to 60%. These depressing statistics can only be changed one school and one classroom at a time.

First, we need to understand why so many students struggle with learning to read. Although students can have difficulties in one or more of the aspects of reading we described previously (phonemic awareness, phonics and decoding skills, oral reading fluency, vocabulary, and comprehension), it is important to say that fluency and comprehension are greatly affected by the student's *ability to recognize known words quickly and to decode unknown words efficiently*. You can spend valuable time working on improving a student's comprehension with little benefit if that student is unable to read the words written on the page. It is hard to *understand* what you can't read.

You should also realize that students who do not spend adequate time engaged in reading text build up a large "practice deficit" compared to their fellow students who spend more time reading. You may have heard of the "Matthew Effect," a term based on the Bible verse that says that the rich will grow richer while the poor lose what little they have. Keith Stanovich (1986) used this term to describe the fact that students who can read proficiently read far more than their peers who struggle with reading. Through the act of reading itself, the good students improve their reading skills while the poor readers do not. Good readers get better, and struggling readers fall further and further behind. New research supports the notion that reading text orally at an appropriate level of difficulty supports the development of fluency and vocabulary, and it builds the wide background knowledge essential for comprehending text beyond the most literal level (Rayner, Foorman, Perfetti, Pesetsky, & Seidenberg, 2001).

Serious Reading Difficulties

There are three basic types of serious reading difficulties. Most struggling readers have problems applying phonics to decode words they don't know. Some can read the words but can't understand what they are reading. Still others have problems processing text quickly enough to understand it.

DECODING PROBLEMS

By far the most common type of reading difficulty is the inability to decode words presented in lists without the support of context. Dyslexia is a severe difficulty of this type (Lyon, 1995; Shaywitz, 2003). The underlying difficulty for a student with this problem is usually phonemic awareness. Some of these students also have trouble remembering phonological information. For example, they may be able to sound out parts of a word but unable to remember the sequence of the sounds in order to blend them into a complete word.

COMPREHENSION PROBLEMS

The second type of reading difficulty is an inability to comprehend text despite being able to read accurately and fluently. Students with this problem normally also have problems with listening comprehension. Their problem lies in remembering, organizing, and using information that they take in through listening *or* reading.

PROCESSING PROBLEMS

There is evidence that some students have still other reading difficulties because they are slow processors of information. It may take them a long time to organize and pronounce responses to oral directions or questions, as well as to pronounce words while reading (Wolf & Bowers, 1999; Wolf et al., 2003).

When Is a Reading Difficulty a Reading Disability?

Here we must say just a word about the difference between a reading *difficulty* and a reading *disability*. This topic is actually the subject of a great deal of debate by educators, researchers, and policy makers. Most states define learning disability by looking at scores from IQ tests and achievement tests. Many experts suggest that the best way to find out which students have true reading disabilities is to provide all young, struggling readers (in kindergarten and 1st grade) with high-quality reading instruction and with extra reading intervention if they need it. Students who still have serious reading problems even after they receive this intense intervention probably have true reading disabilities. They can then be tested with tests of *reading* skills and competencies rather than with IQ and general achievement tests.

What does this mean for the reading coach? It means that each child in the primary grades should be provided with high-quality reading instruction and additional intervention if they need it. It is nearly impossible to distinguish 1st grade students who have what has been called "garden variety" reading difficulties from those with true disabilities until the students have been given *real opportunities to learn*. We will try to clarify this issue in the next section.

The Importance of Instruction

Although there is evidence that severe reading difficulties are associated with factors related to brain function, family history, and early literacy experiences (see Mathes & Denton, 2002), research has found consistently that factors related to early reading instruction play a big role in determining which students will become struggling readers. In fact, the power of high-quality, intensive, and focused instruction in compensating for neurological, genetic, and environmental factors has been underestimated (Foorman, Fletcher, & Francis, 1997; Shaywitz, 2003). For example, recent studies of brain function in students with serious reading disabilities and in young students who are at risk for developing serious reading problems have shown that high-quality, intensive reading intervention actually changes the way a student's brain functions (Simos, Breier, Fletcher, Bergman, et al.,

2000; Simos, Breier, Fletcher, Foorman, et al., 2000)! In studies of brain imaging before and after intervention, Simos and his colleagues found consistently that, after receiving small-group or individual intervention, the brains of students with severe reading problems become like those of normal readers. Instruction has the power to change the way a person's brain works.

Another important finding of recent research is that the "wait to bloom" approach does *not* work. In a delightful children's book by Richard Kraus (1998) called *Leo the Late Bloomer*, a young lion, Leo, has many difficulties. Leo's parents wait for him to "bloom," and eventually, as if by magic, Leo blooms. Suddenly, he can read and write. Unfortunately, in our educational system, a child who is a poor reader at the end of 1st grade has almost a 90% chance of remaining a poor reader at the end of the 4th grade (Juel, 1988; Torgesen & Burgess, 1998) and at least a 75% chance of being a poor reader at the end of the 12th grade (Francis, Shaywitz, Stuebing, Shaywitz, & Fletcher, 1996). The most successful schools actively teach their struggling students instead of relegating them to the back of the classroom or assuming that retaining them in a grade is the obvious solution.

A Three-Tiered Model of Intervention

Many educators and researchers are proposing that schools implement a tiered approach to reading intervention to meet the needs of as many students as possible. In this three-tiered model, the first tier consists of quality classroom reading instruction based on the principles we described in this chapter. Mathes and Denton (2002), in their analysis of some key studies of classroom-level and supplemental reading intervention, concluded that the percentage of students experiencing severe reading problems could be reduced to 7% or less (contrasted with the current 25–40%) just by providing high-quality classroom reading instruction in the 1st grade. In the three-tiered model, if students continue to struggle even after receiving quality classroom instruction, they are provided with supplemental intervention. This may consist of intensive reading instruction offered individually or in small groups in addition to the student's regular classroom reading instruction. For example, Mathes et al. (2005) provided supplemental reading instruction to struggling 1st grade readers in groups of three. This "pull-out" intervention

was taught by highly qualified teachers for 40 minutes each day. In this study, fewer than 1% of the 1st graders in the participating schools remained poor readers at the end of the school year. In the three-tiered intervention model, students who still struggle even when they have been provided with both quality classroom instruction (Tier 1) and intensive supplemental intervention (Tier 2) receive Tier 3 intervention. Tier 3 is intervention of even greater intensity, delivered in smaller groups of students or individually, often for longer periods of time each day and sometimes for many months or even years. In some descriptions of the three-tiered model, Tier 3 intervention is provided in special education. In Resources for the Reading Coach, we provide information about a very helpful booklet on the three-tiered intervention model that was developed at the Vaughn Gross Center for Reading and Language Arts at the University of Texas.

The key role of instruction in preventing early reading difficulties gives us both great hope and tremendous responsibility. The next section of our book lays out a game plan designed to address this responsibility on a school-wide, systems-level basis.

The SAILS Model

Given the wealth of information we now have about how students learn to read and why some become struggling readers, what can we do to help the struggling students become competent, motivated readers? Each school is a unique situation with its own strengths and needs, but there is a lot to be learned from schools that have implemented successful reading programs in the face of significant challenges. Some of these schools serve communities where students often have low rates of reading success (for example, impoverished communities and those in which the native language of many students is not English). Researchers have observed and conducted interviews in schools that have high rates of success despite challenging situations, and they have found that these schools have many common characteristics and practices that can be summarized as key principles for effective school reading programs. If these challenged schools can achieve reading success with their students, others can learn from their experiences.

Helping administrators, teachers, and others follow the lead of these successful schools can present significant challenges to the reading coach. In most challenging situations, it is helpful to have a comprehensive strategy or plan. So we developed a five-part model for improving students' reading skills and outcomes. We call our model SAILS (**s**tandards, **a**ssessments, **i**nstruction and **i**nterventions, **l**eadership, and **s**ustained **s**choolwide commitment) (Hasbrouck & Denton, 2004):

- Adopting standards to focus and guide instruction;

- Using assessments to screen, diagnose, and evaluate the progress of student learning;

- Delivering instruction and interventions designed to meet the needs of each student at all levels of ability and skill;

- Providing leadership to assist with the implementation, evaluation, and improvement of each of the three previous components of the model; and

- Making a sustained schoolwide commitment to help every student achieve success in reading by adopting a no-excuses attitude.

STANDARDS

Standards are clear and public expectations for what students should learn at each grade level. Most states have adopted standards or benchmarks for students, but local school districts or schools can also develop standards. Schools with successful reading programs set clear goals and benchmarks for their students (Denton, Foorman, et al., 2003; Lein et al., 1997; Ragland, Clubine, Constable, & Smith, 2001). Adopting unambiguous and ambitious performance standards is a crucial first step to solving the problem of having some groups of students who consistently get left behind their peers academically. The adoption of goals implies that *all* of the students in the school are expected to learn to read. Carefully developed standards can guide teachers, administrators, parents, and students themselves in making sure that students master the knowledge and skills they should (Haycock, 2001).

It is important to have year-end goals for student achievement, but it is equally important to measure each student's progress toward the goals throughout the school year. When teachers monitor students' progress in meeting standards, they can focus instruction on the needs of individual students. One way to determine whether students are on track toward meeting year-end standards is to set benchmarks in skills such as oral reading fluency.

Reliable norms for oral reading fluency have been developed for fall, winter, and spring of Grades 1–5 (Good, Wallin, Simmons, Kame'enui, & Kaminski, 2002; Hasbrouck & Tindal, 1992). When teachers compare the fluency levels of their students to these norms, they can determine whether the students are making adequate progress. See the Appendix for a table of oral reading fluency norms.

In their study of characteristics of 68 schools with high success rates in reading, Parker et al. (2004) observed that educators in these schools used data from statewide standards-based assessments in a systematic way to analyze schoolwide strengths and weaknesses. Teachers and administrators throughout the schools had a strong sense that test results were not solely a reflection on particular teachers or even particular grade levels but that the results reflected the strength and weaknesses of the schoolwide reading program. The focus on standards was key to improving reading outcomes for individual students and for the school as a whole.

READING ASSESSMENTS

Educators in effective schools consistently use *reading assessments* that inform and shape the instructional programs designed to help students meet established benchmarks (Denton, Foorman, et al., 2003; Lein et al., 1997; Ragland et al., 2001). They implement the four types of assessment we described above: screening, diagnosis, progress monitoring, and outcome assessments (Kame'enui, 2002).

In these effective schools, educators aggressively search for students who need support by screening students in the primary grades and also screening older students who are new to the schools (Denton, Foorman, et al., 2003) to "catch them before they fail" (Torgesen, 1998). Scores obtained from screening measures are compared to benchmark scores so teachers and administrators can see whether a student is probably on track to learn to read successfully or may need specialized intervention assistance to become a skillful reader.

Diagnostic assessment is the foundation of effective intervention and instruction for struggling readers. This is an area where reading coaches can play an important role. They can help teachers become aware of the critical importance of diagnosing students' reading difficulties, of how to administer informal diagnostic assessments efficiently, and, most important, how to use the results to plan and monitor the effectiveness of a program of targeted instruction. Foorman and Moats (2004) summarized critical characteristics of schools that succeed in teaching students to read in kindergarten through 2nd grade despite challenging conditions. They concluded that a key, common characteristic of reading instruction in these schools was that the teachers collect results of student assessments and use them to provide instruction targeted to students' needs.

Teachers in effective schools assess students regularly to monitor their progress toward reading goals and benchmarks based on standards. In the schools described by Denton, Foorman, et al. (2003), the results of progress-monitoring assessments were provided to the principal or another instructional leader in the school, who reviewed the results with grade-level teams of teachers. Together, the instructional leader and teachers examined patterns of student growth and planned strategies for providing instruction and intervention to struggling students.

Finally, educators in schools with high reading success rates pay close attention to the results of outcome assessments that can tell them whether their reading programs are effective. They modify the programs when needed in response to these results.

INSTRUCTION AND INTERVENTION

In schools where nearly all students learn to read, teachers provide reading *instruction* that is based on adopted standards and targeted to address student strengths and needs as identified by assessment data (Adler & Fisher, 2001; Denton, Foorman, et al., 2003; Lein et al., 1997). They also provide supplemental, targeted reading *intervention* when students need it (Adler & Fisher, 2001; Denton, Foorman, et al., 2003; Ragland et al., 2001). The most effective reading teachers in the primary grades do not choose between teaching phonics and providing lots of opportunities to read and write. They provide explicit phonemic awareness and alphabetic decoding instruction to students who need it, emphasize reading for meaning, and provide many opportunities for students to read and write in meaningful ways (Pressley et al., 1996; Snow et al., 1998). Successful reading teachers also know that students are motivated to read when they are able to read fluently with little conscious effort *and* when they

are provided with a print-rich environment with many engaging opportunities to read and write.

Effective teachers are self-reflective and adopt a problem-solving approach when students experience difficulty. Struggling readers do not all learn in exactly the same way or in the same time frame. Teachers who collect progress-monitoring assessment data have a tool to help them make key decisions about their students' progress—or lack of progress. If students are not making progress, these teachers examine their own instruction and make changes in their methods, materials, pacing, or other facets of their teaching. They may re-administer informal diagnostic assessments to find out more specifically what is easy and what is difficult for their students. Effective teachers are flexible and continue to learn about research-based instructional methods in reading, with particular emphasis on reports like those described earlier that present a *convergence* of research evidence.

Effective teachers of struggling readers provide both accommodation and instruction. When teachers provide instruction, they determine what the student can and can't do, and they teach and provide practice on the skills and knowledge the student needs to learn to read. Accommodation means modifying the curriculum, materials, and/or presentation to allow struggling readers to be successful (such as providing a "buddy" to read assignments from the science textbook to a student who has difficulty reading the text alone, or administering math tests orally). Although accommodation is important, it is not enough. Students of all ages deserve to be taught how to read successfully (see Denton & Hasbrouck, 1999).

Schools that make a commitment to providing instruction that supports successful reading for all of their students base day-to-day decisions on this priority (Lein et al., 1997). Some of the decisions include how reading lessons are (1) *scheduled* (e.g., 90 minutes of reading instruction daily for struggling readers); (2) *planned* (e.g., use assessment data to design instruction and decide what materials to use); (3) *organized* (e.g., small or large groups, regrouping across classrooms, tutoring); (4) *delivered* (e.g., explicit, cooperative groups); and (5) *evaluated*, based on scientific evidence of effective practice (Denton, Foorman et al., 2003; Foorman & Moats, 2004). In the 26 high-poverty successful schools studied by Lein et al. (1997), the researchers noted that the basis for making decisions was consistently, "What's best for kids?" (p. 4), and they report that educators in more than one school made comments like, "Money is not going to keep any child from participating" (p. 6). These schools found creative ways to stretch budgets, use parent-teacher organizations for fund-raising, partnering with businesses, and tapping into community resources.

Not only do these schools provide quality classroom instruction, they also provide supplemental intervention to students who need more intensive and individualized instruction. In some of the effective schools studied by Denton, Foorman, and colleagues (2003), some struggling readers received as much as three hours per day of reading instruction. In the schools described by Foorman and Moats (2004), reading instruction and intervention was a schoolwide priority, with increased time spent on classroom reading instruction, small group interventions, specialized tutorials, and extended-day activities available to support student success.

LEADERSHIP

We are defining *leadership* as providing the guidance, support, and structures at state, district, and building levels to allow effective reading instruction to take place. A common characteristic of all schools that have effective schoolwide approaches to reading success is the presence of an instructional leader (Adler & Fisher, 2001; Denton, Foorman, et al., 2003; Ragland et al., 2001). Leadership at the school level, whether provided by a building principal, a reading specialist or coach, a leadership team, or a combination of these, helps ensure the implementation of a schoolwide reading model that provides for consistency, structure, quality curriculum, and effective instruction.

Effective instructional leaders are familiar with research-supported reading instruction. They encourage teacher creativity and leadership, taking advantage of each teacher's talents and experience. They collaborate with teachers and staff in deciding how reading instruction is planned and delivered across classrooms. They insist that these decisions be based on research findings and the success rates of their own students. In several of the schools described by Denton, Foorman, and colleagues (2003), principals met regularly with grade-level teams to review the progress-monitoring assessment data. The teams problem-solved together if students were not on track to meet the benchmarks. In some of the schools, principals went into classrooms to provide teachers with

individualized coaching and to model effective instruction. Expectations for the teachers were high, but they were not working alone. They received the professional development and support they needed to succeed.

Instructional leaders in the effective schools are consistent in their focus on aggressive and continuous efforts to find and serve *all* students who need help to learn to read. They provide the tools and conditions that teachers and support staff need for effective instruction. Reading instruction is a priority when time and resources are allocated in these schools. For example, scheduling supports the need to provide supplemental intervention to those who require it, and teachers are allowed time to collaborate. Teachers are not left to their own devices when they encounter challenges. They can take advantage of effective and sustained professional development, including mentoring, modeling, and collaborative problem solving with reading coaches. The instructional leaders also maintain updated and aligned policies, and there is coherence among state, district, and school standards and curricula so that teachers clearly understand the goals of instruction.

SUSTAINED SCHOOLWIDE COMMITMENT

We define the final component of the SAILS model—*sustained schoolwide commitment*—as a lasting agreement among all school faculty and administrators to adopt a no-excuses intervention model, making a firm pledge to work together to help every student be a successful reader. Beyond providing effective classroom reading instruction, teachers in the successful schools described by Denton, Foorman, and colleagues (2003) had what was described as a "relentless" (p. 259) approach to providing intervention. One principal described a feeling of "urgency" at her school, a total commitment to teaching every child to read. In successful schools, teachers and administrators have a passionate and firm belief that it is realistic to expect all students to achieve state, local, and schoolwide standards (Adler & Fisher, 2001; Denton, Foorman, et al., 2003; Lein et al., 1997; Ragland et al., 2001).

The most effective teachers of struggling readers set ambitious and realistic goals for their students, design lessons to move the students toward those goals, and expect their students to be successful. In the same way, the most effective schools have high expectations for all students and the overriding belief that they all can be successful.

Energy and resources are directed at areas in which students have difficulties. Administrators, teachers, and staff have opportunities to collaborate to address barriers to learning and are eager to learn from each other. There is effective communication across grade levels, programs, and teaching areas. Parents are seen as critical partners. Educators consider referral to special education or retention a last resort, after using multiple intervention strategies (Ragland et al., 2001).

Implementing SAILS.

These five components of SAILS—**s**tandards, **a**ssessments, **i**nstruction and **i**ntervention, **l**eadership, and **s**ustained **s**choolwide commitment—are all important to the successful implementation of an effective reading program in a school. We are aware that there are other considerations, including the overall climate for learning in a school. In challenging situations, the most successful schools maintain a safe, orderly, and positive environment (Foorman & Moats, 2004). To be successful, the SAILS model must be implemented in a positive and caring schoolwide environment, where there is a commitment to the emotional and physical safety of all students.

Conclusion

Reading coaches undertake a demanding role. Working with professional colleagues to collaboratively address the challenging difficulties of struggling readers can be daunting. It is imperative that a coach be well informed with the highest quality and most current knowledge available. We hope this chapter served to reinforce what you had already known about reading, and perhaps extended or deepened this knowledge somewhat. We now move on to the process of coaching. Let's get started!

3

GETTING STARTED

You are recognized as a person in your school or district who knows a lot about effective reading instruction. You may have assisted in a recent curriculum-selection process or served as a mentor to student teachers or a first-year classroom teacher. Perhaps you are already a certified reading specialist. But now your principal or district supervisor has tapped you for this new role—reading coach. That sounds exciting, but how do you get started? Introducing this new role to a school's staff, many of whom have never worked with a reading coach before, can be a real challenge. This chapter is designed to help you with that process.

Roles for a Reading Coach

Reading coaches provide many services to their schools, in both instruction and leadership ("Changing Role of Reading Specialists," 2002). Coaches do all of the things listed here, along with lots of other varied tasks (Dole, 2004; Lefever-Davis, Wilson, Moore, Kent, & Hopkins, 2003):

- Review curriculum materials and make suggestions for adoption or for supplementing instructional resources
- Visit teachers' classrooms and model lessons
- Organize and facilitate teacher study groups to explore relevant topics of interest
- Provide workshops to introduce teachers to new strategies and provide follow-up support for professional development
- Help teachers with the organization and management of their literacy programs
- Advise building or district administrators on how reading research applies to program policy decisions
- Meet with parents who have concerns about their children's reading skills
- Conduct assessments of students' reading and use the results to make instructional recommendations

As we discussed in Chapter 1, we have organized all of these various tasks into the three roles a SFC coach fills:

(1) *Facilitator*, to help effective and skillful teachers continue their success; (2) *Collaborative Problem Solver*, using a strategic and structured process to work with teachers in addressing students' problems that arise in the classroom; and (3) *Teacher/Learner*, sharing effective, proven strategies, methods, and techniques with groups of teachers through professional development.

The decision about which role to use with a given teacher is guided by that teacher's needs at the time, determined through regular contacts with each one of them once the coaching process has begun. We will walk you through the process of getting started as a coach and provide some strategies to make this process a smooth and easy one. The first step in this process is called "entry."

Entry

In the professional literature on coaching and consultation, some attention is usually devoted to the topic of "entry," generally defined as how to get started in coaching or consulting in a school or district. Pipes (1981) defined entry as "the process whereby a consultant comes into contact with, establishes a working relationship with, and begins the analysis of problems presented by the members of an organization when the intent of the consultant is to provide consultation services to that organization" (p. 11). Now, does that help make entry perfectly clear? Perhaps not. OK, let's break this down a bit more.

Pipes is certainly correct that coaching is a "working relationship" focused on an "analysis of problems" presented by colleagues. He also accurately notes that entry is a "process" as opposed to an event. You can't just stand up at a faculty meeting, announce "I'm your new reading coach and here's what I can do for you," and expect all the other teachers to immediately flock to your door to seek your assistance with their reading challenges. It is also important for your fellow teachers *not* to think you are simply going to be walking the halls, politely asking whether they need anything, and generally helping out wherever you can.

WHAT WILL YOU DO AS A READING COACH?

The first step to take in this ongoing entry process is to clearly define for *yourself* the role of reading coach. In Chapter 1, we defined coaching broadly as "*a cooperative, ideally collaborative relationship, with parties mutually engaged in efforts to provide better services for students.*" We also identified four goals for coaches: (1) improve students' reading skills and competence; (2) solve referred problems; (3) learn from each other; and (4) prevent future problems. A new coach should spend some time thinking about this definition and list of goals, as well as any other guidelines available to define the role, such as a job description or any district or state guidelines for the role of reading coach.

Eventually, you will want to be able to articulate clearly what you think a reading coach is and how you plan to provide coaching services to your colleagues. You must be able to describe to other teachers, parents, and administrators:

• The rationale for this new role

• A description of the coaching process

• The tasks you will be doing as a reading coach and services you can provide

• How you will be spending your time during the school day

• How you can be contacted by a teacher or parent who may want to work with you

You will also want to spend some time thinking about the kinds of tasks you will *not* be undertaking, as coaches are often seen as the person who can address every pos-

sible concern related to reading. It is unlikely that your time will allow for that!

WHAT WILL YOUR COLLEAGUES DO?

It will be helpful to have a clear understanding of what role your colleagues will play as they seek out your assistance as a coach. This will help you articulate the coaching process as you introduce your role to them. For example, if you clarify coaching as a professional, cooperative process focused on helping students improve their reading skills, your colleagues will better understand that meeting with you is not a just chance to vent or complain about problem students and challenging parents or to share frustrations about other teachers or administrators.

Coaching is not the correct venue for expressing dissatisfaction with a poor reading curriculum or lamenting the lack of in-service training to help address new challenges in the classrooms. While such concerns may be relevant, and may indeed be discussed briefly (and professionally) as part of coaching, the focus must be on the *students' instructional needs*, and the entire process should be driven as much as possible by objective data rather than the beliefs, frustrations, or assumptions of the participants.

As you work through the remaining chapters of this book, some of these issues will begin to come into sharper focus, which will definitely help you in the process of defining and articulating how you want to work as a reading coach to best serve the needs of the students.

DEFINING YOUR ROLE WITH YOUR ADMINISTRATOR

Of course, you won't be able to define your role completely by yourself. As much as this may sound appealing (naturally, we *all* would like to create and define our own jobs!), it is critical to involve your supervisor in this process. It is entirely possible that your supervisor will indeed ask you to take the lead in defining this new role. Having a reading coach in their building is new territory for most administrators as well. If someone walks into a school building and announces to the principal that he is the new counselor or 2nd grade teacher or P.E. coach or 7th grade science teacher, an administrator generally knows what to expect from that person. When it comes time to evaluate this new staff member, we can expect that the supervisor has guidance from experience and training and can accurately and fairly judge whether that person is performing adequately in his assigned job.

Reading coaches will also have to be supervised and evaluated. If a principal has never worked with a reading coach before, how will he or she be able to make these important decisions? In most cases this won't be a serious problem. However, we know of at least one case where this issue was cause for some concern. A teacher who had previously held a more traditional role in a school, and had consistently received positive annual evaluations, was then moved into a new role as a consulting teacher (with no specialized training, by the way). At the end of the year the administrator believed this teacher's performance in her new role had been inadequate. The teacher was then given a negative evaluation and was terminated. This is obviously an extreme case, and it would have been avoidable by engaging in a process such as we are describing here, to thoughtfully develop and share with your supervisor a clear description of the role of a reading coach and hold ongoing discussions about the role and expectations for performance. We developed an *Evaluation Checklist for SFC Coaches/Consultants* (Hasbrouck & Denton, 2004) that you and your supervisor may find useful. A copy is included in the Appendix.

It is wise for a new reading coach to take the lead in including his or her supervisor in the process of defining the role of coach. Take the time to ask your supervisor questions about how he or she would address some of the questions previously raised:

- What is your rationale for this new role?
- What is your understanding of the coaching process?
- How would you describe the process of coaching?
- Have you had previous experiences supervising a reading coach? If so, were those experiences positive or negative?
- What tasks do you envision that I will do as a coach, and how would you like to see me spending my time during the school day?

These questions will not be able to be completely addressed at a single meeting. For one thing, your new role will continue to develop and evolve over time. As it does, remember to make time for a professional discussion with your supervisor about your role and how well he or she sees you fulfilling it. Treat such continuing meetings as professional discussions, not as time to argue for more resources or complain about having too little time to do your work. As much as possible, bring any available relevant data to this meeting, and treat it as a problem-solving activity. Keep the discussion focused, professional, and nondefensive. Use your best communication skills, and keep notes!

Confidentiality and Professional Ethics

COACHING VERSUS SUPERVISION

One thing that will inevitably arise as a concern to reading coaches is the issue of *confidentiality*. As a reading coach, your role is different from the role of a more traditional teacher. Reading coaches often have opportunities to spend significant amounts of time in their colleagues' classrooms. Coaching often involves observing a teacher conducting a lesson and then providing feedback to that teacher about the quality of teaching. On the surface, this looks much like an evaluation of a teacher's classroom performance. It is *critical* for a coach (and the coach's supervisor and colleagues) to understand the subtle, yet significant differences between coaching and supervision.

While the processes of supervision and coaching do, in fact, appear at times to be nearly identical, one key difference between them is their *purpose*. A primary purpose of supervision is to provide information so a supervisor can make evaluative judgments: Is this teacher performing in a professionally competent manner or not? Of course a good supervisor also works with teachers to help them improve their professional skills, but the key point is evaluation. Coaching, in contrast to supervision, is *never* about making evaluative decisions about professional competence. Coaching is about the well-being of *students*, not judging or evaluating teachers. Coaches collaborate with teachers to help them provide the best possible instruction to every student, at every skill level.

Another difference between coaching and supervision is the requirement for cooperation that coaching has and that being evaluated doesn't have. A coach must be *invited* to observe a lesson and then provide feedback to a teacher. If a teacher is not willing to be observed by a coach, coaching cannot occur—period. Obviously, this is not the case when a supervisor arrives to observe a teacher. While a teacher may have some control and input about when to be supervised, the option of not allowing the principal to watch a lesson being taught does not exist.

Being certain that all participants are fully aware of these essential differences can help you avoid some potential problems down the line.

Some coaches do have duties and responsibilities that require them to work with teachers in a way that mirrors supervision. We consider that coaches in these situations are providing coaching *plus* supervision. We maintain that the coaching role itself should be defined as a voluntary peer-to-peer process.

THE CORNERSTONES OF COACHING—TRUST AND CONFIDENTIALITY

It is essential for your supervisor and your teacher colleagues to understand that your role as a coach precludes you from sharing any information about a teacher's performance that you may learn while providing coaching. Trust and confidentiality are cornerstones of coaching. As we have discussed, coaching can occur only within a cooperative or collaborative professional relationship. As in all human interactions, a professional relationship must be built on trust and mutual respect. A coach perceived by teachers to be a "spy for the principal" or a gossip who talks about one teacher to another will soon be unable to provide coaching services at all. Few, if any, teachers will want to open their classrooms and allow themselves to be observed if they don't believe the coach will maintain a sense of privacy and keep all communication confidential. This includes information teachers may share with you about any of their students or students' families.

This may seem easy to do, but a promise to keep all information obtained through coaching completely confidential can be challenging. Sometimes, coaches are assigned to schools where they have been working in a different role for many years. In such cases, the coaches are likely to have formed various kinds of relationships with others at the school. Perhaps one or more of the teachers are considered to be close friends by the coach, or maybe even the coach and the principal have formed a friendship that extends beyond the school day. However, there may be a couple of teachers with whom the coach long ago got off on the wrong foot, and those relationships may have never improved. In either situation, the coach has a real challenge: restructuring some of these *personal* relationships into different *professional* relationships. There is certainly no reason to give up a friendship with a colleague just to take on the role of reading coach, but it may mean

that the content of some of the conversations will have to change. While a couple of teaching or administrative buddies can vent frustrations and share experiences about fellow teachers, a coach cannot for reasons of professional ethics and to ensure that all colleagues with whom the coach works will be treated equally and professionally.

Another issue we must consider while we are discussing confidentiality takes us back to the clear focus and purpose for coaching—to help every student become a successful reader. A coach is in a school to help every student get the best possible instruction in reading and make the most progress possible. What if, in your role as coach, you observe a teacher who is not providing adequate instruction, or worse? What if you witness, consistently, very poor instruction? Or no instruction? What if you observe a teacher making a hurtful or derogatory statement to a student? Or possibly engaging in physically inappropriate behavior, such as shoving or slapping? Sadly, if you coach long enough, you may eventually observe something just like this. In such cases, it is important for the coach to have at least thought about issues relevant to professional ethics and, ideally, to have discussed such possibilities in advance with a supervisor.

RULES OF PROFESSIONAL ETHICS

Heron, Martz, & Margolis (1996) suggest that professionals who work as consultants in schools—like reading coaches do—develop a clear ethical framework to guide decisions and behavior. The challenging professional environment of conflicting laws, regulations, and procedures, and the often high emotions raised by complex issues such as student academic success, make this a top priority for reading coaches. Some topics these authors raised include recognizing your professional limitations, needs, and strengths; confining practice to your own competence and limits of training and preparation; ensuring that recommendations you offer as a coach have a solid empirical basis whenever possible; and keeping abreast of new professional developments (Heron et al., 1996).

Heron and colleagues (1996) also discuss how personal values may at times contribute to unethical professional behavior. They cite an example that may be relevant to a reading coach: What if a coach who is philosophically biased against direct instruction in phonics uses his or her influence to coerce a colleague or parents to reject phonics instruction for a student? Heron et al. contend that coaches must be sure to keep their values out of the coaching process and to rely instead on data and well-validated research findings to guide their recommendations. They also suggest a set of questions a coach may use in the kind of professional self-analysis that will lead to ethical professional behavior:

- *Will my actions produce the maximum benefit for all concerned?* Know the limits of your own training and experience, along with reasonable time limits for meeting goals. Know when it is appropriate to request assistance from others or remove yourself from a situation in which you will probably not be able to offer appropriate services.

- *Will my actions communicate how I want others to behave toward me and other professional colleagues, parents, and students?* Coaches must model appropriate, respectful, considerate, and professional behavior while engaging in coaching-related activities.

- *Does my daily professional practice adhere to local, state, or national standards for ethical behavior, laws, and policies?* (See Corey, Corey, & Callanan, 1993; or Greenspan & Negron, 1994, for further guidance in professional ethics.)

As part of defining your role with your supervisor, spend at least a few moments discussing issues related to professional ethics, as well as the procedures that must be followed about confidentiality. Of course, behavior that is clearly abusive must be reported immediately in accordance with your school, district, or state regulations. We hope you never have any such experience as a reading coach, but it is far better to have at least considered the possibility in advance, should such event ever occur.

Building a Caseload

We hope you now have an understanding of how to get started as a reading coach. After beginning the process by defining your role as a coach for yourself, your colleagues, and your supervisor, the next step is getting to work! As we mentioned earlier, you can't make this happen by just standing up at a faculty meeting to announce what it is you can do for all of these professionals! There are still a few other steps you will want to take.

WHICH TEACHERS WILL WORK WITH YOU?

Eager and open.

In most schools there will be some teachers who are eager to begin working with you as soon as they hear you describe your new role as a reading coach. The most eager are, typically, beginning teachers in their first few years in the classroom. When most of us think back on our experiences as beginning teachers, we remember how overwhelmed and isolated we sometimes felt. Novice teachers can benefit greatly from the support of a reading coach. Many new teachers, in fact, are quite skilled and have been well prepared by their college courses. They need only some general guidance and encouragement. Others may be confused about important issues such as how to organize their classrooms to provide both whole group and small group instruction to a wide range of students, how to effectively use the school's reading curriculum for their assigned grade levels, how to provide the extra instruction needed by some of their lower-performing students, how to administer or interpret the results of diagnostic assessments, and others.

Eager but resistant.

Another group of teachers who may be eager to use your coaching services can be quite different to work with. There are some teachers who believe that any classroom problem they have has little or nothing to do with their own actions but rather is caused by "a problem student who won't do the work," "neglectful parents," "those primary grade teachers who just aren't doing their jobs getting students ready for 4th grade," "the completely inadequate materials we were given to teach from," "that principal who is always riding my back to do a better job," and on and on and on. You get the picture. Although these teachers are often enthusiastic about the chance to work with a coach, you may find that somehow they really don't want to hear suggestions about things they may need to do differently.

Reluctant but not resistant.

There may also be a couple of other groups of teachers, and neither group will be likely to beat a path to your door the day you put out your "open for business" sign. The first group contains the veteran teachers who are experienced and successful educators and who have gotten along just fine without coaching services in the past. They may be feeling justifiably confident about how they are teaching reading and may see no immediate need to seek out your services.

Reluctant and resistant.

The other group is comprised of those teachers who are just reluctant to try any new program or service. There may, in fact, be some among them who could definitely use some help in improving their instructional practices but are resistant to making changes or simply anxious about having another adult in the classroom watching them teach.

WHY SHOULD TEACHERS WANT TO WORK WITH YOU?

There are some specific techniques that can be effective with teachers from each of the four categories described in the prior section, but we'll start with some general suggestions for laying a foundation for your work as a reading coach. First of all, don't panic or spend too much time worrying about whether anyone is ever going to want to work with you as a coach. Trust us on this one. There is a typical scenario that plays out for almost all reading coaches: In the beginning, all coaches worry because only a few (eager and open) teachers have sought out their services. Then, usually around early January or so, the concern is the opposite: "I'm swamped with requests for my time! Help! Too many people want coaching! What should I do?" We'll have suggestions for that second concern in a bit. For now, let's drum up some business for you.

1. *Advertise and market your services.* You can start by taking that definition you developed to describe your role as a reading coach—the rationale for coaching, a description of the coaching process, and a list of some of the services you can provide—and communicate it to your colleagues. Make sure everyone hears about the new role you will be playing and how you see yourself working with them all to help improve their students' reading outcomes.

We all know that teachers are busy people. Our experience has been that simply making an announcement about this new role as one item in a full agenda for an after-school faculty meeting, when everyone is tired anyway, will probably not get the attention

of anyone but those eager and open teachers. Follow that announcement with more information. Some coaches we've worked with have found it constructive to openly advertise their services to get the ball rolling. Some coaches have created clever one-page flyers (attention-grabbing graphics, catchy slogans, easy-to-read at a glance) that they put in teachers' mailboxes or even post around the school in conspicuous places (over the faculty room microwave, for example). Besides once again reminding teachers about *what a reading coach is* and the kinds of *tasks and services a coach can provide*, such printed information should also state your *schedule* and *when*, *where*, and *how* a teacher can reach you so you can get started on helping the students become better readers.

2. *Start small; work with a willing colleague.* Don't worry if only one or two teachers express an interest in working with you. Your caseload will increase over time. You probably want some experience under your belt, anyway, before the really challenging cases come! If no one calls, sends you an e-mail, or fills out your nifty referral forms, you may have to go to them! Start with those eager and open novice teachers. Stop by their classrooms before school or during a prep period; just start chatting and asking a few general questions. These kinds of contacts will often lead to a request for some "advice," which can ultimately move toward becoming a more formal coaching opportunity.

3. *Continue advertising and give credit to others.* As you begin working with other teachers and problems begin to be solved and concerns successfully addressed, it might be helpful to let others know about these accomplishments. Remember the issues of confidentiality, however. You may *only* spread the word about a successful coaching outcome if the teacher you worked with agrees to have his or her experiences shared publicly. Some teachers will be reluctant to let others know they sought assistance from a reading coach, even if the results were positive. As time passes, and your role as the coach becomes a more commonplace component of daily school life, this reluctance will be greatly reduced.

However, whenever a teacher is open to sharing a coaching success story, be sure to stress the *collaborative* nature of the process. As tempting as it may seem to be viewed as the "all-powerful guru of reading" with a "magic bag of tricks to solve all possible reading problems," such an image is likely to set you up for a fall. Emphasize the *shared* process of coaching, and credit the efforts of the teacher who did the actual work with the student. Reducing the "expert aura" will result in creating a sense of confidence and trust among your colleagues, essential for building the cooperative and collaborative professional relationships needed to provide effective coaching.

4. *Don't separate roles.* A final suggestion for drumming up business and forming collegial relationships with your fellow teachers is to try to keep your role in the school similar to theirs as much as possible. Coaches have to engage in activities that sometimes look more like an administrator's than a teacher's. Coaches typically spend at least some time outside of a classroom setting when they are not working directly with students. Coaches move from classroom to classroom. Their schedules may be much more under their own control than the schedules of most teachers. This kind of flexibility can make some of your colleagues a bit envious. To defuse any possible resentment that arises, we recommend that you seek ways to stay professionally aligned with other teachers. For example, make sure you find ways to participate in the duties and tasks that most teachers undertake, perhaps morning bus duty, serving on committees, monitoring hallways, bringing snacks to the faculty meetings, or even taking turns cleaning up the staff room. Carey (1995) recommends that coaches attend open houses at their schools, parent-teacher association meetings or other meetings, and get-togethers with school faculty and staff. Teachers will be far more open to working with you if they see you as "one of them" rather than as some kind of administrator or supervisor.

Which Role to Use?

Now that you have introduced yourself as the reading coach and have begun meeting with some teachers to discuss their problems or concerns, you may be wondering how and when to start performing those roles of coaching we introduced to you previously: Facilitator, Collaborative Problem Solver, and Teacher/Learner. You will make that decision on a case-by-case basis, reflecting the needs

of your colleagues. To figure out what those needs are, we suggest that you try to initiate some kind of contact with each teacher you work with, at least once a month, regardless of the teacher's interest or readiness. By staying in contact and showing openness to working with every teacher, you may find that even those reluctant teachers who at first did not want any assistance, and even those who were initially resistant to working with a coach, may eventually decide that working with you is worthwhile. Coaching can occur only when a professional relationship has been established. It is really hard to start a relationship of any kind if there is no contact with the people involved!

At these monthly check-ins, ask three key questions about each teacher's reading program:

1. What is working well for you?

2. Do you have a concern about the progress of any of your students?

3. Do you have any questions or suggestions for me?

If things are going well for a teacher, you may serve as a Facilitator. Determine if there is anything that teacher is doing that you should learn about and perhaps share with other teachers. Use these opportunities to encourage the teachers and find ways to support their work. Even the most gifted teachers need support and reinforcement at times (Anderson, Major, & Mitchell, 1992). However, if a teacher identifies a concern about a student or group of students, you can move into the Collaborative Problem Solver mode. This process is fully described in Chapters 5–7.

If you find that a number of teachers seem to share the same concern, consider putting on your Teacher/Learner hat, and think about designing some kind of professional development activity. This may be the most strategic and efficient way to help out with concerns that are being raised by more than one individual teacher. For example, if several of your colleagues feel the need to incorporate more phonemic awareness into their instructional programs but are unsure what materials or strategies to use, or if several teachers have found that their students are having difficulty reading and understanding content area readings (in social studies, science, health, etc.), suggest putting together an after-school workshop on effective phonemic awareness instruction or on evidence-based suggestions for helping students develop content area reading strategies. Coaches can design and deliver these kinds of professional development activities themselves or work with the principal or district to bring in a consultant or trainer to address a specific topic. Another way to determine whether professional development is needed is through regular visits with your building principal and other reading leaders and doing a collaborative analysis of student performance data. If there are any patterns or evidence of low performance, staff development and support may be indicated. We will provide more detail on this topic in Chapter 8.

Conclusion

The process of defining and beginning a new role within the kind of system you will find in a school building or school district happens over time because the role evolves as the participants engage in the process. Given this, you may want to consider seeking input about the role of reading coach from your colleagues as time passes. Informal chats about how they feel about your coaching, or more formal data collection, such as a survey or questionnaire, may provide you and your supervisor with valuable information about ways to improve the delivery

4

TIME MANAGEMENT AND COMMUNICATION

Let's take a moment to revisit our definition of a reading coach from Chapter 1. We characterized a reading coach as an experienced teacher who has a strong knowledge base in reading, has experience providing effective reading instruction to students, can work effectively with peer colleagues to help them improve the reading outcomes of their students, and who receives support for providing coaching. In Chapter 2, we focused on the foundational knowledge a reading coach needs. Chapter 3 provided an overview of the roles of an SFC reading coach, ideas for getting started, and a discussion of some critical issues related to working as a coach in a school setting.

Here in Chapter 4, we'll get more specific. We'll focus on two essential tools for helping an experienced reading teacher become a coach who works effectively with peers and parents: *time management* and *communication*.

Time Management

One challenge that reading coaches can expect to face as they make the transition from their previous positions is the new issue that arises from having a schedule that is, in fact, somewhat more open-ended than that of a traditional teacher. Coaches often have a certain degree of flexibility in setting their own schedules: deciding when to do things like visit a teacher's classroom, schedule an assessment of a student, or meet with a parent. This can be a great perk of becoming a coach, and after years of having your schedule dictated almost entirely by external considerations (the start of the school day, bus schedules, lunch, recesses, and break schedules) and managed by the ringing of bells or buzzers, this flexibility can feel quite liberating! The problem begins to arise, eventually, when your schedule starts to fill . . . and overfill! How do you get everything done in a reasonable number of hours?

GENERAL TIME MANAGEMENT ISSUES

One of the first things to consider as you begin to deal with scheduling is the notion that effective time management is a professional act. It is something you will need to master if you want to be considered a skillful, qualified, and capable coach. Unfortunately, the reality of time management is that it doesn't get you any additional time. Good time-management skills simply help you displace less critical tasks with more important ones.

A realistic place to start thinking about professional time management is to consider how some time issues are under our control while others are not. We must accept those aspects of a schedule that cannot be changed—*externally generated time problems*—such as mandatory meetings, other teachers' schedules, and the like. What we can begin to consider getting under control are those *internally generated time problems* that include procrastination, disorganization, "task-hopping," and allowing ourselves to become overcommitted.

USING A SYSTEMATIC PROBLEM-SOLVING PROCESS

Skillful time management is not magic. As you well know, there are only so many minutes in an hour, and hours in a day. You can't create more time. Recall how Roger Kroth (Kroth & Edge, 1997) reminded us that in schools, no matter how hard we try, there is never enough time to accomplish all of the important work we have to do. However, what you *can* do is use the time that is under your control as efficiently as possible. To accomplish this, consider using the four-phase, systematic problem-solving process that we describe below (and discuss in greater detail in Chapter 5). The four steps of this process are:

- *Phase 1:* Problem Presentation and Analysis
- *Phase 2:* Data Analysis and Intervention Development
- *Phase 3:* Implementation
- *Phase 4:* Evaluation

Phase 1: Problem Presentation and Analysis.

To start developing an effective time-management system, start with a baseline description of your current time-management processes. The baseline can point you toward the time-related concerns that you really need to address. To determine where you are now in time management, ask yourself whether you are spending some of your valuable professional time (1) engaging in nonessential work; (2) attending unnecessary meetings; (3) dealing with general disorganization in your paperwork or materials; (4) spending time with people who end up taking too much of your time; or (5) participating in activities that are not related to your professional performance goals.

To address these issues, you can collect data and use it to develop an action plan for improving your own time-management system. Collecting time data can be as simple as keeping a journal or informal log that you summarize at the end of the day or week to help identify problematic areas. We've also developed a more formal system for tracking and analyzing time called the *3T-SR: Teacher Time Tracking in Special Programs for Reading Teachers and Specialists* (3T-SR) (Hasbrouck, Parker, & Denton, 2003). The 3T-SR is an instrument for monitoring a reading teacher, coach, or specialist's time in professional activities. The 3T-SR can be used for several purposes:

- Accountability (How is time being spent by the reading coach? Is enough time being allocated to cover essential services?)
- Program planning and evaluation (Are coaches spending their time as productively as possible?)
- Self-monitoring to develop an effective personal time-management system

The 3T-SR is available in the Appendix at the end of the book.

Phase 2: Data Analysis and Intervention Development.

The second phase in a systematic problem-solving process involves carefully examining the data you have collected and developing a plan for making desired changes in your time management. Analyzing your data helps you develop a "problem formulation," in this case, a clear idea of the time-related problems you want to address. If things are really out of control, you may need to list your problem areas and prioritize them to see which ones you want to tackle first.

After getting a handle on what the real time-related concerns are, the next step is to set some goals: How do you want to distribute your time across professional activities? What are your professional priorities? What do you want to achieve at the end of each week? Identifying one, two, or three goals may be appropriate. These goals should be realistic. If you are currently spending close to two hours a day managing paperwork and materials, setting a goal to reduce this to no more than 15 minutes a day is probably unrealistic, at least right away.

It may be appropriate to set some interim goals that are more immediately achievable. Make your goals as concrete as possible. Specify *what you will achieve* in a *specific time period*: "My goal in four weeks is to be spending no more than 50 minutes on average each day on my paper and materials management." Finally, decide how to determine whether you have achieved your goals in the allotted amount of time. For example, you may decide that after four weeks you'll once again spend a few days using a log or journal (or the 3T-SR) to give you new data about how you are doing now in managing your time.

To develop your time-management intervention plan, take a careful look at your goals and ask yourself what you must change in your daily or weekly routine to achieve them. Do you need to spend a few hours organizing your filing system? Do you need to get rid of some of the books and materials you have cluttering your office? Can you delegate some of the paperwork that is taking so much of your time? Perhaps there is a more efficient computer-based system that could be implemented? To help you brainstorm ideas for tackling the things you want to change, it may be worth your while to read some time-management books or visit some Web sites that have ideas on how to get organized. You can also attend a workshop or simply ask your most organized friends and colleagues to share their favorite ideas and strategies.

Once you have a set of good ideas, narrow the list to approaches that will work for *you*. It will be a waste of time (which you certainly want to avoid!) and a big frustration if you try to use someone else's best tactic that just doesn't suit your own individual style. Perhaps your computer-whiz friend told you excitedly how her personal digital assistant (PDA) was the key to her amazing productivity. But using a PDA might not be the answer for you if you get nervous even approaching a computer keyboard.

After selecting some approaches you *do* want to try, write down an action plan. It also may help to develop a timeline: What tasks will you undertake first? What will need to be accomplished by the end of Week 1? Week 2?

Phase 3: Implementation.

The next phase in this problem-solving process is to implement your action plan for intervention. Because you put your plan into writing, and perhaps even developed a timeline, you now have a tool to help you determine whether you are fully implementing your plan and making progress toward your overall goals. During implementation, you will need to make some interim decisions about how the plan is working and determine whether to make some modifications along the way. If you have decided to tackle your organizational challenges by using a new computer-based organizer to rearrange all of your files and then learn that the software you need is back-ordered, you'll have to adjust either your plan or your timeline.

Phase 4: Evaluation.

At the end of the predetermined time period for improving your own time management, collect and analyze some new data to assess how you are now spending your time. These findings will help you decide what your next steps should be. If all or some of your goals have been met, perhaps you will want to set some new ones. If your goals were not met but you are making steady progress, you may just want to stick with your plan awhile longer. If you are still far from making the changes you'd hoped for, perhaps you need to review the list of ideas you generated in Phase 2 and consider rewriting your action plan or modifying your goals.

USING TIME-MANAGEMENT STRATEGIES FOR DEFINING YOUR ROLE AS COACH

There is clearly some work involved in becoming an efficient time manager. It is quite possible that you may need only to fine-tune your current time-management strategies as you begin your new role as reading coach, without using the four-phase problem-solving process. However, one area where coaches often find a need for this more formal course of action is the ongoing process of defining their role as reading coach.

Recall how in Chapter 3 we presented "entry" into a new system as an ongoing process? We also mentioned that even if the amount of work you begin doing as a coach is rather small at first, your workload is likely to grow . . . and grow? As this starts to happen, we strongly advise that you return to this time-management problem-solving strategy. It can generate concrete data to use when holding professional discussions with your supervisor about how you are spending your time.

As your role develops and expands, and the full benefits of having a reading coach in the building becomes more obvious, your supervisor will probably begin to think of more tasks that you could do—all of which you readily agree will truly help improve students' reading outcomes in your school. It is also likely that at this same time more and more teachers, and perhaps even some parents, have learned what a valuable resource a reading coach can be in helping them work with their students or their children. At some point, you may begin to feel overwhelmed and also sense that you just cannot stretch out your time any further and continue to perform in a professional manner. To address this concern, it is not very effective to simply stop by the principal's office and shout, "You've got to help me! I just have too much work to do!" This is especially ineffective if you just happen to stop by the office when the principal is also feeling buried by workload demands! We have a better approach than creating an uproar, one that is much more likely to make a real difference in getting your supervisor to pay attention to your concerns.

Rather than just dropping by, make an appointment with your supervisor. Pick a time of day when things in the office tend to have calmed down a bit. Bring along some time-management data you have collected over the past week or so to document just exactly how much time you are spending on various tasks. (For this kind of high-stakes discussion about time management—which can have an impact on your job definition—we suggest you consider using a formal system such as the 3T-SR (Hasbrouck et al, 2003) for monitoring time, rather than just a journal or log. The 3T-SR has been validated as an accurate data-collection system and provides an easily interpreted graph of the ratio of time to tasks.

Begin your discussion by acknowledging that you have heard your supervisor's requests for you to take on additional tasks and that you agree that these tasks are important and valuable. Your discussion could go something like this:

> Thank you for making time to meet with me. I know how busy you are. I read your e-mail outlining your ideas for new responsibilities you'd like me to assume as part of my work as the reading coach. I agree with you that all of the tasks you listed are very valuable and are ones that really do need to be done. I'm also flattered and pleased that you believe that I would be able to do these important jobs for our school. I do feel confident that I could do them well, and I would sincerely like to add these tasks to my role. However, because of our frequent conversations, I know you understand how busy I already am. In fact, I've collected some data over the past two weeks to document how I am currently spending my time. [Show the graphed results of your personal time survey.] Given that you are my supervisor, I'd really appreciate your guidance and input about what tasks I should stop doing, or cut back on, so that I'll have sufficient time to add these new

responsibilities to my workload. Or perhaps there are some suggestions you could offer about how I could be doing my work more efficiently?"

A conversation such as this is very different from a stressed-out gripe session about how overworked and undervalued you are, isn't it? This kind of calm, rational, data-based professional discussion can be very enlightening to both you and your supervisor. It can be the beginning of an important discussion about what a reading coach should be expected to do and which resources can be used to help get all of the important tasks accomplished. (*Note:* It may also be helpful to have your supervisor have an opportunity to read this book—or at least Chapter 10: "A Note to Administrators Who Work With Reading Coaches." That final chapter is a synopsis of the entire book, with emphasis on the importance of having the administrator and coach work collaboratively to define—and redefine—the coach's role and responsibilities.)

Communication

Coaching is an important and challenging job. Skillful coaching requires the mastery of many important skills, along with a substantial professional knowledge base. Most knowledgeable educators agree that a key foundational skill for a coach is the ability to listen, understand, empathize, and share information effectively with colleagues. This is the skill of *communication*.*

A RELATIONSHIP SKILL

It may seem strange to see a section on communication in a book for reading coaches. Clearly, someone who has been asked to take on the role of coach is a person who has already shown a mastery of communication skills. Communicating is a part of daily life. It is vital for both establishing and maintaining relationships. We all learned how to talk, listen, respond, and converse with others long ago and have many years of practice under our belts. You may even have taken a course in communication skills somewhere along the way and are now familiar with the basic terms of communication such as active

---

* We are aware that interpersonal exchanges are governed by specific cultural influences and expectations. It is imperative for coaches and consultants to be aware when attempting to engage in formal communications with peers, colleagues, or parents from a different cultural or linguistic background that there is a need to "establish and maintain sensitive and responsible cross-cultural interactions" (Harris, 1991, p. 27). Our book addresses communication skills most used in the majority culture in the United States, with acknowledgment that variations on some of our recommendations might need to be made for working with those from culturally and linguistically diverse backgrounds.

listening, paraphrasing, summarizing, and open-ended or closed-ended questions.

A PROFESSIONAL SKILL

We have a good reason for including an overview of communication skills in our book. While most of us do, in fact, have perfectly adequate communication skills for daily life, the work of a coach frequently requires the use of strategic and well-practiced communication skills to help you first establish a professional relationship with a colleague and later facilitate communication with someone who may be feeling deeply frustrated, angry, anxious, suspicious, irritated, confused, or embarrassed. We developed this section of our book to assist you with situations such as these.

Here is an important rule of communication: The more *tense and high stake and confusing* the situation, the more you need to be *skillful* and *formal* in your communication. This is true in professional situations, as well as personal ones. A skillful and formal manner of communicating uses the same basic skills of listening and responding as we use in the normal, daily conversations we all have, but it becomes more *focused* and *intense*. And, in those inevitable tense and high-stake situations, you need to have rehearsed your advanced communication skills well. Having simply attended a three-hour workshop on effective communication a few years ago will not help you much when you are faced with a furious parent or a frustrated and apprehensive colleague. It is certainly helpful to be aware of what good communication skills are, but that is just the first step. It is essential that you spend time learning the skills and give yourself time to practice them by rehearsing some challenging situations that might come up.

NONVERBAL COMMUNICATION TECHNIQUES

We'll start our overview of communication skills by discussing how to present yourself physically in formal communication. Egan (1994) reminds us that high-stake or tense interpersonal transactions require an "intensity of presence" (p. 91). If you are perceived as being deeply attentive during such interactions, you transmit positive messages about the importance of the other person and how much you value what he or she is saying to you. A disengaged presence can promote distrust and hesitancy. The way you orient yourself physically during formal communications can contribute to this sense of disengagement.

THE SOLER TECHNIQUE

We've adapted the acronym SOLER (*s*it squarely, *o*pen posture, *l*eaning forward, *e*ye contact, *r*elaxed) from Egan to describe the "microskills" used to attend to the person with whom you are communicating:

- **S**: *Sit squarely* in front of the other person. If possible, arrange to sit so there is no desk between you, although it may be that when you are meeting with another teacher in his or her own classroom, that teacher may at first feel more comfortable while seated at the desk. Try to not to twist in your seat as you chat. Facing another person directly is associated with a nonverbal message of engagement and availability.

- **O**: Maintain an *open* posture. Avoid crossing your arms or legs, or allowing an angry or anxious expression to be revealed on your face. Of course, simply crossing your legs does not prevent you in any way from attending to a personal interaction fully. What is important, however, is how your posture and gestures are *interpreted* by those you are coaching.

- **L**: *Lean forward* slightly as you speak and listen. Egan (1994) notes that "in North-American culture, a slight inclination toward a person is often seen as saying, 'I'm with you, I'm interested in you and in what you have to say'" (p. 92), whereas leaning backward can imply lack of engagement or even boredom.

- **E**: Maintain *eye* contact. People engaged in deep, meaningful conversation almost appear to have "locked" their eyes on each other. In a professional conversation it is important to find the right intensity for eye contact. It is not negative to glance away occasionally (such as taking a look at your notes or the folder of information you brought along), but make sure your eye contact suggests real interest and involvement. The amount and intensity of eye contact has definite cultural implications. If you are coaching or consulting with members of culturally or linguistically diverse groups, you will need to adapt this and some of the other recommendations regarding the use of communication skills (Harris, 1991).

- **R**: Throughout the process, try to be as *relaxed* as possible. Bolton (1979) calls this "relaxed alertness," suggesting that you are relaxed and comfortable but also caring and attentive. If you can communicate a sense of calm, you can greatly influence the mood and direction of the conversation. This ability to stay relaxed while fully engaged in intense and at times emotionally challenging professional conversations comes only from practice and rehearsal.

As you begin to master the SOLER technique you can also become aware of any adjustments or censoring of a reaction you may have to do during a conversation. If you feel yourself beginning to tense up or feel angry or threatened, perhaps scowling, crossing your arms, or leaning back away from the other person, use that moment as an opportunity to ask yourself about where those negative reactions are coming from and think about positive ways to deal with those challenges so you can keep the communication moving ahead.

NOT JUST LISTENING, *ACTIVE* LISTENING

The most important single skill involved in communication is the act of listening. Skillful communicators do not just hear the words being spoken; they work hard to understand the *meaning* of what is being said, interpreting the stated words and the unstated, nonverbal communication. A cartoon once captured this well with the following statement: *"I know you believe you understand what you think I said, but I am not sure you realize that what you heard is not what I meant."* A goal for a skillful coach should be to hear the meaning behind and between the spoken words.

Using a process known as *active listening* enhances purposeful, focused listening. Active listening is more *dynamic and engaged* than passive. Westra (1996) suggests that engaging in active listening requires starting with a certain attitude or mind-set about the communication process. An active listener must be and do the things we list here (which, by the way, are a great list of attributes for a successful reading coach!). An active listener must:

- Have empathy
- Be authentic
- Postpone interpretation
- Suspend judgment
- Stay attentive to the speaker
- Have patience

USE MINIMAL ENCOURAGERS (VERBAL AND NONVERBAL)

While someone is talking, it can be helpful to use what Bolton (1979) calls "minimal encouragers," neutral verbal and nonverbal indications that acknowledge you are following what is being said. These have also been referred to as the "grunts and groans" of conversation. The most common of the *verbal* minimal encouragers are probably "Uh, huh" or "Mm-hmmm," which both imply, "Please continue—I'm listening and I understand what you are saying." Most people have their own favorite sets of minimal encouragers, such as "I see," "Oh?" "Really?" "Right," or "Go on." Nodding while maintaining a neutral or serious facial expression is probably the most common of the *nonverbal* encouragers.

Good communicators also must have the *patience to wait* through pauses and silences. Most "listeners" simply talk too much. Silence can be necessary to allow the speaker to collect thoughts, reflect, or sort out options about what to say and how to say it. As an active listener, you can use periods of silence to review your SOLER position and communicate empathy and attentiveness.

MORE VERBAL LISTENING SKILLS

There are several more types of verbal responses that are typically recommended as part of effective listening: *reflecting, paraphrasing, asking questions, summarizing, avoiding jargon,* and *avoiding unnecessary interruptions.*

Reflecting.

One recommended verbal response is *reflecting,* which can be defined as a response that focuses on the speaker's feelings (or *affect*) by providing feedback about what he or she appears to be experiencing. The listener offers a guess or hunch, based on cues obtained from the speaker's presentation, both verbal and nonverbal. A reflective response is nonjudgmental and concise. For example, if a teacher is relating in great detail about all the various ways she has attempted to help one of her students improve his reading fluency with little or no effect, a reading coach might reflect, "Gee, you've really worked hard trying to help Lenny. Seeing no improvement in his fluency must have made you feel very frustrated." You are not commenting on the quality or appropriateness of the interventions the teacher has tried. You are only acknowledging that she has worked hard and is probably feeling a bit discouraged. Skillful reflecting can help verify a speaker's emotional state and help the speaker become more aware of the feelings a situation is generating. This can be a big step in establishing trust; it's good for a teacher to be thinking, "That coach really hears what I'm trying to say—the coach *gets it*." Once a teacher knows his or her feelings have been "heard," that teacher may be more ready to move past the emotional reactions and on to a thoughtful, rationale process to tackle the problem.

Paraphrasing.

Another skill in active listening is *paraphrasing*, a succinct response that restates the essence of the speaker's content in the listener's own words. Paraphrasing can convey that you are carefully attending to what is being said and are seriously attempting to follow it. A skillful paraphrase is condensed and concise, a statement of the essential facts and ideas of the speaker's message rather than the feelings. A paraphrase can help cut through the "clutter" of presented details and highlight the fundamentals. It is critical to avoid parroting (an exact repetition of the speaker's own words), which usually inhibits rather than encourages continued conversation. An example of a good paraphrase is:

> TEACHER: I know that we are supposed to be collaborating and working together, but I'm just not sure I can work with Regina's special education teacher. He only has an alternative certification and he's already told me he has no experience working with kids with reading problems like Regina's.
>
> COACH: OK. I think I see. You're concerned about having to work with the special education teacher because you are concerned about the quality of his professional preparation and his lack of experience.

Asking questions.

During active listening, it also may be necessary to ask questions. As a coach, you are listening for a specific purpose: to help guide your colleague through a collaborative problem-solving process to improve students' reading outcomes. In a later section on interviewing, we'll tell you in detail how to obtain information strategically and efficiently to develop an appropriate reading intervention plan. Here we will mention just a few general questioning procedures for use in active listening. One type of questioning is *clarifying*, whereby listeners ascertain that

the message being sent by the speaker is being correctly interpreted. A clarifying question may follow a paraphrase: "Did I get that right?" A listener may also need to check if a reflection of feelings was correct. This is called a *perception check*. Some questions can be used to seek *elaboration*: "Can you tell me a bit more about the types of things you've already tried with this student?" This is an example of a *closed-end question*, asked to obtain specific information. This type of question attempts to elicit a limited response. The purpose of an *open-ended question* is to begin a conversation, to start the flow of shared information, without direction or an agenda. An open-ended question could be: "Please tell me your concerns about Kelly's reading."

Summarizing.

As a conversation continues, there will be moments when it is important to *summarize* the important bits of information that have been offered so far. Summarizing is a method of tying together the most relevant ideas at key moments in the conversation. Summaries can be especially important when information has been shared in a rather fragmented manner, which is common when emotions are running high. A summary should be a fairly brief restatement of the important themes, issues, and feelings that have been expressed. The listener can use the summary to share some tentative conclusions and receive feedback to make sure the conclusions are accurate. A well-constructed summary can help the speaker see an integrated version of the concerns and issues that have been shared. In the formal problem-solving process, summarizing is a way to bring closure to one phase of the process and make the transition to the next phase. Summarizing helps move the process forward in a productive manner.

Avoiding jargon.

During active listening in a coaching situation, it is important for the coach to *avoid using jargon* or professional terminology that may not be familiar to the speaker. In this same vein, avoid using slang as well. This can be an issue especially for younger beginning teachers who may developed have a relaxed manner of communicating among their peers at college and may find themselves using informal (and unprofessional!) slang phrases such as, "So, I hoped that, you know, we could, like, find some time to get together?" or "I kinda wanted to ask you some questions . . ." or "I was talking with her mom and she goes, 'I don't want to talk now,' and I go, 'Well, we need to talk sometime,' and she goes . . ." If you feel you may be using these kinds of informal slang terms in your speech, tape-record yourself or ask a trusted colleague to give you some honest feedback.

A major purpose of professional conversations for a reading coach is to build collaborative relationships with the goal of helping to address students' academic problems. Using words that are unknown, unclear, or possibly intimidating to the speaker could serve to make the speaker feel uncomfortable, unimportant, irrelevant, or incompetent. This is clearly not what a coach should be trying to achieve. Monitor your own language choices and be sure to encourage the speaker to stop you at any time you may unconsciously use a term or phrase that may be unfamiliar or unclear. A coach can encourage such behavior through modeling. For example, if a speaker uses a word or term that may be unclear, use that as an opportunity to stop the conversation and ask, "I need to ask, what do you mean when you say your student's parents are just wacky. Can you clarify what you mean by 'wacky'?"

Avoiding unnecessary interruptions.

An active listener also knows that it is important to *interrupt as infrequently as possible* with questions or reactions. This, of course, needs to be balanced with the responsibility to manage the problem-solving process efficiently and effectively. This responsibility may at times require the coach to interrupt to cut off the speaker. When a speaker is beginning to ramble, speaking about things that are not relevant or helpful to the problem-solving process, repeating information already shared, or seems unsure how to terminate the conversation, a coach can "interrupt" in a purposeful way, perhaps by reflecting the speaker's feelings, paraphrasing, asking questions, or summarizing strategically: "Let me interrupt here. I think I have a good idea at this point about what your concerns are, and I'm watching the time. You mentioned that you needed to be back in your classroom by 2:45 and we're getting close to that time. Let's see if I can summarize your concerns correctly."

LEARNING TO BE A SKILLFUL COMMUNICATOR: PRACTICE MAKES PERFECT

Most of the time you won't be using communication skills in such a formal manner. As a coach, you will frequently hold conversations with colleagues, parents, and administrators without thinking twice about how you are sitting or standing or whether you should summarize or paraphrase what was just said. However, there will be circumstances when you are faced with a communication challenge, where someone has strong emotions or passionate beliefs about a topic that needs to be addressed. When these situations arise, be sure you have practiced all these critically important skills and are so comfortable and confident that using them feels effortless. When you have to stop and think about what to say next or how to respond to what a colleague or parent just said, you have stopped listening.

ROLE-PLAYING YOUR WAY TO SKILLFUL COMMUNICATION

In our training sessions with coaches over the years, we have found that the very best way to become a skillful communicator is through role-playing, ideally in a group with three participants. Find a couple of willing colleagues (perhaps other coaches from your district?) who also want to improve their professional communication skills. To begin, each person who is participating should independently read the "Communication" section in this chapter. Then, get together to identify, define, and discuss the components of skillful communication: active listening, nonverbal communication skills, SOLER, reflecting feelings, paraphrasing, asking questions, summarizing, avoiding jargon, and avoiding unnecessary interruptions.

After studying the information on communicating, set aside 45 minutes to an hour so the three of you can meet for a practice session. During this session, each person takes one turn in three different roles: *Coach*, *Colleague/ Parent*, and *Observer*. The Coach and Colleague/Parent engage in a dialogue, discussing an emotionally charged situation presented by the Colleague/Parent. The Observer monitors this conversation and notes the Coach's use of key communication skills.

Each participant should come to the practice session with a scenario relevant to situations that a reading coach may encounter and be ready to perform as the person in the scenario who is seeking support or assistance from the Coach. The person seeking help could be a parent who is seriously concerned about the instruction his or her child is receiving in a reading class, a teacher who is angry at the principal about the lack of support for using a certain commercial reading program, or a teacher who is overwhelmed by a low-performing student who is also engaging in challenging behaviors. It is ideal for the participant taking on this role in a scenario to have personally experienced this situation or one like it and to be able to share some details while playing out that role. The scenario is not shared with the Coach or the Observer ahead of time. All details of the situation are shared only through role-playing, as the Coach asks questions of the Colleague/Parent. Remember, the scenario should have enough details (real or imagined) to enable a conversation of about 10 minutes.

After about 10 minutes, the Observer tells the participants that time is up, and the Coach brings closure to the dialogue. The Observer then leads the Coach and the Colleague/Parent through a structured, three-way debriefing that should last about 5 minutes. After debriefing, everyone switches roles, and the process begins again with a new scenario.

This type of practice works best if everyone participating makes a serious effort to stay "in role." If the Colleague/Parent, the Coach, or the Observer interrupts the conversation to make a comment such as "I feel so silly" or "Wow, you sure are reminding me of a parent I worked with a few years ago!" the practice opportunity will be seriously diminished.

Playing the Colleague/Parent role.

When you take on the role of the Colleague/Parent, you get a chance to show off your hidden theatrical talents! Remember, the purpose of this session is primarily to provide the person who is role-playing the Coach an opportunity to practice using good communication skills in a potentially challenging condition. The Colleague/Parent should display emotions such as anger, frustration, aggravation, discouragement, pessimism, helplessness, and confusion as honestly and realistically as possible. However, try not to be so "over the top" that the Coach is presented with an impossible situation.

Playing the Coach role.

When you role-play the Coach, you simply need to practice your best communication skills by listening and responding appropriately as the Colleague/Parent shares concerns. The Colleague/Parent needs to feel as if he or she has been heard. This is *not* the time to try to figure out how to "solve" the problem being presented to you. As you role-play, think of this kind of initial dialogue with a Colleague/Parent as an information-gathering opportunity, as well as a chance to build a professional, collegial relationship. In Chapter 5, we will talk about engaging in a systematic problem-solving process, and in Chapter 6, we'll discuss how to gather information to solve problems. For now, your task is simply to listen and respond.

The Coach begins the role-playing with introductions. ("Hi. I'm Natalie Donahue, the reading coach. I was told you wanted to see me. I have about 10 minutes to visit with you right now. Is this a convenient time?") Follow this with an open-ended question to give the person playing Colleague/Parent a chance to provide you with background information. ("So tell me, what's going on with your daughter?") From there, ask additional closed- or open-ended questions to obtain additional information and provide clarification or elaboration. Spend 10 minutes or so responding to the answers, as appropriate, with paraphrasing, summarizing, reflecting feelings, and other techniques. Remember to practice your SOLER posture and to use some minimal encouragers. When the time is up, or the dialogue has come to a natural end, the Coach brings closure to the conversation, perhaps by summarizing what has been shared and making suggestions about what might happen next. ("Thank you for taking the time to let me know about this situation. I think that I may be able to be helpful as we identify some possible next steps to take.")

Role-playing the Observer.

The Observer has three responsibilities: (1) monitoring the time during the practice session; (2) observing and taking notes about the Coach's communication skills; and (3) facilitating the debriefing session. During the conversation, the Observer takes detailed notes about the communication skills the Coach is using. You may want to use a photocopy of the *Communication Skills Practice Form* (see Appendix) to organize your note-taking. The more specific and concrete you can make your notes, the more helpful they will be for the other participants. After about 10 minutes, the Observer lets the Coach know that time is up so the Coach can end the conversation appropriately.

When the Coach has wrapped up the session, the Observer immediately leads the participants through a structured, three-step debriefing process that usually lasts about 5 minutes:

- Step 1: The Observer starts by asking the Colleague/Parent: "How well did you feel the Coach listened and responded to your concerns? What skill did the Coach use most effectively in communicating with you? Do you have any suggestions for the Coach?"

- Step 2: The Observer shares observations made from the notes and offers comments about what the Coach did well. The Observer also makes suggestions for ways the Coach may improve next time.

- Step 3: The Coach has the opportunity to share impressions about the conversation. After the debriefing is complete, the roles are switched for a new scenario until all three participants have played all three roles.

REHEARSE YOUR COMMUNICATION SKILLS FOR THOSE CHALLENGING CONVERSATIONS

Even skillful, experienced professional communicators feel the need to keep their skills well practiced. If you know that a potentially difficult conversation with a teacher, administrator, or parent has been scheduled, it is quite appropriate to rehearse the situation ahead of time. Ask a friend, spouse, or peer to spend a few minutes role-playing with you. Or just run some possible dialogues in your head and try out responses. Don't let these rehearsals take you so far that you have memorized pat answers. This gets in the way of careful listening. Instead, use rehearsal

times to assure yourself that you will be able to handle strong emotions or other communication challenges.

POSTPONING CONVERSATIONS

Good, productive communication cannot occur when one or more parties remains angry. Problems will not be solved when participants are so frustrated that their purpose in meeting with you is simply to express rage or vent anger. It is perfectly appropriate for you to end any conversation in which you feel threatened or unsafe or in any situation where it appears that a participant wants only to express aggravation. In such a situation, the professional response is to reschedule the session. If you feel you are in physical danger, remove yourself immediately from the scenario or move to an area where others may be available to provide assistance. For instance: "Mrs. Kingston, I can see you are still very angry about what has been happening with Joshua's teachers. I sincerely am interested in working with you to solve this problem to your satisfaction, but I don't believe we can make any progress today when you are so upset. Perhaps you could accompany me to the office where we can see if the principal may be available to hear your concerns?"

Conclusion

Learning how to manage your time and how to communicate skillfully and purposefully will greatly enhance your ability to provide excellent coaching services to your colleagues, administrators, and parents. Using time efficiently and communicating effectively with a wide variety of people will allow you to focus on the important task of coaching: helping all students become the best readers they can be!

5

SYSTEMATIC PROBLEM SOLVING

In Chapter 3, we talked about how one of three roles of an SFC reading coach is that of Collaborative Problem Solver. In our work with coaches and consultants since the mid 1980s, we have found it extremely useful to have a problem-solving process in our "bag of tricks" to help coaches fill this important and challenging role. A structured process provides coaches with a strategy for working with a colleague to tackle a range of problems, from the relatively simple, everyday kinds of concerns to the extremely complex problems—as many reading challenges are—involving academic, behavioral, and social-emotional concerns that often extend beyond the walls of a classroom into the school, home, and community.

A generic process for problem solving has long existed (for examples, see D'Zurilla & Goldfried, 1971; Gick, 1986; Hayes,1989; Krulik & Rudnick, 1984; Rubenstein & Firstenberg, 1987; VanGundy, 1987; Voss, Tyler, & Yengo, 1983) and has been used across many disciplines including business, mathematics, chemistry, engineering, and social sciences. In this generic model, four steps have been identified:

1. Identify the problem to be solved

2. Develop a solution

3. Implement the solution

4. Evaluate the effectiveness of the implemented solution

What occurs in each phase of the problem-solving process is fairly self-explanatory. The first phase involves accurately identifying what the problem actually entails. Once a clear and precise definition of the concern has been developed, the second phase is to design a plan to solve the problem. The plan then needs to be implemented and, finally, an evaluation should be conducted to determine the degree to which the problem has been solved. Simple, right?

Well . . . yes, at times it is, in fact, fairly simple. But while a four-phase process to tackle problems sounds rather straightforward, in the real world things quickly get more challenging because the problems themselves can be quite complex. This is certainly true when we think about the kinds of challenges that reading coaches face. Academic issues are frequently multifaceted, and to fully analyze most reading problems, a coach must consider all of the contributing variables. These can include the quality and nature of instruction; curriculum materials; skill and experience of the teacher; classroom environment; any disabilities or learning problems a student may have; the effect of the academic problem on the student's behavior, motivation, and self-esteem; and more. Just knowing about a four-phase problem-solving process is certainly not sufficient.

Systematic Problem Solving

Systematic Problem Solving (SPS) involves moving from problem to solution using a traditional four-phase process: (1) problem identification and verification; (2) problem formulation and intervention development; (3) intervention implementation; and (4) evaluation (see Figure 5.1).

The problem-solving process that we have developed for reading coaches also involves four phases, which mirror the more generic SPS. However, in our work with coaches and consultants over the years, we've adapted and customized each phase to more precisely match coaches' specific problem-solving needs. Our SPS for coaching proceeds though the following four phases:

1. Problem presentation
2. Defining the problem, setting goals, developing a plan
3. Implementing the plan
4. Evaluation and next steps

(*Note:* Before a teacher involves a coach or consultant in a student's academic, behavioral, or social-emotional concern, it is necessary to have contacted the student's parents. Parents should be involved whenever there is a concern about their child's performance at school. Some schools or districts may have a specific written policy about obtaining parental permission before even considering the development of an individual remedial or intervention plan for a student. Be sure you know what the policies and procedures are regarding parental notification before you begin SPS.)

In the Student-Focused Coaching model, collaborative problem-solving forms the basic structure for all coaching processes. It is the framework that a coach should use to address all his or her work with colleagues. A collaborative problem-solving process often begins with a brief overview of how SPS will proceed. Many teachers assume that in your role as coach, you will simply listen to their descriptions of problems and then immediately provide a "prescription," or solution, for solving them. Although there may be some occasions when you can quickly give advice or suggest a plan of action to a teacher (we'll discuss this later in this chapter), in most cases you'll find that you are much more successful if you follow some version of the more detailed SPS procedure. A coach may find that in some cases it is best to use the SPS process only as a framework or roadmap for problem-solving that is not shared with the teacher. As you incorporate this process in your coaching, you will be able to determine when to make the process more "public" and when to keep the SPS process working behind the scenes.

In this chapter, we will present SPS as a process that involves a coach working with one teacher who shares a concern about one student. We want you to be aware that the process can work equally well in other situations. You can also use SPS to work with a teacher who has a concern about a *group* of students. This includes a concern about students in a teacher's lowest reading group who are not making progress or a concern about a content area class (such as science or social studies) where some students are struggling with the reading and writing requirements of the course. Yet another model for using SPS includes a coach working with a parent and a teacher together, often called conjoint consultation (Hughes, Hasbrouck, Serdahl, Heidgerken, & McHaney, 2001). The direct participation of parents in a strategic problem-solving process can be powerful, especially for problems that involve behavioral or social-emotional concerns.

PHASE 1: PROBLEM PRESENTATION

The first phase of the SPS process begins when a teacher (or parent or principal) who seeks your assistance as a reading coach tells you about a concern. This usually occurs during a meeting the teacher schedules with you, perhaps after school or during a shared planning period.

Get the facts of the case.

The problem presentation meeting between the teacher and reading coach usually takes the form of an interview. (*Note:* Chapter 6 provides detailed information about the process of conducting interviews with teachers, as well as with students and parents.) The teacher describes the current status of the problem, shares information about the student who is having the difficulty, presents a bit of history about when the problem started, and describes what has been tried so far (if anything) to address the problem. The teacher may also provide other details that can help you get a more complete picture of the concern, such as whether the student is receiving any special services or significant details the teacher may have about the student's academic background or family situation.

Using data from observations or assessments to direct and facilitate educational endeavors has been shown to be a key tool used by schools whose students achieve outstanding success in reading (Denton, Foorman, & Mathes, 2003; Parker, O'Neill, Hall, & Hasbrouck, 2004). Some schools require referring teachers to bring such data to an initial discussion with a coach about a student's academic problem. This can include information from an informal academic assessment that may address such things as:

- How often does the student complete assigned work? Always? Usually? Sometimes? Rarely? Never?
- Is the quality of the work satisfactory?

- Does the student do well in one subject but not in another?

It can also be helpful to analyze some of the student's work samples or even review the results from an informal reading inventory (IRI) that includes oral reading fluency data, which has been shown to be a highly accurate indication of a student's overall reading performance (Fuchs, Fuchs, Hosp, & Jenkins, 2001). (We recommend that you consider reading "Intervention D: Academic Assistance" in Sprick, Sprick, & Garrison [1993] for more helpful details about how a coach and a teacher can use an academic inventory. Chapter 6 also provides a guide for collecting information for SPS.)

Obtain relevant current and historical information.

Problem solvers understand how important it is to get as much background information as possible. Be prepared to ask specific questions to get a sense of the status of the problem. These questions may include:

- Is the student's reading challenge currently getting worse? Better? Is it pretty stable?
- What interventions have you tried?
- Have the student's parents been involved?
- Have other teachers been involved?

Obtain relevant contextual information.

Along with the specific, concrete details of the case, a coach must be fully attentive to other information that is presented, sometimes between the lines. While some of the critical contextual details may be obtained by skillfully asking questions, some of the more sensitive information may have to be gleaned through careful observation of a teacher's body language, the choice of words, where the pauses or hesitations are made when presenting the information to you, and the sense of ownership or blame regarding the problem. A coach must pay special attention during the Phase 1 interview to gather critical contextual information about the teacher's tolerances, philosophy, background, skills, teaching style, and so on. In training coaches and consultants, we describe this as having your special "coaching antenna" turned on while working through problems with your colleagues. Of course, all of this is most important in your first collaboration with a teacher. Once you have established a professional relationship, you will already have a sense of

this kind of background information when you collaborate in the future.

Keep in mind that in the next phase of SPS, you will collaborate with the teacher to develop an intervention plan designed to specifically address the teacher's concern. If such a plan is going to be effective, no matter how carefully it has been designed, it must first be implemented. Developing a plan that does not adequately reflect the teacher's personal philosophy of instruction, a plan that could not be easily implemented because of the way the teacher has organized the classroom, or a plan that requires specific knowledge, training, resources, skills or experience that the teacher does not have would probably result in a plan that never gets off the ground, let alone one that can be used effectively (Voss et al., 1983; Witt, 1986).

Veteran versus novice problem solving.

This problem presentation phase is a crucial one in the SPS process and frequently requires more time and skill than you might initially think. Swanson, O'Connor, and Cooney (1990) and Gick (1986) identified some of the differences in the ways veteran and novice problem solvers approach a presented concern. Experienced and skillful problem solvers know that a key to their success is to be certain that all efforts are directed to the actual problem, not a "supposed" problem or a "proxy" problem. Novice problem solvers can find themselves intimidated or even nearly panic-stricken very early in this phase, in part because within moments of hearing the problem being described, they often begin a frantic mental search for "*The* Solution" to the problem. Sometimes they may even begin to carry on an anxious internal dialogue: "Oh, yikes! I've never had to deal with a problem like this one before. I have *no idea* what should be done about this! What am I going to say to this teacher? Why did I ever think I could be a coach anyway? I'm a complete fraud and the teacher is soon going to figure this out." Anyone who is busy thinking thoughts such as these and feeling this apprehensive about what solution to suggest cannot be listening intently to the factual information being presented, let alone attending to the more subtle contextual information!

Veteran problem solvers approach this SPS phase very differently. To begin with, experienced problem solvers know that there is never, ever "*The* Solution" to any problem, so they waste little mental energy trying to come up with one. These pros also know that it is their responsibility as the expert problem solver to direct the process carefully and not rush through any of the steps. Although one goal of coaching is always to solve the referred problem, achieving this goal is not the problem solver's responsibility alone; it must be a shared responsibility. And, importantly, the veterans also know that the problem being initially described to them ultimately may not even end up being the targeted concern. So why worry now about a possible solution? These veteran problem solvers stay cool, calm, and collected throughout this process.

The coach with two brains!

One way even beginning coaches can emulate the veteran problem solvers is to approach the problem presentation phase of SPS using two different "brains." The task of the "first brain" is to listen intently to all of the information being presented. This brain reminds us to use our best communication skills:

- Use the SOLER position
- Reflect feelings
- Paraphrase content
- Ask questions to clarify
- Check perceptions
- Seek elaboration
- Summarize at transitions
- Avoid jargon and unnecessary interruptions

Using that first brain, the coach carefully and fully attends to the content of what is being shared. The coach accepts the information being presented as the speaker's vision of the problem and understands that to ultimately address this issue effectively, the coach must have clear picture of the presenter's *interpretation* or *perception* of the concern, regardless of its accuracy. This first brain is also the one using a special coaching antenna, which is busily noting any subtle clues to things like the teacher's belief systems, tolerances, and philosophy.

In contrast, the coach's "second brain" is taking almost the opposite approach. This brain is maintaining the stance of the ultimate skeptic and remains thoroughly unconvinced of the presented information: "Yeah, yeah . . . *maybe* this student's reading is really as low as the teacher is saying; *maybe* the problem is just inadequate curriculum materials; *maybe* this teacher has tried everything in the book before calling me in to help. I'll believe it when I see it for myself." Staying at least somewhat dubious at this stage of the process can help guide a coach to remember to fully explore the true nature of the problem, understanding that teachers or parents who have had to live with a challenging problem for a period of time may have lost their perspective about the facts and may be so emotionally involved that they have difficulty staying objective or presenting relevant details in an objective, unbiased manner.

Hidden agendas.

At times you may find yourself working with a teacher whom you feel may be carefully editing the information being shared with you. Perhaps a teacher is trying to paint a picture of the situation that is somewhat different than objective reality. At times, a teacher may want you to help with a hidden agenda and for a variety of reasons may not want to discuss this openly. For example, a teacher may truly believe that a student has been inappropriately placed in his or her classroom and should be moved to a full-time special education setting or another alternative placement. What this teacher wants is ultimately to have the student removed but is reluctant to say this to you directly. Instead, the teacher may give you a mixed message, saying aloud: "I'm hoping that by working with you I can find some way to help Gerald improve his reading" while thinking: *"If this goes the way I hope it will, Gerald will be out of my classroom soon."*

At times, teachers may not believe that some of their problems can or should be addressed by a classroom intervention. They may believe that some problems are in fact unsolvable due to external conditions, such as a student's home situation, racial or cultural background, or another situation that is not politically correct to discuss openly. A teacher might be reluctant to say, "Well, you and I both know that Maria's reading skills are not going to get any better no matter what we try. Her parents don't even speak English, and Maria told me neither of them even knows how to read. Anyway, none of the kids who live in that apartment complex behind Wal-Mart ever do well in school, ever."

It is certainly challenging to work with teachers who have a hidden agenda or strongly held negative beliefs about students or their families. We have found that just engaging in a skillfully managed SPS process can sometimes bring some new awareness and an attitude shift to some teachers. However, it also may be necessary at times to confront a teacher and challenge that teacher's ideas about what some students can or cannot do. A challenge is not picking a fight but an invitation for a colleague to reexamine some internal thinking or external behavior that seems to be self-defeating, harmful to others, or both, and ultimately to change those patterns (Egan, 1994). Keeping that skeptical "second brain" and your coaching "antenna" actively engaged will help you cope with these rare situations.

Developing questions or hypotheses.

To move the initial activity of presenting a problem to targeting the problem, the coach needs to be mentally formulating a list of questions or hypotheses about the presented information that will have to be addressed. You will be developing this mental list at the same time you are listening to the teacher's version of the concern. While your "first brain" is listening attentively to the factual information, the "antenna" are busy picking up any subtle background issues, and the "second brain" is reacting with suspicion to each piece of information presented. Whew! There's a lot going on here!

These questions or hypotheses you are forming are important because they will help guide you and the teacher to collect additional, important information to either help confirm the problem as presented or provide an alternative vision of the concern. Either way, before beginning the next phase of the process, the coach knows that in almost every case additional data will help the overall outcome to be successful. Table 5.1 provides some examples of questions (Q) or hypotheses (H) that you may come up with while listening to a teacher present a student's reading problem.

Certainly, some of the questions that form in your mind during the problem presentation should be asked directly during this initial meeting, or at least you can use questions to probe to see whether a hypothesis seems to be confirmed or should be rejected. For example, if a teacher says "Joshua cannot read any of the materials I'm using in my classroom," and you hypothesize that this teacher may have little experience teaching students at this grade level, you can simply ask a direct question about this: "Am I right in thinking that this is your first time teaching this grade level? Have you had any previous experience teaching kids at this level?" However, some of the questions or hypotheses will best be addressed by data collected outside of this meeting. For instance, if the teacher says: "I know Robin can do the work. She's just not trying hard enough," perhaps you might formulate

Table 5.1   Questions or Hypotheses Formed by the Coach

Teacher Comments	Questions or Hypotheses
"Joshua cannot read any of the materials I'm using in my classroom."	Q: What is Joshua's current reading level? Q: Is the problem primarily a decoding problem, a comprehension problem, or a combination of both? H: This is the first year this teacher has been teaching 4th grade. Perhaps this teacher has little experience with students whose reading skills are below level.
"I've tried everything I know to help Abigail, and I don't know what else to do!"	Q: What kinds of interventions have been tried? For how long? With what kind of results? H: Perhaps the teacher's knowledge of effective interventions is limited. H: Perhaps the teacher did not adequately implement a potentially effective intervention (too short a duration, an instructional program not accurately conducted, or another reason).
"I know Robin can do the work. She's just not trying hard enough."	Q: Is this a "can't do" problem or a "won't do" problem, or a combination? H: Perhaps this teacher doesn't know about ways to modify or adapt curriculum materials for students who are struggling readers.

this question in response: "Is this a 'can't-do' problem or a 'won't do' problem?" The best way to answer this question may be to complete a classroom observation or conduct a 1:1 interview and assessment with Robin herself.

Final Steps in Phase 1: Problem Presentation.

At this point, you should move toward bringing closure to this phase of the SPS process. Part of your responsibility as a coach is to manage the entire problem-solving process skillfully. Remember that until more objective data can be collected, information obtained at this stage can only reflect the teacher's *perceptions* about the problem. Spend just enough time on this to provide a general sense of the teacher's view of the problem and a focus for the next steps.

Before wrapping things up it is appropriate to (1) briefly summarize your understanding of the presented concern; (2) ask the teacher whether your summary is correct; and (3) ask whether the teacher wants to add any additional information. Then make a plan to collect any additional information you both agree will be needed to facilitate the development of the final, accurate problem definition in the next phase of the process. In most cases, especially if you are working with a teacher for the first time, this will usually involve conducting a classroom observation, which is always a rich source of the critical contextual information necessary for problem solving. (In Chapter 6, you will find detailed information on how to conduct and debrief classroom observations and collect other key data for problem solving.) We also suggest that you find ways to develop a collaborative approach to this problem by involving the teacher in the data collection process, as appropriate. Below is an example of how a coach might close this meeting during Phase 1: Problem Presentation, following a teacher's summary of the presented problem:

> "OK. It looks like I have a pretty good understanding of James's reading concerns. I certainly don't want to take up more of your valuable time than is necessary. As I explained earlier, the next step will be to schedule another meeting where we can start discussing what we can do to help James. Before we have that meeting, I usually find it very helpful if I schedule an observation of James's reading lesson. This gives me some important firsthand information we can use to make some good decisions about

how to help improve things for James. I'd also like to have a chance to visit with James and perhaps conduct some informal assessments to nail down what may be going on. You mentioned that you haven't talked to his teacher from last year. How would you feel about contacting the teacher to see whether you can find out whether James was also having problems last year and whether she tried anything that was particularly helpful? I also think it would be helpful for you to take some notes during the time you are working with James on his reading, noting errors he's making or other things you are noticing about his reading. When we get back together, we can discuss what we've both learned and then set some goals and develop a plan of action. How does that sound? OK, what time looks good for you to have me come into your class to watch James's reading group?"

If the teacher pushes you for a solution or advice, try to fend off the request with the reminder that it would be foolish for you to offer a suggestion without fully understanding the specifics of the problem. Point out that reading challenges are often complex. Jumping to a conclusion can often result in jumping into confusion!

PHASE 2: DEFINING THE PROBLEM, SETTING GOALS, DEVELOPING A PLAN

The second phase of the SPS process is perhaps the most involved because there are three parts to this phase: (1) defining the problem based on an analysis of comprehensive and concrete data; (2) helping the teacher to set some realistic and achievable goals; and (finally!) (3) developing an intervention plan to address the concern and reach the identified goals. This third part also includes designing an evaluation to assess the effectiveness of the intervention and mapping out a plan for how you, the coach, can support the teacher during the time the teacher is implementing the plan in the classroom.

Remember, the role of coaching in collaborative problem solving includes managing the SPS process skillfully. There are lots of important tasks involved in Phase 2. Try to find a way to complete all of them carefully and completely, being mindful of the time constraints of the teacher. Phase 2 may need to be divided across a couple of meetings, depending on the complexity of the problem being addressed.

Defining the problem.

Look at the data collected. The coach begins this next part of the SPS process by determining whether the plan to collect additional data was carried out. If not, the meeting should perhaps be rescheduled. If sufficient information has been collected, it should then be shared and analyzed collaboratively by the teacher and the coach. It is helpful to both model the problem-solving process to the teacher and to continue to build the important collaborative relationship by thinking aloud as you examine any newly collected information, asking the teacher to voice opinions: "Hmmm. This is interesting. What do you think about this?"

If the collected data included a classroom observation, begin the analysis of that information by asking an important question: "Was the day I was in your classroom to observe James's reading group fairly typical?" If the teacher does not consider that the observation was conducted on a typical day, that teacher will not believe the collected data, so don't waste too much time presenting it. In such a case, have a conversation about why the day was not a regular day, and perhaps schedule another observation. If the teacher does consider that the day of the observation was reasonably similar to a typical day, you can go ahead to present the information. Start with some positive comment about what you saw, if possible. As you present the information, you may find that the teacher begins to have an "ah-ha!" moment about what is going on. Because classroom observation data can be so powerful and informative, it is possible that this alone can give the teacher some ideas for the next steps.

Present and reflect upon any other collected information. Try to keep the focus on the key elements—those points that will lead to an accurate problem definition—rather than simply presenting and reviewing every piece of data. All the findings you share must be easily understood and interpreted by the teacher. You may find it helpful to translate data into a more easily interpretable format. Transforming data (such as the number of errors made while reading or results from a phonics-screening test) into charts or graphs can make data more easily understandable.

As you listen to the teacher present any collected information, be sure to clarify or modify inaccurate or incomplete statements to assure an adequate understanding of the information. Direct the focus to the conditions most relevant to the problem. The teacher may need help in understanding or interpreting the data so that the next part of the process goes smoothly. For example, if you collected some "on-task/off-task" data that shows the student was off-task during 23% of the observed reading lesson, or that the student is performing at the 45th percentile on a comprehension measure, it may be helpful to provide some information about what these figures mean and how to determine their significance to the problem you are working on with the teacher.

Analyze collected data

All this new information was collected to help more clearly define the student's reading problem. Interpreting the data involves a careful look at the information broadly to see if there are patterns or clues to why a problem developed in the first place and why it may be continuing. As the coach, you need to help the teacher note and understand the significance of any such patterns or clues so that you can form an accurate problem definition.

During this analysis, you must be sensitive to the teacher's sense of pride. Conduct your analysis of the collected information skillfully, in a manner that never is perceived as accusing or blaming teachers for their actions or lack of action, or implying fault. The focus of the discussion and data analysis must be on the influence and impact of the teacher's actions on the student. For example, instead of implying that a teacher is not skillful because a student was assigned to read materials that seemed far too challenging, you might say: "Based on the assessment I conducted of James's current reading level, it appears that his instructional level is actually lower that you probably suspected. We'll have to look at the difficulty level of the materials he is trying to read. Making some adjustments there may be part of the plan we develop together."

After you and the teacher have reviewed and analyzed all of the information you both collected, take the lead to summarize what you've both observed, and state a concise, accurate, and complete definition of the problem. This problem definition may or may not match the original problem definition from Phase 1. It must reflect a synthesis of the review of the collected data that you and the teacher have just completed. You may need to narrow the problem or focus on one part of a complex cluster of problems in order to develop an effective intervention plan. You should also present the definition as a proposal that is open to amendment, revision, and input from the teacher: "After looking over all of this information, it appears that James is having problems with his reading because of some underlying skill deficits. He is reading almost two years below grade level, and we identified some problems with both decoding and fluency, both of which are affecting his comprehension and his motivation. Is this your sense of the situation? Is there anything you want to add? Do you think we might want to target one of these skill areas to address first?"

Setting goals.

The next part of SPS involves developing some specific goals: In what ways can we expect the student's reading to improve if we plan and carry out an effective intervention? Moving the focus of the conversation with the teacher away from the worries and concerns about "the problem" and thinking instead about some potential positive outcomes can be a relief, and it starts the process of coming up with a plan from a more encouraging and constructive place.

Developing a plan.

We have now reached that point in the SPS process where a coach works with a teacher to help develop a plan to address the identified concern. It should be clear by now how the SPS process helps you, the coach, approach problems or concerns like a veteran problem solver. You've completed a thorough analysis of a problem and verified issues by collecting objective data. A target problem has been identified, and some reasonable goals for the student have been developed. Now you are in a good place to begin developing a plan for the teacher to use to help the student achieve those goals.

Providing support

While developing the plan, it is important to include a process for the coach to both help ensure that the plan is being correctly implemented and provide support and assurance while the teacher attempts to make changes in the current patterns of interaction with the target student. If teachers had known how to implement these new ideas already or could do them easily and consistently, they might not have needed any help from a coach in the first place! Part of the process of developing the intervention plan includes deciding how, as reading coach, you will support the teacher during the implementation phase.

Developing the evaluation plan

The success of an intervention should be determined by evaluating the degree to which each targeted goal was reached. Evaluations can be *formative*, providing information during the implementation of the intervention, or *summative*, providing information at the conclusion of the intervention only. In most cases, it is helpful for the evaluation plan to provide both of these kinds of information. The coach can use formative data to help support the intervention, while summative data is probably most helpful in determining the degree to which the goals have been met.

Some goals for the target student may be less concrete, such as an "improved attitude about reading." Achievement of some of these goals may be judged by developing an evaluation scale. For example, if a student currently "has a poor attitude about reading," you could develop a 5-point scale (with 5 being a very positive attitude and 1 being an extremely poor attitude). Suppose you and the teacher rate the student's current attitude as 2. Your goal would be to raise it to 3 or 4. On the other hand, some broad, general goals, such as "improved confidence about her reading" may best be reconfigured as more measurable goals, focusing on what observable behavior changes would show evidence of "improved confidence," such as more books being completed or increased participation in class discussions. (See Chapter 7 for more information about developing evaluation plans.)

Final steps in Phase 2.

As in Phase 1, the coach should wrap up this part of the SPS process by (1) briefly summarizing the definition, goals, and intervention plan (including the plan for collecting evaluation data); (2) asking the teacher whether your summary is correct; and (3) asking whether the teacher wants to add any information. (See Chapter 7 for detailed information on setting goals, developing an intervention plan, and supporting teachers while the intervention plan is implemented.)

PHASE 3: IMPLEMENTING THE PLAN

Now the teacher takes over. For the length of time specified in the intervention plan, the teacher implements the new teaching method, uses additional instructional materials, and sees that the student receives tutoring or whatever help was specified in the plan of action. Along the way, any formative evaluation data that was specified in the evaluation part of the plan gets collected.

In Phase 3, you will take a background role, but this is a role of vital importance: You will provide support to the teacher so that the developed plan gets implemented accurately and completely and that data collection is conducted as planned. Even though a plan may specify what to do for a specified period of time, the coach and teacher should be making decisions along the way. The teacher should certainly be taking note of what is happening daily in the classroom. The coach may also visit the classroom to see how things are proceeding. Based on these kinds of ongoing informal observations, along with analysis of any formative data that is being collected, the teacher and coach together can determine whether the intervention should be continued, modified, or ended for some reason.

In most cases, it will be appropriate to let the intervention run for the predetermined length of time and then complete the final phase of the SPS process, Phase 4: Evaluation and Next Steps. If the intervention plan needs to be modified or adapted, however, there is no need to repeat the entire process. Rather than restarting with a problem presentation, you and the teacher can revisit the information collected in Phase 2 and determine whether more information needs to be collected, the problem definition needs to be revised, the goals need to be modified, or some components of the plan itself should be changed. The SPS process has given you a lot to work with.

PHASE 4: EVALUATION AND NEXT STEPS

At the end of the implementation period, the teacher and coach sit down with all the information that was collected, which may include both formative and summative data. Together, the coach and teacher analyze this information and use the results to make a decision about next steps. Should the intervention be:

1. *Terminated?* (All goals were met at a satisfactory level.)

2. *Continued?* (Progress is being made, but not all of the goals have been reached.)

3. *Restructured?* (Perhaps some of the goals were achieved, but a new plan must be developed to address other goals. Perhaps little or no progress was made, and the current plan must be revised or an entirely new plan developed.)

Even if you and the teacher find that all of the goals have been achieved, there are still a couple of decisions that must be made. If the teacher believes that the original concern has been sufficiently addressed and feels no need for continued coaching at this time, you can shake hands or give each other a hug, praise each other's "good work well done," and move on, hopefully leaving a positive professional relationship in place, and perhaps some new learning or new understanding for both participants. However, it may be that even if the concern that caused the teacher to seek out your assistance in the first place has been completely resolved, a teacher may have other reasons to continue working with you. The teacher might want to address some different issues, perhaps involving the original target student. There may be other problems or other students that the teacher might want you to help with. Then, the SPS process begins again, back to Phase 1: Problem Presentation through the next three phases. Often, the second time through the SPS with any teacher goes much faster because a trusting collegial relationship has been established, and you both have a much better sense of each other's philosophies, knowledge base, and so on.

Figure 5.1 Development of an Intervention Plan Using the SPS Process

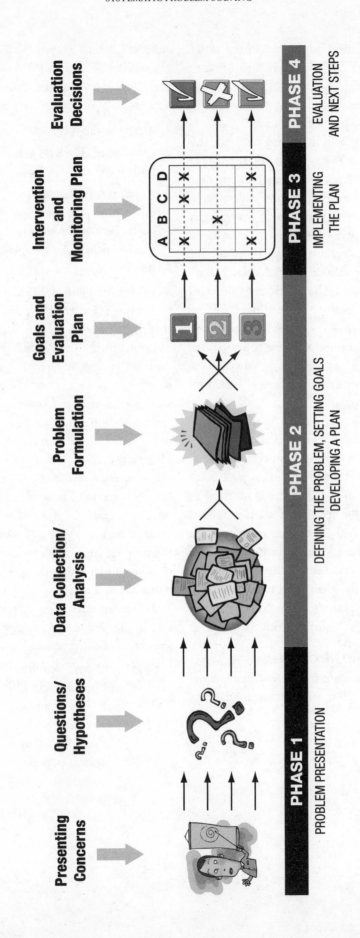

Managing the SPS Process

SPS is a collaborative process. It is successful when both the coach and the teacher fully commit to working together to help address a student's concern. However, the roles of the two participants in this process differ. The teacher is primarily responsible for helping describe the concern and presenting the critical contextual information. The teacher is usually also the person who carries out the plan that is developed to solve the problem. The coach helps decide what additional information is needed to fully define the target problem, leads the development of the intervention and evaluation plan, and supports the teacher during the implementation of the plan. The coach also has an additional responsibility: to manage the problem-solving process effectively.

Managing the SPS process involves using time management and skillful communication, along with being attentive to larger goals, which include helping a teacher learn how to engage independently in a systematic problem-solving process when future problems with students arise. The *Consultant Evaluation Rating Form (CERF) Training Manual* (Hughes & Hasbrouck, 1997) identifies 14 key communication and relationship-building skills that a coach or consultant should use when leading a collaborative problem-solving process such as coaching:

1. Makes the problem-solving process overt.

2. Effectively manages each session (sequence, focus, amount of time spent on each step).

3. Facilitates a collaborative partnership with the teacher.

4. Demonstrates effective nonverbal communication.

5. Maintains a professional yet warm demeanor.

6. Uses precise and appropriate language; avoids unnecessary or undefined jargon.

7. Appropriately reflects and validates expressed emotions and feelings.

8. Allows the teacher to tell his or her own story without unnecessary interruption or excessive questions.

9. Uses open- and closed-end questioning procedures appropriately to obtain information.

10. Seeks clarification, as necessary.

11. Accurately and appropriately paraphrases content.

12. Shares or presents only accurate information.

13. Encourages teachers to view the problem in a new light, as appropriate.

14. Acknowledges and accepts the teacher's efforts to address the concern.

The *CERF* manual (Hughes & Hasbrouck, 1997) describes the process involved for each step of a systematic problem-solving process, as well as the 14 communication and relationship components in great detail. It would be helpful for a coach or a coach's supervisor to use the *CERF* manual to help learn these skills and evaluate the implementation of SPS by a coach.

Streamlined Problem Solving

In this chapter we have described a multistep process coaches can use to address the sometimes quite complex problems that can arise in school settings. It is obvious that completing this process can involve a significant investment of time. Those of us who work in schools know all too well that time is often in short supply and, of course, it needs to be used wisely. It is also true that not every concern that come your way as a coach will need to be addressed through such a systematic and complete process as SPS.

TEAM PROBLEM SOLVING

Sometimes it can be more efficient for a group of people to tackle problems, rather than having a coach work 1:1 with an individual teacher. Some schools have implemented a process where a team of teachers and often other school-based professionals such as special educators, school psychologists, reading specialists, and counselors collaborate to address students' behavioral and/or academic concerns. Such teams have been given many different names, including student study teams, teacher assistance teams, school guidance teams, schoolwide alternative program teams, instructional consultation teams, mainstream assistance teams, and intervention teams (Kampwirth, 1999; Nolet, Tindal, & Hasbrouck,

1991; Sugai & Tindal, 1993). Teams have been used to address students' problems because (1) the more people at the table working on a problem, the wider the diversity of possible solutions; (2) research on school restructuring has identified the benefits of collaboration and teamwork; and (3) ideas generated by a team can sometimes spread and have a broader impact than a single teacher and a single student (Kampwirth, 1999).

However, as anyone who has tried solving a problem in a group well knows, the potential benefits of any kind of team problem-solving approach can be easily outweighed by some serious difficulties. These can include the challenge of simply finding the time on the calendars of a group of very busy professionals for scheduling regular opportunities to meet. Other difficulties can include the tendency of some individuals to dominate a situation, the length of time it can take to allow everyone to fully participate in a group process, the greater potential for the discussion to drift off topic, and the different individual working styles of each participant that may create some frustrations within the group.

One way to capture both the benefits of a using a systematic problem-solving process with a group of professionals and simultaneously addressing each of the potential pitfalls is to use a structure that controls the time and roles of each participant. Sprick et al. (1993) outlined a process they call *Team Problem Solving: An Efficient 25-Minute Process*. This process begins by assigning specific roles to three participants: Leader, Timekeeper, and Recorder.

The Leader's responsibility is to manage the group process. The Leader makes sure that each person on the team has an equal opportunity to participate, that the team stays focused on each step in the process following the specified order of topics, and that the amount of time allocated for each step is adhered to. The Timekeeper's role is to inform the Leader when the time for each step has expired. The Recorder has the primary responsibility of recording the key agreements at each step of the process and getting copies of the final plan to all relevant parties. Each person who takes on one of these roles also participates in the process. Sprick et al. (1993) suggest that the teacher presenting his or her concern about a student not serve in any of these roles.

The *25-Minute Process* walks participants through a process that mirrors SPS, starting with an overview of the problem and any related background information, defining the problem to be targeted and setting a goal, brainstorming some proactive strategies to address the problem, and finally creating an intervention plan with specified evaluation strategies. This process has been used successfully by many schools looking for an efficient way to have a group of school-based professionals available to address students' problems in a strategic and effective manner. We highly recommend that reading coaches give serious consideration to helping to establish a problem-solving team in their buildings as one tool for developing a schoolwide approach for helping every student be successful.

INFORMAL COACHING SUPPORT

Karen Carey (1995) wrote a wonderful article about the realities of providing coaching or consulting "in the real world." She said that coaches and consultants in schools need to be taught a problem-solving method that is feasible in real-world settings. Carey mentioned the need for coaches and consultants to understand the limited time available to teachers who have too many students with too many problems. She also talked about learning to coach "on the fly," "on the way in from the parking lot in the morning, while walking to mailboxes, down hallways, and during playground duties" (p. 399). These are important and wise suggestions!

Conclusion

In this chapter we outlined a highly systematic process so you will have a technique that you can use to approach any kind of problem that comes your way. At the same time, we want you to function as a coach in a way that addresses the needs of the people with whom you are working. When time is short and a problem is straightforward, you may want to consider moving more quickly through a problem-solving process. On the other hand, when a problem is long-standing and complex, or you are providing coaching support to a teacher you've never worked with before, you may want to follow the SPS process to the letter. That is your call. We have no intention of giving you only one, lockstep approach but to load up your professional toolbox with several effective options for the Collaborative Problem Solver role of coaching.

6

GATHERING INFORMATION

For some students, the road to becoming a competent reader is relatively smooth. Others stumble over obstacles along the way that keep them from reaching their potential. Some obstacles are related to the students themselves; some are related to the kind of instruction the students are getting. Frequently, the obstacles spring from interactions among the teacher, the instruction and materials, and the students. Being an effective coach means identifying and getting a handle on those complex relationships so you can put on your Collaborative Problem Solver hat and apply the process of Systematic Problem Solving (SPS) that we talked about in Chapter 5.

This chapter will tell you how to gather the information you need to clarify problems and overcome the learning barriers that cause students to struggle with reading. As you remember, in Chapter 5 we adapted and customized the four phases of SPS just for reading coaches. Much of the information gathering you'll be doing as a coach occurs in Phase 1 of our SPS process: Problem Presentation. This chapter will also tell you how to give useful feedback to the teachers you work with, which happens in Phase 2: Defining the Problem, Setting Goals, Developing a Plan.

The first step in choosing a process to use in information gathering is to think about the questions you want to answer. These questions should guide any interviews, assessments, and observations you do. You might need to know things like:

- When does Eric seem to have the most trouble with reading?

- What aspects of reading are hard for Santiago?

- Is Kiara actively engaged during reading class?

- Why does Tyrell seem bored when asked to do reading assignments?

- Does Mr. Shepherd target the needs of the struggling readers in small-group instruction?

- Does Rosa struggle to read when she is doing her homework?

- Does Mrs. Aguirre have routines in place so that students know what to do when their work is done or when it is time to change to a different activity?

The techniques we describe in this chapter will help you answer questions like the ones we have just listed so you can get an idea of the obstacles that struggling readers in your school are facing.

Gathering Information Through Interviews

Much of the information you need will come from interviewing teachers, parents, and students. Your initial teacher interview will allow you to clarify the presenting problem. But interviewing one teacher is sometimes not enough. Often, different people have different views of the same situation. Face-to-face meetings can help the reading coach understand multiple perspectives and define the presenting problem in order to set goals and develop a plan.

INITIAL TEACHER INTERVIEW

Many times, a classroom teacher seeks help from a reading coach because of concerns about an individual student or a small group of students. At other times, ongoing assessments of student progress may indicate that the reading skills of a particular student are not improving at the expected rate. In either case, interviewing the student's regular reading teacher can help the coach answer two types of questions. First, it can reveal details about the nature of the difficulties the student is having and the times and situations in which problems occur. Second, it can open a window into the classroom teacher's perception of the student and the student's reading difficulties. This kind of interview frequently occurs in Phase 1: Problem Presentation.

You might want to review the sections of this book on "entry" (Chapter 3) and on communication skills (Chapter 4) as you prepare for a Problem Presentation interview. You will want to make the teacher feel comfortable with the interview process by establishing a relationship of trust based on your sincere respect for the teacher's ideas and feelings. To a large degree, your nonverbal communication expresses your openness to the teacher. The SOLER (**s**it squarely, **o**pen posture, **l**eaning forward, **e**ye contact, **r**elaxed) strategy we talked about in Chapter 4 will help you remember how to assume a posture that communicates listening and openness. Both your verbal and nonverbal responses to the teacher's comments and questions will help determine the success of the interview.

This is also an opportunity to review the SPS process with the teacher. Teachers who bring their concerns to a coach are seeking assistance and solutions. They may believe that the process begins and ends with this initial meeting: They tell you about the problem, you listen carefully, and then you present them with a fully formed solution on the spot! It is important to clarify how the problem-solving process will proceed so the teacher will not have incorrect expectations.

While you want to establish a warm and congenial tone at this first meeting, don't allow the interview to drift off course and become a friendly chat or the kind of conversation about students that typically occurs in the teacher's lounge or workroom. Remember, your goal is to establish and maintain a professional problem-solving relationship that results in improved reading outcomes for students, as well as to obtain key facts and context information. Sometimes this means you must skillfully redirect the teacher's responses and refocus on the reading difficulties of the student.

It can also be helpful to start this initial interview with some agreements about the length of time to spend on this step in the process. As the person in charge of managing the problem-solving process, including the amount of time spent, the coach needs to be aware of the time constraints of all participants and plan to spend only as much time as necessary gathering the information and establishing a collaborative relationship. Teachers often work in situations that keep them somewhat isolated from other adults, and when they have a chance to share their problems and concerns with someone, especially a skillful listener, they may want to extend the session longer than may be productive. You may want to begin with a statement such as: "I'm glad we found this time to talk about your concerns about James. I have about 30 minutes now. Will that work for you?"

The most productive interviews are usually somewhat structured. Planning your questions will help you keep the interview on track. At the same time, the questions you ask should be open-ended and not easily answered with a simple "yes" or "no." This will give the teacher the freedom to express both observations and opinions concerning the student and the feelings accompanying the relationship between student and teacher.

The questions in an initial teacher interview may relate to observations the teacher has made about the struggling student. Here are some examples:

- When does James seem to have problems? Can you describe them? Do you think he has trouble reading unfamiliar words? Is he reading in a smooth and fluent way? Does he understand and remember what he reads?

- What reading assessments have you administered? What have you learned about James's strengths and needs in reading?

- Is there a particular time of day or situation when James seems to do better or worse? Does he respond best to large-group, small-group, or individual instruction? Is he able to complete work independently?

- Have you noticed anything that makes you think that James may have trouble with his vision or hearing?

As you interpret the teacher's responses, keep in mind that the responses reflect the teacher's *beliefs* about the student's reading problems. These beliefs may or may not be supported by other information you gather. The teacher interview provides the presenting problem, which is an important piece of the puzzle but does not necessarily explain the student's difficulties completely or accurately.

This phase of the first interview should end with a brief summary of your understanding of the concerns presented by the teacher, asking the teacher whether your summary is correct, and asking whether the teacher wants to add any information. For example, you might say, "It sounds like you are concerned because James doesn't finish his independent work in reading class and doesn't pay attention during reading instruction. You also seem to be concerned about the quality of his work. His grades in reading are low, especially on assignments to read a passage and answer questions about it. Did I get this right? Is there anything you need to add?"

Finally, you and the teacher should agree on whether more information is needed. You will want to determine what might be a good time, or times, for you to observe James during his reading class. You may ask the teacher to make notes about specific things he or she observes related to James's performance or to collect work samples. You or the teacher (or both) may plan to administer some reading assessments to determine the knowledge and skills James needs to learn. Before you leave the room, make a plan to meet again after this information has been collected. Once the parent or student interviews, work samples, assessments, and/or observations have been completed, meet again with the teacher to define the problem and develop the intervention. (Chapter 7 describes the steps involved in developing interventions.)

INTERVIEWS WITH THE PARENT

Many of our comments about teacher interviews also apply to interviews with parents. Parents know their children well, and your respect for them and openness to their input will go a long way to establish a productive and cooperative relationship. Careful attention to communication skills is especially important when you interact with parents. People who work in schools have their own ways of doing things, and even their own language (with words like *on-task*, *high-stakes tests*, or *objectives*), that may be unfamiliar or even a little threatening to some parents. Some parents may have had unpleasant experiences when they were in school and may have cautious or even negative reactions to some aspects of schooling.

All parents, including those whose cultures or languages are different from the mainstream, should be encouraged to communicate in ways that make them feel comfortable. It is beyond the scope of this book to provide a discussion of working with diverse families, but this is an important consideration for the reading coach (see Harris, 1991).

It is just as important to prepare for the parent interview as for the teacher interview. The questions you ask parents may include:

- Does James have any vision or hearing problems that might affect his reading? Are there any physical difficulties or medical conditions?

- Do you notice James having a problem with reading at home? Does he have trouble when he is doing his homework?

- How long have you noticed these problems? Is this something that has just started happening this year, or has he struggled with reading for quite a while?

- What kinds of things does James say about reading or about school?

INTERVIEWING STUDENTS

Sometimes the best way to find out what is not going well for students is simply to ask them! When you visit the doctor, you are normally asked to talk about how you have been feeling. Doctors use this information along with information gathered from tests and their own observations. In much the same way, conducting structured interviews with students may provide you with insight into their attitudes toward reading, their feelings of confidence in their own reading ability, and the times and situations when they have the most trouble. Once again, use communication strategies that encourage the student to feel comfortable about talking with you.

Gathering Information Through Assessments

Obtaining information from teachers, parents, and students is normally not sufficient to define reading difficulties fully. You will almost always need more information. Specifically, what skills and strategies has the student mastered? What additional instruction or intervention may be needed? If a student is struggling to learn to read, the most basic, direct observation is to administer diagnostic assessments. An obvious first step is to ask the student's reading teacher to provide any available assessment data, as we discussed above, but it may often be necessary to administer more assessments.

In Chapter 2, we described the roles of assessment in the primary reading program. In this chapter, we will discuss the specific components of reading assessments that can help you identify a student's needs. See our Resources for the Reading Coach section for information about several assessments that we have found useful.

PHONEMIC AWARENESS

There are several published and informal assessments of phonemic awareness, the key skill that is so closely associated with learning to read. Students have a very hard time breaking the code if they can't hear the individual sounds in spoken words and blend the sounds to form words. Those two skills—segmenting a word into its phonemes, or sounds, and blending phonemes to form a word—are critical in reading acquisition. It is beyond the scope of this book to provide details regarding phonemic awareness instruction, but we suggest that students who are having a very difficult time reading words presented to them in lists should be assessed to determine whether they have difficulty with phonemic awareness. In tests of phonemic awareness, students may be asked to provide a word that rhymes with a given word, blend together sounds to make a word, or say the separate phonemes within a word pronounced by the tester, among other tasks. These tests are administered orally, and the student does not normally look at printed letters or words during the assessment.

PHONICS AND DECODING

It is important to assess students' ability to use their knowledge of phonics to read unfamiliar words. You can assess this knowledge several ways, including having students:

- Identify sounds associated with letters or letter combinations.

- Read words presented in lists.

- Read nonsense words. (This is a way to make sure that students are sounding out an unfamiliar "word" rather than recognizing part or all of a word at sight.)

- Read connected text while you note the kinds of errors they make.

As we explained in Chapter 2, many struggling readers, even in grades three 3 and above, have difficulties reading unfamiliar words in lists. A classroom reading teacher may describe mainly comprehension problems, but keep in mind that students can't understand text if they can't read the words. Many comprehension problems are the result of decoding problems. It is relatively quick to ask students to read a list of real words or nonsense words to decide whether they might need further assessment of their phonics knowledge and decoding skills. One tool that we recommend is the *Quick Phonics Screener* (QPS) (Hasbrouck, 2003). Information about this tool is included in the Resources for the Reading Coach.

ORAL READING FLUENCY

Think about how it sounds when a good reader reads out loud. Skillful reading is both accurate and quick. Good oral reading sounds natural, not rushed, but not too slow. Good readers respond appropriately to punctuation, and their voices express the meaning of the passage they are reading. The oral reading of the struggling reader may sound slow and labored. It may be choppy, with each word read separately rather than grouped into phrases or sentences. Often, it sounds "flat" or is in a monotone, with very little expression. Struggling readers may skip words that are hard for them, and they often appear not to notice periods at the ends of sentences or other punctuation marks. This kind of nonfluent reading has been shown to limit readers' ability to comprehend what they read.

You may want to review the description of the assessment of oral reading fluency in Chapter 2. Keep in mind that fluency problems are often related to word identification problems. In other words, fluent readers can recognize many words at sight, and they can quickly apply phonics knowledge and recognize familiar patterns to read words that are unfamiliar. Before assuming that a student simply has a fluency problem, assess that student's decoding or phonics knowledge. One useful tool to monitor oral reading fluency is the *Dynamic Indicators of Basic Early Literacy Skills* (*DIBELS*) (Good & Kaminski, 2003), which contains several passages at the 1st through 6th grade levels. A Spanish version of the *DIBELS* is also available. Another set of tools for benchmark screening and progress monitoring are the *Reading Fluency Benchmark Assessor* (Read Naturally, 2004) and the *Reading*

Progress Monitor (Read Naturally, 2005). Intervention Central (www.interventioncentral.org) offers some non-standardized passages that can be used for informal assessments of fluency or monitoring students' progress.

READING COMPREHENSION

The ultimate goal of reading is, of course, making meaning from text. Some students seem to read fluently, and even expressively, but are unable to understand and/or remember what they have read. Comprehension is one of the most difficult components of reading to assess. One of the best tools for a teacher or coach to use to assess a student's reading comprehension is the informal reading inventory (IRI), in which students read aloud passages of increasing difficulty and verbally answer questions about the passages. By administering an IRI, you can determine the level of text the student should read during reading instruction (the approximate instructional level), the level of text that he or she can read independently (the independent level, the appropriate level of difficulty for homework assignments), and the level of text that is too difficult for the student (the frustration level). Students who are consistently asked to read frustration-level text tend to develop habits like guessing or skipping words or waiting for the teacher or other students to tell them difficult words. They may also have behavior problems resulting from repeated failure and frustration. An IRI can give you valuable information about a student's ability to understand and draw conclusions from text that is easy for them (independent level) and from passages that are at just the right level for reading instruction. You can also calculate a fluency score on an IRI by timing the first 60 seconds of a student reading at the instructional level.

SEQUENCE OF ASSESSMENT

With so many reading components that may need to be assessed, it can be hard to decide which assessment to do first. Time is always limited, so we want to be sure to gather only enough data to allow us to move on to instruction and intervention where we need to spend most of our time. For beginning readers, we advise starting with tests of phonemic awareness, letter recognition, letter-sound knowledge, and a few simple high-frequency sight words. For students who are able to read simple text passages, you may want to start with an IRI to determine overall reading levels and find out whether there are pat-

terns in the kinds of words that are hard for the students and whether they can comprehend text. Many IRIs also include a measure of fluency. If the student is reading below grade level, we recommend that you (or the student's teacher) administer assessments of phonics/decoding, such as the QPS (Hasbrouck, 2005). If the student has severe decoding problems, follow this with a test of phonemic awareness.

Gathering Information Through Observations

Reading difficulties are rarely, if ever, caused *only* by conditions in the student. For example, if students are easily confused, the kind of instruction and feedback they receive can have a big effect on their ability to understand concepts and apply skills in reading. To fully understand students' reading difficulties, how to improve the instruction they receive, and the interactions between conditions in the classroom, the instruction, and the student, it is important to observe during reading instruction.

OBSERVING THE STUDENT IN THE CLASSROOM

The kind of observation you conduct depends on the questions you want to answer. If you want to try to identify specific situations in which the student seems especially frustrated by reading tasks, you may want to conduct a functional (or ABC) observation that tracks what happens before (**a**ntecedent) a **b**ehavior and after (**c**onsequence) the behavior (Sugai & Tindal, 1993). If you want insight into a student's off-task behavior during reading instruction, you may record the amount of time the student is on-task, off-task, or disruptive during different instructional formats (e.g., situations in which the teacher instructs the *whole group* while they are expected to listen or times when the teacher observes students while they read out loud). In our experience, these *two kinds of observations* are likely to provide you with useful information about the student's interaction with the teacher and the classroom environment during reading instruction and reading-related activities.

We suggest you follow a basic plan to prepare for a classroom observation. The seven steps in the process are to:

1. *Select an observation format* to match the kind of information you need. For example, if you need to get a

general sense about how the target student is behaving in the classroom, a functional (ABC) observation may be just the ticket. If more detailed information is needed about the relationship between the instruction and the behavioral outcomes, you may want to use the *Activity Structures Observation Strategy-Revised* (ASOS-R; Denton, Parker, & Hasbrouck, 2004). This tool is available in the Appendix. If, however, this is your first visit to the classroom, you may just want to jot down some anecdotal notes about how the classroom is set up, how reading instruction is scheduled, what other students do while the teacher is teaching small groups, and so forth.

2. *Review the directions for conducting the observation you select.* Be sure you feel comfortable with collecting information using this format. (You may need to do some practice observations first, perhaps in the classrooms of teachers you've worked with in the past.)

3. *Decide how many times, and for how long, you will observe.* It is normally better to observe in the classroom more than once. If you observe only one time, you might choose a day on which the teacher or student is not feeling up to par or when the class activities are not typical. Normally, you get a more accurate picture if you conduct two or three 20-minute observations rather than one 50-minute observation.

4. *Schedule a time* for the observation with the teacher. Be sure to observe at the time of day and during the class when the teacher has indicated that the student has the most difficulty. Before you conduct a more formal observation, it can be helpful to go into the classroom for a brief (five- to ten-minute) informal observation with two goals: getting a general sense of how the classroom works and letting the students (and the teacher!) become used to having you in the room so that they will behave naturally when you conduct the main observation. If your target student is easily distracted, it may be necessary to conduct more than one of these brief classroom observations to get them used to your being there. Be sure the teacher knows that he or she has the option to ask you to reschedule an observation if, for example, the student is having a bad day and not acting normally, or if the teacher does not feel well.

5. *Prepare the teacher* for what you will be doing. Some teachers find it difficult to be observed by an outsider,

especially when that person takes notes throughout the observation. Be sure that the teacher understands the purpose of your observation. Stress that you will be observing the *student* and will share your observations with the teacher. Also, assure the teacher that you will not discuss what you observe with anyone else, including the principal or the student's parents. Those frequent, short, informal visits to the classroom before the formal observation may go a long way to help the teacher, as well as the students, feel more comfortable with your presence in their room.

6. *Assemble your materials.* Take your computer or a clipboard to hold any paper observation form, as it is unlikely that a desk or table will be available. Some types of observation also require a stopwatch. You will also need two pens or pencils. (It's always a good idea to have a backup!)

7. *When you enter the classroom for the observation, find a place to sit where you are as unobtrusive as possible.* Make sure you have a clear view of the teacher and the student you are observing. In some classrooms, students move from one area of the room to another during a lesson. Be prepared to change your position, if necessary, so you can see the teacher and student. Knowing where to position yourself is another good reason to do at least one early visit to the classroom before conducting your formal observation.

OBSERVING STUDENT-TEACHER INTERACTIONS

If you want to collect information about how a student responds to situations in the classroom during reading instruction or activities that involve reading, conduct a functional (or ABC) observation (Sugai & Tindal, 1993). We have included an ABC Observation Form in the Appendix. As we noted earlier in this chapter, the ABC stands for *antecedent, behavior,* and *consequence.* We are going to explain exactly what each of these words means.

Let's start with *behavior,* because students' behavior is often linked to academic problems. Let's suppose that you are working with Jessie, a 5th grade boy who told you during a student interview that he feels embarrassed when he is asked to read out loud in class. When you assessed his oral reading fluency, you found that his reading is very slow and labored for a student his age. Jessie's teacher reports that he is often highly disruptive during social studies, science, or reading class when students are taking turns reading the text out loud. This behavior may be linked to Jessie's difficulties with fluent oral reading. Another student, Samantha, is a 2nd grade girl, whose teacher complains that Samantha doesn't pay attention to reading lessons and rarely finishes assigned independent work according to instructions. From your assessment of Samantha, you know that end-of-first-grade text is at her frustration level. You suspect that her behavior during reading class may be linked to her reading difficulties.

Remember, your primary goal as the reading coach is to help improve students' reading outcomes, not to help the teachers handle behavior problems. Remember also, though, that students who have academic difficulties often demonstrate problem behavior in the classroom. We are suggesting that it may be helpful to observe student behavior to help you understand the possible obstacles to reading growth that students may face in their classrooms and to develop interventions that may help make reading instruction more successful for specific students.

Now let's talk about the word *antecedent*. An antecedent is something that happens just before a behavior and appears to be linked to the behavior in some way. The antecedent may or may not cause the behavior. Here's a simple example: When the doorbell rings (antecedent), my dog barks (behavior). Pushing the button on the doorbell does not somehow flip a switch in my dog's throat causing her to bark, but she has learned that part of her "job" is to let me know when someone is at the door. In our previous story about Jessie, a situation in which students in the class are asked to read out loud seems to be an antecedent to Jessie's disruptive behavior. There seems to be a connection between the two.

The third letter in ABC stands for *consequence*. A consequence is something that happens *after* a behavior and is linked to the behavior. This is the same as talking about the consequences of your own actions. Consequences can be positive or negative. Positive consequences are also called rewards or reinforcements. If I decide to have dessert when I go out to eat, I am rewarded by the enjoyment of the treat. Another consequence is not so rewarding—I put on another pound! In our story about Jessie, we find during an ABC observation that his teacher usually sends him to a time-out room when he disrupts the class. Going to time-out keeps Jessie from having to read orally in front of his classmates. Since this strategy "works" for

Jessie, he keeps using it day after day: It is a consequence that rewards or reinforces his behavior and makes it more likely that he will behave this way again in the future.

OBSERVING ACTIVE STUDENT ENGAGEMENT IN DIFFERENT INSTRUCTIONAL FORMATS

Some observation strategies allow the observer to record student behaviors at regular time intervals. One such tool is the *Activity Structures Observation Strategy—Revised*, or ASOS-R (Denton, Parker, & Hasbrouck, 2004). This tool allows the observer to compare the on-task behaviors of a particular student with those of a classmate or a group of classmates and to compare student engagement in different types of classroom activities. This strategy helps you determine whether problems are limited to the target student or are prevalent in the classroom as a whole and possibly due to the teacher's instructional or classroom management difficulties. Another strength of the ASOS-R is that it results in a graph that can be used to illustrate for the teacher the percentage of time that the target student and other students were on-task, off-task, and disruptive—while the teacher was using different instructional formats. These formats include teacher behaviors—lecturing, giving directions, conducting a demonstration, asking questions, evaluating student work or performance, answering questions, observing students, or nonacademic activities (e.g., discipline, interruptions)—and the size of the instructional group—large group, small group, or individual instruction. Forms you will need to conduct the ASOS-R can be found in the Appendix.

OBSERVING READING INSTRUCTION

As we described in Chapter 2, research in reading over the past 20 years has provided us with a great deal of insight about the kinds of instruction that are most beneficial to struggling readers. If the instruction has the qualities shown in the following list, it will probably be effective for most students in the classroom. Some will need more intense, supplemental instruction based on the same principles and delivered in small groups in addition to regular classroom reading instruction.

Reading research has shown that beneficial instruction:

- Is based on assessments of a student's strengths and needs and is targeted to teaching what the student needs to learn

- Is purposeful and designed to teach essential objectives

- Includes instruction focused on the essential components of reading, including phonemic awareness and phonics (in the early grades and for older students when needed), fluency, vocabulary, and comprehension strategies

- Is explicit and systematic, purposefully teaching students key concepts and skills

- Makes use of quality instructional materials, including text that is at the student's instructional reading level

- Is delivered using effective communication skills

- Provides many opportunities for practice with monitoring and feedback from the teacher

- Includes many opportunities to apply concepts and skills in reading and writing connected text with scaffolding and feedback provided by the teacher

- Is provided in large groups, small groups, and individual formats, depending on the particular tasks

- Actively involves all students for a large percentage of the lesson

- Is delivered with warmth and enthusiasm in a classroom with established routines and expectations

The qualities in the prior list can guide the professional development that you, as the reading coach, provide to teachers and others in your school. We devote Chapter 8 to professional development, and that chapter describes a plan for providing workshops and ongoing modeling and mentoring to teachers based on their needs in areas related to effective reading instruction.

THREE USEFUL TOOLS FOR OBSERVING THE TEACHER

We have three formats to suggest for observing reading instruction—the *Literacy Instruction Feedback Template* (LIFT) (Denton, 2004a), the *Student Success—Teacher Strategy Observation* (SS-TS) (Denton, 2004b), and the *Scale for Coaching Instruction Effectiveness* (SCIE)

(Hasbrouck & Parker, 1995). These tools can be useful for providing teachers with feedback *after* they have received professional development and support in implementing effective reading instruction in their classrooms. Besides providing a framework for coaching classroom teachers, the observation tools can provide the reading coach with feedback about the effectiveness of the professional development in the school.

The LIFT observation.

LIFT (Denton, 2004a) is a brief observation form that is directed specifically at the implementation of explicit instruction in the reading classroom (see Chapter 2). The LIFT form provides space to record observations of the teacher's instructional strategies and the students' responses to classroom reading instruction. A copy of this observation tool is included in the Appendix.

SS-TS observation.

The SS-TS (Denton, 2004b) is similar to the LIFT in some ways, but it places more emphasis on the interaction between student and teacher behaviors. We have included a copy of the SS-TS in the Appendix.

SCIE observation.

The SCIE (Hasbrouck & Parker, 1995) is designed to enable peer coaches—such as a reading coach—to provide feedback to teachers on specific components of instruction. The purpose of the feedback is to help teachers identify aspects of their instruction they would like to improve and then set goals for making those improvements. The SCIE can be used in observations of instruction in any subject at any grade level. Research studies using the SCIE have shown it to be highly valued by teachers as a tool for professional growth (Hasbrouck & Christen, 1996) and useful in improving the skills of beginning teachers (Hasbrouck, 1997).

The SCIE involves having a coach observe a teacher's entire lesson, from start to finish, while taking detailed notes. The lesson should be at least 20 minutes in length. After completing the observation, the coach will complete the SCIE protocol, rating each of 51 items on a two- or three-point scale. As soon as possible after the observation, the coach meets with the teacher to go over the SCIE ratings together. The coach explains each rating, tying it to specific elements observed in the teacher's lesson.

After this debriefing, the teacher can decide to set a goal or goals for instructional improvement. The coach then works with the teacher to determine how to provide support for achieving these goals. For example, if the coach noted that the teacher's lesson did not seem to be focused on an appropriate instructional objective (i.e., SCIE item A1a: Lesson Planning & Preparation: "Selecting Appropriate Objectives/Purposes for a Lesson"), the coach may find some resources for the teacher to use to learn how to set appropriate objectives (perhaps a book, workshop, or some resources on the Internet).

Using the SCIE to provide coaching for instructional improvement should be considered an *advanced* coaching tool. As a reading coach, consider using the SCIE only when you have established a strong, positive, trusting professional relationship with the teacher and when the teacher fully understands the SCIE's purpose and has specifically requested this kind of observation. A SCIE observation follows much the same format that an administrator does in making evaluative judgments about a teacher's instructional skills. All parties involved *must* understand clearly that the purpose of the SCIE is to help the teacher identify some specific goals for improving instruction. The purpose is *not* to make any kind of evaluative decisions that would influence hiring, retention, or promotion. The results of the SCIE would be considered highly confidential, to be shared only with the coach and the observed teacher. We recommend that before you observe a teacher using the SCIE, the rationale for the SCIE (setting personal goals for instructional improvement) and the procedures be included in the professional development you provide the teachers. The SCIE is also available in the Appendix.

OBSERVING INTERACTIONS AMONG THE TEACHER, INSTRUCTION, MATERIALS, AND STUDENT

Other observation tools are designed to capture information about classroom ecology and routines. Rating scales and checklists may be constructed to describe the physical, instructional, and social environment in the classroom. Cohen & Spenciner (2003) suggest that observations of the physical environment include such things as lighting, noise, distractions, temperature, comfort of the student, arrangement of the seating, and general layout. The instructional environment includes such elements as access to and adequacy of materials, instructional methods (especially active versus passive involvement), expectations and demands, modifications, grouping, and scheduling. Perhaps the most complex aspect of the classroom environment is the social environment. This includes the nature of interaction between teacher and student, the way the teacher handles behavior management, peer interactions, and the general atmosphere and classroom climate.

Framing these elements of the classroom environment as questions can help guide your observations. Some questions about key aspects of the physical, instructional, and social environments that may affect a student's reading outcomes are:

- Is the noise, temperature, or lighting making it hard for the student to concentrate and learn?

- Is the student's seating placement in the classroom conducive to learning?

- Does the teacher use high-quality materials as part of effective instruction?

- Does the student have access to the materials?

- Are the materials appropriate for this student?

- Does the instruction appear to be purposeful and based on objectives?

- Is the instruction directed at teaching skills and concepts related to the critical reading domains: phonemic awareness, phonics, fluency, vocabulary, and comprehension?

- Do the instructional strategies implemented in the classroom promote mainly active or passive student involvement?

- Do the teacher's expectations and demands appear realistic and conducive to learning?

- Does the teacher provide modifications, supports, or scaffolding to ensure a high rate of student success?

- Are the grouping formats appropriate for the instructional objectives?

- Is reading instruction scheduled for a sufficient period of time each day and at times when students are more likely to be attentive?

- Does the teacher communicate warmth and enthusiasm toward the students and the subject matter?

- Do the students appear to be aware of classroom routines, rules, and consequences?

- Are most of the students in the class on-task?

- What is the teacher's reaction to behavior issues?

- Are the rules clear and consequences applied consistently?

- Do teacher-student interactions generally appear positive?

- What is the ratio of teacher comments that are positive, neutral, and negative?

PROVIDING FEEDBACK TO TEACHERS AFTER OBSERVATIONS

When you find yourself thinking about getting together with a teacher to offer feedback based on your information gathering, you'll know you've entered Phase 2 of our coaching SPS: Defining the Problem, Setting Goals, Developing a Plan. As you prepare to meet with a teacher after conducting a classroom observation, keep your role as a reading coach in mind. Remember that your ultimate goal is *to improve students' reading skills and competence.* Your role is not supervisor, but coach, which means that your job is to engage with the teacher in systematic problem solving to support the reading growth of *students* in the classroom.

At the beginning of the postobservation conference, make it clear to the teacher that your purpose in conducting the observation was to observe the target student within the classroom and to collect information that might support you and the teacher as you work together to help the student succeed. You might begin by relaying a personal story about a time when "a second set of eyes" revealed aspects of your teaching you never realized were there—a time when you were observed by a colleague and received helpful feedback.

Once you have established a focus on the *student* as the purpose of the observation, continue by asking the teacher if the observation was conducted on a "typical" day. It is important to get this information ahead of time so the teacher cannot later explain away what you observed with the statement, "But that *never* happens!" And, in fact, if the observation was conducted on an untypical

day, you need to know that so you can schedule another observation.

At this point, you can begin to describe the student's behaviors you observed in the class. As you talk about things you noticed the student doing or saying, link these observations to the strategies the teacher was using at the time. For example, you can talk about antecedents to student behaviors that you recorded during an ABC observation, the percentage of time the student was on-task during different types of activity formats during an ASOS-R observation, and observations you recorded about the student during a LIFT observation.

Try to restrict this description to student behaviors that are directly relevant to success in learning to read. If factors related to the physical or social environment in the classroom (described in the prior section) appear to be strongly related to the student's reading problem, you will need to discuss some of these factors. However, we suggest that your main emphasis be on the learning environment—access to appropriate and high-quality materials including text on the student's instructional reading level, instructional methods, especially active student involvement and the elements of explicit instruction, ambitious but realistic expectations and demands, and the effective use of grouping and scheduling. Often, when you target instruction to student needs, make sure that appropriate text and scaffolding are provided to support student success, and involve students actively in the lessons. Behavior problems solve themselves without the teacher focusing directly on them.

One mistake made by many beginning coaches (and one we made ourselves at first!) is to try to give the teacher too much feedback at one time. We suggest that the coach provide at least three points of positive feedback to the teacher, reinforcing the effective aspects of the lesson. Then choose only one or two important areas in which the teacher might make changes.

Remember, you can't "fix" everything at once by providing a list of all imperfections! Frame your feedback as "just reporting the facts" of what you observed. Avoid judgmental statements. Always try to convey to teachers an attitude of respect for them as professionals. Ask for teachers' opinions. Ask why they make certain instructional decisions during the lesson. Teachers often have good reasons for choices they make while teaching, even though they may not be readily apparent to the observer.

Convey to the teacher that you are partners in helping the student grow. Remember the important message that coaching is about the kids!

Sometimes supporting student growth means that you need to support teacher growth. If teachers have several areas of need, work with them continually over time, using several types of professional development, including modeling. We're going to describe some of these types of professional development in Chapter 8.

AN ALTERNATIVE APPROACH TO OBSERVATION AND FEEDBACK

As we've just discussed, there are advantages and disadvantages of observing teachers and providing them with feedback about lessons. A serious drawback of traditional classroom observation is that teachers may feel as though they are being supervised and may become defensive. Showers and Joyce (1996), in their description of peer coaching, offer an alternative approach. They describe a study of peer coaching in which observations of lessons were not followed by feedback. In this study, two teachers would cooperate in planning lessons, observe each other teaching the lessons, and then reflect together on both lessons afterward. We suggest that this approach may be useful for the reading coach. When a coach and teacher co-plan lessons, observe each other teaching, and discuss both lessons afterward, the coach has the opportunity to model three key dimensions of teaching—planning research-based reading instruction based on assessment results; providing effective, explicit, targeted instruction

(see Chapter 2 for a description); and reflecting on one's own teaching afterward. The observation tool should be selected carefully, and the coach and teacher should observe each other using the same tool. The LIFT observation may be helpful for this kind of observation. The coach may teach first in order to model certain aspects of explicit instruction. Having the teacher focus on these particular elements should heighten the teacher's sensitivity to them. The coach's observation of the teacher can then provide valuable information about the continuing needs of the teacher. To implement this approach, the reading coach must be willing to reflect about both strengths and weaknesses of his or her own lesson. This kind of openness can go a long way in encouraging teachers to trust the coach and to take the risks that go along with change.

Conclusion

Our focus on helping students become better readers must be supported by useful, reliable information about student strengths and needs, the nature of the reading instruction they receive, and the complex interactions and conditions that exist in the reading classroom. Providing effective coaching depends on your ability to identify and understand these conditions in order to help students and teachers overcome obstacles to progress. Interviews, assessments, and observations are the reading coach's tools for gathering this important information.

7

DEVELOPING, SUPPORTING, AND EVALUATING READING INTERVENTIONS

As you know, wearing your Collaborative Problem Solver hat as a Student-Focused Coach involves using Systematic Problem Solving (SPS), which we have customized for reading coaches and that you learned about in Chapter 5. SPS will guide you and a classroom teacher or other colleagues in helping a student who is struggling with reading. You also learned (in Chapter 6) details about some procedures, tools, and strategies you can use to gather the information needed to identify and define a problem, which occurs in Phase 1 and early Phase 2 of SPS and lays the foundation for an effective intervention.

Now we are going to discuss some procedures that a coach—working collaboratively with colleagues—can use in Phases 2, 3, and 4 of SPS to set goals, develop a plan, support the teacher, and (finally) evaluate the effectiveness of an intervention to help improve a student's reading.

Setting Goals

Once a presented problem or concern has been identified and defined (starting in Phase 1: Problem Presentation, and finalized in the early stages of Phase 2: Defining the Problem, Setting Goals, Developing a Plan), there's more to do in Phase 2. You can now move the process to *setting goals*. As we mentioned in Chapter 5, identifying the goals before working on the plan of action refocuses all participants on where they are going rather than where they have been. This step can bring a wave of positive feeling and optimism to the process and provide a clear path to follow in intervention development. The goals set at this point can also serve the evaluation process in Phase 4 of SPS, where the success of the intervention is determined and decisions are made about next steps.

HOW TO SET GOALS

Goals should be linked directly to the problem definition that targeted the area of primary concern. Setting two to four goals is usually best. The goals should be at-tainable given the resources available, which include time, money, and people who can help, as well as the planned length of the intervention. It would be unreasonable, for example, to set a goal that a 4th grade student, currently reading at the 1.5 grade level, will be reading at the 3rd grade level in five weeks. It is also unreasonable to make perfect scores a goal (100% correct on all written work; zero errors in oral reading). Most human beings cannot consistently achieve at a perfect level!

Teachers may begin the discussion of goals by talking broadly about their hopes for their student. They may say they would like the student to "develop a better attitude toward reading" or "feel more confident about reading." It's usually a good idea to reconfigure these general goals as more measurable ones, focusing on the observable behavior changes that would show evidence of "a better attitude" or "more confidence." For example, you can determine whether a student reads more books or increases participation in class discussions.

Some goals may involve a clearly described "baseline," the level at which the student is currently performing, and specify a desired performance level for the end of the intervention period. You can determine baseline levels by reexamining some of the observation or assessment data that was collected after Phase 1. Goals that are developed from baseline data can be stated using clear, concrete descriptions of where the student is currently performing and where you can expect him or her to be performing within a set period of time. For example, if James's teacher begins by stating that she'd like to see James become a better, more confident reader, you might work with her to develop some goals that may look like these:

GOAL #1: James is currently reading at about the 2nd grade level based on results of an informal reading inventory. Our goal is for him to be reading at a 3rd grade level in six months.

GOAL #2: James correctly identified 14/30 (47%) vowel combinations on an informal phonics assessment. Our goal for him is to correctly identify at least 27/30 (90%) vowel combinations six weeks.

GOAL #3: James's oral reading fluency score on unpracticed 2nd grade materials is currently 68 words correct per minute. Our goal for him is to have a score of 80 words correct per minute in six weeks in 2nd grade materials.

GUIDING THE GOAL-SETTING PROCESS

If the teacher with whom you are working has little previous experience developing goals for students, this step in the process may require some direction and leadership from you. However, to maintain the sense of collaboration, clearly explain the rationale for setting goals at this point in SPS, and continue to seek input and suggestions from the teacher throughout the goal-setting process. While the content of the goals may come from the teacher (e.g., "I just want April to be a better student and start getting better grades."), you may have to guide the teacher toward developing a more concrete, measurable goal (eventually, something like: "April will increase the accuracy of her reading seatwork to an average of at least 80% and will turn in her completed assignments at least four out of five days."). The coach should explain that establishing concrete goals is important because it helps guide the development of the intervention plan and also helps motivate both the teacher and the student with a "fixed target." It will also facilitate the eventual evaluation of your efforts.

UNSTATED GOALS

In addition to the openly identified goals, there may be times that the coach wants to set goals that are left unstated. Such goals may include desirable changes in a teacher's attitudes or behaviors, such as having a teacher become more positive or patient with students, or increasing a teacher's skill level in using assessment data to make instructional decisions. Although such "covert" goals can be an important part of the SPS process for a coach, they are not goals you discuss openly with a teacher unless that teacher has expressed an interest in them. If this is the case, you may want to gently broach the possibility of having the teacher set some personal goals along with establishing goals for the student: "While we were analyzing the data I collected during the classroom observations, you expressed some concern about the low ratio of positive to negative statements that I recorded during the times I visited your room. I wonder if you might be interested in working toward increasing your positive statements and interactions? Might that be something you'd like to consider for setting as a goal for yourself to work toward?"

DEVELOP AN EVALUATION PLAN

The success of an intervention should be determined by evaluating the degree to which each goal was reached. If the goals have been well defined, developing an evaluation plan goes quite smoothly. As we mentioned in Chapter 5, evaluations can be *formative*, conducted as the intervention is being implemented, or *summative*, completed at the end of the intervention period. Many evaluations collect both types of information. Formative data can be used to help support the intervention, and summative data is important for the final decisions about the overall success of the intervention plan.

The coach can take the lead in developing the evaluation plan by suggesting one or two possible evaluation strategies to consider. Determining whether the student's goals have been achieved might involve using some of the classroom-based measures described in Chapter 6 that can be used to collect the data for defining and analyzing the original presenting problem, including informal reading inventories, phonics screeners, classroom observations, assessments of oral reading fluency, or perhaps a standardized measure such as the *Woodcock Reading Mastery Test*. Standardized measures are best used for assessing growth over a longer period of time, generally a year or more. There are informal assessments that can measure improvement over shorter periods of time. For more information on the use of informal measures for assessing skill growth and goal attainment you can look for books or workshops about curriculum-based assessment or curriculum-based measurement. (See the Resources for the Reading Coach section for some suggestions.)

Solving Problems Like an Expert! Developing an Intervention Plan

Novice coaches sometimes believe that problems are solved by identifying *the* key (magic?!) intervention strategy. More expert problem solvers understand that a consistent and skillful implementation of one or more possible strategies will probably lead to improvement, as long as the strategy is supported by evidence of effectiveness and is linked logically to the targeted problem and goals.

It is vital that you work with the teacher to develop an intervention plan that *can*, and probably *will*, be implemented in the classroom. Carefully designing a great intervention plan that never gets implemented will not help improve a student's reading. Researchers have identified some circumstances that contribute to the successful implementation of intervention plans:

1. The teacher *believes* that the intervention will be effective.

2. The intervention does not require lots of *time* or *material* resources.

3. There is a *match* between the theoretical underpinnings of an intervention plan and the teacher's *philosophies* and *beliefs*.

4. The *intrusiveness* of the intervention on the normal classroom routines and schedules is *minimal*.

5. The teacher has a *sense of control* of the situation (Gutkin & Conoley, 1990; Witt, 1986).

Keeping these circumstances for success in mind when developing a plan will go a long way toward ensuring that the teacher will implement it successfully. Now, begin developing your plan with a thoughtful and deliberate exploration of possible strategies to use to reach the goals you have identified rather than with a frantic search for *the* right answer or that elusive "magic bullet."

DEVELOPING A LIST OF INTERVENTION STRATEGIES

Brainstorming can be a great way to generate a list of possible strategies. It is nice for a teacher to have a "menu" of ideas from which to choose, but realistically there are times when there is only one feasible or acceptable strategy to consider. You can kick off the brainstorming session by saying something like, "Now that we have an idea of what goals we'd like to see James achieve, let's think of some ways we can help him meet these goals. Do you have any ideas about something you might like to try?"

And once again, if the teacher has had little experience in developing or using effective intervention strategies, the coach may need to take the lead in this process, perhaps by suggesting one or two possible strategies: "Thinking about the fluency goal we set for James . . . have you ever used a repeated-reading strategy in your classroom? There are some really good ways that this can be used to make a big difference in a student's accuracy and rate. Would you like some more information about what this could look like as part of a plan for James?"

Sources of strategies.

The wealth of resources and experiences that you undoubtedly have brought to the position of reading coach will be the primary source of strategies you can suggest to a teacher. The information we gave you in Chapter 2 can remind you of key factors that should be in place in research-supported instruction. Our Resources section is also a good source of ideas for possible intervention strategies.

However, while coaching has four goals—improve students' reading skills and competence, solve referred problems, learn from others, and prevent future problems—these are *goals*, not mandates. As a coach, you are a *resource* for effective ideas and strategies, not the provider of *the* perfect solution!

No single person can possibly know everything about how to help every student. Skillful, confident, professional coaches acknowledge their own level of training and expertise, as well as the limits of their knowledge and skills. In every profession, ethical standards require that a practitioner provide *only* advice and engage in activities that are in their skill sets and levels of expertise. As a coach, you need to be open to turning to other experts who may have different and/or specialized knowledge and skills that are different from yours. Many students who have reading problems also have significant behavioral and emotional needs. Quite a few come from families that face tremendous stress. A reading coach cannot be expected to have a bag of tricks or a handy magic wand to remedy all of these situations. But a coach should be prepared to call on the expertise of others when a situation warrants it.

Evaluating the suggested strategies.

Each intervention strategy you generate together with the teacher must be evaluated. Strategies under consideration should be judged on several dimensions to determine the general likelihood of their being effective. Again, it is quite possible that the teacher has little or no experience in evaluating intervention strategies, so be prepared to guide this process. Each strategy should:

- *Match the problem definition and specific goals*
- *Be appropriate* for the situation (match the age/skill level/needs of the student)
- *Be feasible* (match with the demands of the context and the available resources)
- *Be aligned with the philosophies and beliefs* of the teacher
- *Be minimally disruptive* to the normal routines of the classroom
- *Have evidence* of effectiveness

"I tried that but it didn't work."

The teacher may have already tried to implement a version of some of the very intervention strategies that you think should be considered as part of a new, collaboratively designed plan of action. The teacher may be reluctant to try again, believing that she has already attempted that particular solution and determined for herself that it wasn't effective. However, it is possible that the techniques or strategies the teacher tried may not have been used consistently or accurately, or were used for an insufficient period of time. If the teacher was trying to use a strategy for the first time, it's possible that more training, guidance, or support was needed to implement the strategy effectively. The coach may need to discuss why those "already tried but failed" strategies should perhaps be reconsidered and how those strategies can be adjusted to be more successful.

Selecting strategies to implement.

Once some possible strategies have been identified and evaluated, the teacher can select some to try. Although the coach can have input, it is important for the teacher to feel empowered to make the final selection of strategies.

After all, the teacher is the one who has to implement the plan in the classroom. The teacher has to believe the plan can work and that he or she can use the strategies effectively. A coach may need to help the teacher select a reasonable number of strategies to implement at any given time. You can point out that the list can be revisited in the future if any of the strategies selected are not as effective as was hoped or prove to be too challenging to implement in the classroom.

Developing the Plan of Action

Now it's time to develop a plan for implementing the strategies. The plan must be quite specific about how the intervention will be carried out: *who* will *do what* to implement each strategy; *how* these actions will be taken; and *when*, or *how often*, or *for how long*. Remember to include steps for notifying the student and the parents about the plan.

In some cases, the teacher may need some training to be able to successfully implement one or more of the selected intervention strategies. This may involve observing a demonstration by the coach or another teacher, or attending a workshop or in-service. If such training, guidance, or preparation is needed, it must be specified as part of the overall plan. There may also be data-collection forms, charts, or self-monitoring forms that must be created and copied in order to implement the plan. Your plan should list the person(s) who will be responsible for locating or preparing these materials, and the date they will be needed. This level of specificity will help ensure a consistent and accurate implementation of the plan. It is usually helpful for the coach to take detailed notes about the final plan of action and offer to write up the plan and distribute copies to everyone who may be involved.

WRAPPING UP INTERVENTION DEVELOPMENT

Once the goals have been set, the evaluation plan is in place, and a detailed intervention plan has been developed and written down, the coach should finalize this phase of the SPS process by briefly summarizing the definition of the target problem, the identified goals, the plan for collecting the evaluation data, and then reviewing the written plan of action. Following your summary, invite the teacher to add any information or make any corrections needed.

It is always a good idea to present the finalized plan with a balance of *optimism* and *realism*. We hope the teacher feels empowered by the SPS process and has confidence that the collaboratively developed plan has a good chance of helping the target student achieve the specified goals. However, it is important for the teacher to have realistic expectations. A significant period of time and sustained effort will probably be required before you can see improvement in a student's reading skills. Every plan is, at best, a good-faith effort to help students make some gains in their skills. A good plan, developed with care and evaluated following the SPS guidelines, is an important step in the right direction. It is never an ironclad guarantee of success.

Providing Support to the Teacher

Many interventions require at least *some* change in the teacher's behaviors or routines and may involve the teacher in new and untried procedures. During the discussion of the intervention, the teacher will probably get excited about the new ideas being discussed and the awareness that help for the student is on the way. In all of this enthusiasm, the teacher may honestly feel able to complete each of the tasks identified in the intervention plan. But upon returning to the demanding routines of the classroom, the teacher may be, in fact, a bit unclear about procedures or unable to complete some steps of the plan.

Even the most carefully developed and well-designed intervention plans—those viewed enthusiastically by teachers during the planning process—may not be implemented successfully. This happens for a variety of reasons. Maybe the teacher did not understand sufficiently how to do part of the intervention or did not have the skills or resources (time, money, materials, assistance) to carry it out. Another possible reason for an unsuccessful implementation is that there are rarely instant and positive changes in students' problems when an intervention is first implemented. Teachers may become discouraged and stop prematurely or modify the intervention plan in a manner that lessens its chances for success.

As the coach, you can avoid these pitfalls if you understand the need to support the teacher's implementation of the plan. Providing support often involves "checking in" periodically with the teacher, either in person, by phone, or by e-mail, to see how things are going and providing help, advice, guidance, and encouragement. It is almost always crucial to begin this support just *before* the initial implementation of the plan. If the teacher has decided to be ready to begin the plan on Monday, make a note to check in on the preceding Thursday or Friday, or even over the weekend, to see whether the teacher has everything in place to begin implementing the plan successfully. Be sure to check in again Monday afternoon or Tuesday morning to see how things went on the first day.

The frequency and intensity of the support should match the complexity of the intervention and the expertise and experience of the teacher in implementing interventions. In most cases, the greatest amount of support is needed in the early stages, and support can taper off after things are successfully rolling along. Obviously, inexperienced teachers attempting to implement complex interventions will require more frequent and intensive monitoring than experienced teachers implementing less complex interventions.

Evaluating Outcomes

If the evaluation component of the intervention plan contained plans for conducting formative assessments, the coach should be checking to see if this data is being collected. The information collected formatively—which includes such things as the student's self-monitoring forms, curriculum-based measurement graphs, and scores from weekly progress checks—can be reviewed periodically by the coach and teacher together to allow them to make decisions along the way about whether a component of the intervention should be *continued as is* (adequate progress is being made toward the achievement of the specified goal), *modified* (progress toward the goal is slow or nonexistent), or *phased out* (the goal has been achieved!). At the end of the specified intervention period, any summative evaluation procedures specified in the intervention plan should be completed and that information analyzed collaboratively by the coach and teacher. Again, this data can be used to guide collaboration on decisions about whether to terminate, continue, or restructure the intervention plan.

If, anywhere along the way, it appears that changes in the intervention plan are needed, you can work with the teacher to determine the following: Should those changes involve doing basically the same procedures but perhaps a bit more intensively? Or a bit more frequently? Does the procedure need to be used more systematically? Does the teacher need a bit more training or support?

Suppose the plan involves having the target student work for 15 minutes, three times a week, with a peer tutor to practice oral reading. If the formative evaluation data seems to indicate that progress is insufficient, it doesn't necessarily mean that the idea of tutoring should be abandoned. Perhaps you and the teacher should consider having the tutor work with the student for 20 minutes each session rather than 15. Or maybe the tutor can come an extra day or two each week. It could be that the materials used in the tutoring sessions need to be examined—they may be a bit too easy or too difficult to help the student. It is also important to watch the interaction between the tutor and student. How about looking at how the tutoring sessions themselves are going? Have the sessions become a time for friendly visits rather than focused, intensive practice? Is most of the tutoring time being spent getting ready, finding materials, or in some other activity besides oral reading? Consider such factors before scrapping the idea of tutoring.

If it appears that some new ideas or approaches should, in fact, be considered, you do not have to restart the entire SPS process again. Simply go back to the notes you took during Phase 2 and look at the original list of possible strategies that was developed. It may now be time to consider including one of those ideas in the plan of action. Be sure to provide the teacher with any training or support necessary when modifications or additions are made to the plan.

Another consideration to make in the evaluation process is whether the original goals were realistic. There are times when a coach and teacher may have been overly optimistic about how much growth or skill improvement would be realistic to expect from a student. It may be that the goal itself, rather than the intervention plan, should be modified. Lowering a goal or extending the time period for goal attainment can feel discouraging to all participants, but sometimes it is the most logical step to take. If a goal must be changed, it is important to present that to the student in a way that is as encouraging as possible: "James, you have been working very hard on your reading. I'm so impressed with your efforts. You know that we had hoped to be moving you up to the next level of materials by now, but I think it will be best to stay at this level for a little bit longer. I know what a hard worker you are, and I just guessed that you'd get up to that next level a bit faster. You *will* get there if you keep working this hard. It will just take a bit longer than we thought."

Examining the evaluation data may also indicate that one or more of the original goals has been achieved. Congratulations to everyone! This is an exciting moment to be sure. However, this rarely means that the larger goal of helping the student become a skilled reader has been achieved. If the general goal of a teacher was to help a student become a more competent and confident reader, making gains in reading level, reading accuracy, and reading fluency can justifiably be seen as important steps in that direction. However, once one or more of the initial goals has been achieved, it may simply be time to develop some new goals, revise the plan of action, and begin on the next step of this important journey to help the student truly become a good reader.

Conclusion

Your job as a reading coach is to do your very best work as a competent and caring professional to help teachers help their students. You cannot hold yourself or allow others to hold you to any higher standard than that. You are not a miracle worker or a magician. Some of the challenges that face teachers are not easily addressed. Problems that reflect issues and concerns that are beyond your expertise will be brought to you as a coach. As a Collaborative Problem Solver you are professionally obligated to help the teacher develop a plan that has a good chance for success, not one that is guaranteed to solve the targeted problem.

8

TEACHING TEACHERS: PROVIDING EFFECTIVE PROFESSIONAL DEVELOPMENT

I hear and I forget, I see and I remember, I do and I understand.
—Confucius

We have said that the SFC reading coach has three important tasks in a school—to be a Facilitator, a Collaborative Problem Solver, and a Teacher /Learner. In Chapters 5, 6, and 7, we described using the process of Systematic Problem Solving (SPS) to address concerns in the school that affect student reading achievement. This chapter will be devoted to the topic of professional development, the important role of Teacher/Learner.

The goal of effective professional development is not that teachers learn how to "go through the motions" of implementing an effective instructional strategy. They must *understand* the strategy enough to be able to know *when* and *how* to use it to support student learning and practice it enough to be able to apply it flexibly (Showers, Joyce, & Bennett, 1987). This kind of understanding takes time. So our definition of professional development goes beyond the traditional workshop and includes meetings with small groups of teachers, study groups, and observation and coaching of individual teachers as they learn to integrate effective instruction into their everyday teaching routines.

We say that the coach is both a teacher and a learner because, in a very real way, the coach learns from every teacher with whom the coach interacts. Sometimes the lessons are about providing good instruction, sometimes they are about interacting with all different kinds of people, and sometimes they are lessons in patience. Beyond learning from the teachers, the coach has a responsibility to keep learning about practices supported by the best possible research in reading instruction. The coach should continue to read and study, seek out professional develop-

ment opportunities, and access the support of colleagues and outside resources.

We'll be discussing different approaches to professional development in this chapter. Beyond all that information, we'd like for you to remember the following:

The Three Commandments of Professional Development

1. Focus on student outcomes and plan accordingly.

2. Promote instructional practices that are based on the best available research.

3. Plan all aspects of professional development in a purposeful, unified way.

Traditional Approaches

The first thing teachers generally think of when they hear the words *professional development* is probably a vision of a visiting "expert" who comes to the school, delivers a one-day workshop, and leaves, never to be seen or heard from again. Unfortunately, this has been the traditional model of professional development implemented in our schools. We know from research what teachers have known for years: This way of providing in-service continuing education for teachers (which we have not-so-affectionately called "one-shot wonders" or "drive-by professional development") doesn't work very well. Teachers may get an overview of a particular teaching approach, pick up some useful ideas, or even "make and take" some things to use in their classrooms, but they rarely learn enough in these one-day events to make a real difference in their instruction or to affect student outcomes. Besides, these workshops are often what we call "sit and get" sessions (or "stand and deliver" from the perspective of the person providing the workshop), in which teachers sit for hours and listen to a protracted lecture peppered with a few activities. There is considerable evidence that this traditional, short-term workshop approach does not normally result in improved instruction or student outcomes (see Showers & Joyce, 1996).

Professional Development Is Teaching

The key to effective professional development is the realization that it is a form of *teaching*. At the beginning of this chapter we included a Confucius saying that illustrates the importance of active involvement in learning. We humans learn new skills and absorb new concepts best when we can see demonstrations and models, actively participate and practice what we are trying to learn, and have ample opportunities for practice over time with feedback and guidance as we apply the new learning. Sound familiar? It actually sounds a lot like the description of effective instruction for students learning to read, doesn't it?

HOW IS TEACHING TEACHERS LIKE TEACHING STUDENTS?

Providing instruction to adults is, in some ways, like teaching students but different in other key ways. First, we'll discuss some characteristics of *all* effective instruction, particularly instruction that is meant to teach new skills or change the way people (children or adults) have been doing something.

Effective instruction responds to the needs of the learner.

Just as the effective reading teacher assesses the strengths and needs of his or her students and teaches what they need to learn to become competent readers, the effective reading coach assesses the needs of reading teachers in the school. This assessment can take many forms, including classroom observations, meetings with teachers to talk about their needs, questionnaires, or more formal needs assessment procedures. Sometimes a need becomes apparent from patterns of student performance on assessments. For example, if few students in the 3rd grade are making sufficient progress in oral reading fluency, developing a workshop to present and provide practice in effective strategies for teaching fluency may be warranted. Researchers have recommended that teams of teachers work together to examine the results of student assessments, reflect on their own teaching, discuss their experiences and perspectives, and collaboratively seek solutions to common problems (Birman, Desimone, Porter, & Garet, 2000; Guskey, 1995; Learning First Alliance, 2000; Showers & Joyce, 1996). As teachers engage in this kind of cooperative planning and problem solving, needs that might be addressed in professional development will probably emerge.

To better understand cooperative planning and problem solving, one group of researchers met regularly with small groups of teachers over the course of the school year (Schumm & Vaughn, 1995). In order to include the teachers in the planning process, the researchers had teachers identify their needs in a two-step format. In one meeting the teachers brainstormed topics they would like to focus on in future meetings. This brainstorming session was audiotaped. After the meeting the researchers created a list of all the possible topics. During the next meeting, teachers received a copy of the list and ranked the topics according to their own needs. Future meetings addressed these topics in order. Interestingly, this study was conducted in more than one school, and teachers in different schools all came up with pretty much the same list of topics. But it was important to give them ownership of the process that came from the needs assessment.

Effective instruction may take place in different grouping formats.

Just as the effective reading teacher may provide instruction in large- and small-group formats—and sometimes individually if a student has particular needs—the effective reading coach sometimes conducts workshops for groups of teachers who have similar needs, sometimes works with small groups of teachers at a particular grade level, and sometimes works individually with particular teachers, modeling effective instructional strategies and observing teachers in their classrooms. The SPS process can be a form of professional development when individual or small groups of teachers work collaboratively with the coach to improve reading outcomes for a student or group of students.

Although the particular approach to professional development taken in a school should be determined by the needs of teachers in that school, we suggest that the program begin with a schoolwide workshop for reading teachers. This kind of workshop can give the "big picture." It can be followed by regular meetings with grade-level groups (or groups formed in some other way). In these meetings, groups share what is working in their classrooms and offer suggestions to each other and participate in training developed by the reading coach. They may also participate in a book study. (In our Resources for the Reading Coach section, we include a list of books that may be appropriate.) In the small-group sessions, teachers learn and practice such things as instructional strategies and how to administer assessments and use assessment information to guide instruction. Teachers may also participate in group problem-solving processes, which we describe in Chapter 5. These regular small-group meetings would often be followed by coaching provided to teachers in their classrooms.

Regardless of the content of the professional development or the number of teachers in the group, remember that people are usually motivated to learn new concepts and skills that are practical and relevant to their situations. This means that the reading coach should always be conscious of the needs of the teachers in the school, especially as the needs of the teachers connect with the needs of the students.

Effective instruction in new skills or strategies includes modeling or demonstration.

Simply put, reading or hearing about a new instructional strategy just isn't as powerful as actually *seeing* a demonstration of it. In professional development, this modeling and demonstration takes the form of role-playing during workshops and showing videos of effective instruction. But the important advantage of the reading coach over the providers of more traditional professional development is that the coach is in the school for the long haul. The coach can model effective instruction in the classroom of an individual teacher with that teacher's own students, and this modeling can take place several times if needed. This kind of modeling is powerful if done in the spirit of sharing ideas. Klingner, Vaughn, Hughes, and Arguelles (1999) found that some of the teachers who had participated in a yearlong professional development program focused on reading-related interventions were still implementing the strategies they had learned three years later. These teachers said that one of the factors that made it possible for them to incorporate the strategies into their teaching routines was having the researchers or other facilitators actually demonstrate the strategies in the teachers' own classrooms.

It can be equally powerful to have teachers observe each other (see Learning First Alliance, 2000; Showers & Joyce, 1996). The reading coach may cover one teacher's class while that teacher observes another teacher who is already implementing components of effective instruction. Pairs of teachers may observe an expert teacher and discuss the lesson. Sometimes this expert teacher may be located at a different school. Cross-school observations by teams of teachers may be a strong motivator for growth and change. Another model we have found useful in coaching some teachers is to accompany a teacher (who we'll call Teacher 1) to observe in another teacher's classroom (Teacher 2). As Teacher 2 provides instruction, the coach is able to point out particularly effective instructional strategies to Teacher 1 in "real time"—as the class is going on. We will discuss peer coaching in greater detail later in this chapter.

When people learn new skills, they need opportunities to practice with feedback and support.

Humans are creatures of habit in many ways. When we are used to doing something in a particular way, it can be hard for us to make changes. Most of us have routines for several activities in our lives, such as morning tasks—brushing teeth and getting ready for work—that we execute in very much the same way each day (or at least each workday). There's nothing wrong with having routines. They provide a framework within which we can make important choices. But sometimes we have habits that we would rather change (eating certain foods or biting fingernails, for example) but that are very difficult to break. Anyone who has tried to make real long-term changes knows that it can be challenging.

Even if teachers understand and embrace a new instructional strategy, and have seen and tried it out during a workshop, it normally takes quite a lot of practice to integrate it into their regular teaching routines. Showers et al. (1987), who studied professional development and peer coaching extensively, concluded that teachers need to implement a new practice in about 25 teaching episodes before it is integrated into their repertoire of strategies and they are likely to continue to use it. Even more practice is required to refine the strategies and to be able to use them flexibly to respond to particular student needs. Besides the time spent actually practicing implementing a new strategy, teachers need time to reflect on new concepts and skills. A report of the Learning First Alliance (2000) suggests that professional development might include as many as 80 to 100 hours per year dedicated to study, collaboration, and observation.

But it is not enough to have teachers simply practice new ways of teaching. Teachers need feedback and support as they apply what they have learned. One of the most important characteristics of effective professional development for teachers is continuous coaching or mentoring over time (Guskey, 1995; Joyce & Showers, 1981; Learning First Alliance, 2000; Showers & Joyce, 1996; Showers et al., 1987). It is less important that teachers receive feedback on how well they are executing a teaching strategy than on the quality of the instructional decisions they make as they integrate the strategy in different situations in pursuit of specific goals (Joyce & Showers, 1981). It is not only important that teachers learn new skills but that they learn when to apply them and how to modify them in response to the needs of their students. This represents a deep level of learning in which teachers engage in continuous problem solving as they respond to the needs of their students.

How Is Teaching Teachers Different From Teaching Students?

Although providing continuing education to teachers is like teaching students in many ways, it is also different in some important ways. The key difference: Teachers are *adults*! There are some key characteristics of adult learners that the reading coach must keep in mind. First, remember that adults "come to the table" with accumulated knowledge, attitudes, and beliefs based on their life experiences. Keep in mind that the background knowledge and attitudes of the teachers you are working with may be different from yours. Remember to value these diverse experiences while you offer new approaches. Later in this chapter we will discuss the importance of communicating the reasons and even the theories behind new instructional practices. This is important because teachers may need to consider new beliefs and attitudes that are different from those they previously held. Other important characteristics of adult learners are that they are independent and motivated by their personal needs and goals. They learn best when the content is practical, is relevant to them, and addresses their particular needs.

So what *are* the needs of adult learners? Maslow (1987) described a progression of human needs from the most basic to the most complex. His theory says that the lowest levels of needs have to be satisfied before higher-level needs can be met. His hierarchy of needs, from the lowest to the highest level, is:

1. Physiological or survival needs (food, water, shelter)
2. The need for safety
3. The need for love, affection, and a feeling of belonging
4. The need for self-respect and for the respect of others
5. The need for self-actualization (to become everything the person is capable of becoming or to feel successful and fulfilled)

What does this mean to the reading coach? It means that when you plan professional development activities, it's a good idea to keep the needs that Maslow described in mind.

First, be sure the teachers are comfortable. They will be less likely to benefit from the experience if they are very tired or hungry, or too hot or too cold. Although professional development often takes place after school out of necessity, this may not be the time most conducive to learning. If you must work with teachers after school, think about providing snacks. Acknowledge that you know it's the end of a long day and teachers may be tired.

Be sure the teachers feel safe. The concern is not so much physical safety but emotional safety. The teachers must have a sense that they can ask questions, make comments, and try out new instructional strategies without feeling embarrassed or belittled.

The teachers will be more likely to continue to participate in professional development and learn from each other if they have a sense of belonging to a group. It's important to build a feeling of being a team, so it can be very helpful to meet with the same groups of teachers over time. Sometimes this feeling of community can be enhanced by providing some opportunities for socializing as a group. You might start each meeting with refreshments and a brief time for interaction and chatting among teachers about how things are going in their own reading lessons. Most important, all of the teachers need to feel welcome and know that each one of them has an important role in the group.

Adults (and children too!) have a need to feel respected. Always keep this in mind as a reading coach. All of the teachers in the school must feel that they are important and respected members of a professional community. Sometimes it can be challenging to convey this feeling of respect to a teacher who may need to make changes in order to support greater student growth. For some help, refer back to Chapter 4, where we discuss communication skills in depth.

Adults are motivated by the need for self-actualization: the need to "be all that they can be." Teachers need to feel that they are competent and that their students benefit from their efforts. Teachers are also typically motivated by the need to make a contribution to society. Part of the need for self-actualization is the desire to learn. Remember to ask the teachers what they want to learn about teaching reading and to assess their needs through your observations and through analyzing student assessments.

Teachers are most likely to implement new instructional strategies well and continue to use them over time when the strategies are practical (not too complex or time-consuming) and, most of all, when the teachers believe that their students are successful (Borman et al., 2000; Gersten, Chard, & Baker, 2000; LeFevre & Richardson, 2000; Stanovich & Stanovich, 1997). Showers et al. (1987) summarized findings of nearly 200 studies on staff development and concluded that teachers' initial attitude toward a particular program *is not as important as their judgment of its effects on their students.* Teachers may need to learn the basic concepts and skills of a new approach before they can really buy into it. Teachers are

also much more likely to integrate new teaching strategies into their regular routines if they receive coaching as they begin to apply the strategies in their own classrooms. (Of course, that's where the reading coach comes in!)

As you provide professional development to teachers (including individual coaching and modeling), it is important to keep these characteristics of adult learners and sources of motivation in mind. Your efforts are much more likely to result in success if you treat the teachers with whom you work with respect and keep in mind their needs to feel fulfilled, engage in positive social relationships, and make a difference for students.

Characteristics of Adult Change and Growth

Reading coaches who provide professional development should keep in mind that change can be difficult and that it typically happens in stages and takes time. In their summary of literature on professional development relating to reading, the Learning First Alliance (2000) concludes that school change should take place according to a long-range vision that may include three to five years of work, with student outcomes showing greater growth each year. Following are some other aspects of the change process that the reading coach should keep in mind.

1. *Don't try to change too much too soon.* Guskey (1995) cautions the person organizing professional development to "think big, but start small" (p. 5). If teachers are asked to make a large-scale change, it is unlikely that they will do it. Successful professional development programs should have long-term goals based on gradual change over time, with attention to introducing new practices in such a way that they will not require large changes or a lot of additional work. Yet it's important that teachers not feel that the professional development process is trivial or a waste of time. The best chance for success exists when people are asked to make changes that require a sustained effort over time—but not such large changes that they become defensive and cope by refusing to implement the new practices as designed. However, the long-term approach must not become a fragmented succession of programs. Long-term professional development should include explicit descriptions of how separate strategies can be integrated within a unified framework.

2. *Changes must be realistic.* Keep the "reality principle" (Gersten & Woodward, 1990, p. 8) in mind. Changes that you ask teachers to make must take into consideration the realities of the classroom. Teachers are most likely to adopt new practices—and keep using them—if they are concrete, practical, manageable, and not overly demanding of time (for either planning or instruction).

3. *Effective change takes place at the individual and school levels* (Guskey, 1995). Real school change cannot occur unless it is implemented in individual classrooms by individual teachers. At the same time, teachers will be more likely to implement and sustain new approaches if they feel that other teachers and administrators are on board. Attempting to implement changes without the support of peers and supervisors is very risky. Failure could mean embarrassment or even reprimand. (We discuss the importance of facilitating a school-wide environment to support sustained change in Chapter 9.

4. *Self-reflection and self-evaluation are important* (Learning First Alliance, 2000). This should begin with teachers' evaluation of student assessment data. Some assessments, such as repeated monitoring of oral reading fluency, lend themselves to graphing the results over time. The graphs make it easier for teachers to locate patterns of growth—or lack of growth—in their students' reading. It can be especially helpful for teachers to meet in collaborative teams to examine and discuss student outcomes. Ideally, teachers will recognize their needs for professional development in particular facets of reading as they discuss the assessment results. The reading coach may participate in these collaborative team meetings and skillfully—that is, respectfully, gently, mainly by asking questions—guide the conversation to help teachers clarify their needs.

Elements of Effective Professional Development

Showers et al. (1987) suggest that, for teachers to learn a new instructional practice and apply it successfully in the classroom, they must have opportunities to:

• *Understand the theory and rationale for the new content and instruction.* As adult learners and as professionals,

teachers need to understand the *reasons* for making a change in their teaching, the *relevance* of the new content and instruction to them, and the *likelihood* that the change will result in *increased student success.* One group of researchers analyzed the professional development that had been received by eight teachers in one school who still implemented a peer-assisted learning strategy they had learned 10 years earlier. They noted that the teachers had first participated in a workshop that was practical and let the teachers see the "big picture" of the theory, research, and concepts that supported the teaching strategy. This initial training was followed by ongoing support and coaching as teachers applied the strategy in their classrooms. The researchers suggest that teachers may be dissatisfied with continuous coaching when they have not been given this "big picture" first (Baker, Gersten, Dimino, & Griffiths, 2004).

• *Observe a model in action.* All new instructional methods and skills should be modeled clearly, either in a workshop or in teachers' classrooms.

• *Practice the new strategy in a safe context.* This normally refers to practicing with other teachers within a positive environment, normally through role-playing during a workshop or small-group session.

• *Try out the new practice with peer support in the classroom.* The reading coach provides support and feedback during classroom observations (or facilitates peer coaching), providing further modeling as necessary. Teachers who are in the process of adopting a new instructional method or strategy should have the opportunity to discuss their successes and frustrations with peers or with the coach.

Nearly all teachers can receive some benefit from workshops if they include a presentation of the theory underlying a new instructional strategy, demonstration of the new strategy, the opportunity to practice it during the workshop, and prompt feedback (Showers et al., 1987). They are more likely to refine their use of the strategy and continue to implement it if these elements are included in regular meetings rather than one-time workshops and if they receive some form of coaching as they attempt to apply it in their classrooms.

WORKSHOPS

The key to providing effective workshops is planning. As a reading coach, you will need a framework to help you in the planning process. The one we provide next is certainly not the only way to organize a workshop, but it may be useful as you plan the sequence and format of professional development in your school:

1. Establish a purpose for the session and give teachers the "big picture."

   - *Talk about the benefits of the approach, process, or strategy.* Let the teachers know what they are likely to gain by learning and using the new approach.

   - *Link to needs the teachers have identified.* Let the teachers know that you take their needs seriously by focusing on areas of need that they have identified and linking the workshop to these needs.

   - *Focus on student outcomes.* Talk about patterns of student strengths and needs that teachers have identified through assessments and about the potential of the new approach or strategy to help support the growth of their students.

   - *Create links to research.* A discussion of the potential benefits of the approach should include a description of the research supporting it. Research may sound a bit dry, but it is really just the stories of past success with the approach (even research that uses statistics to analyze test results is telling a story about a group of students and their growth). It's important to make links to research so that teachers know why they are being asked to implement particular strategies. (See Chapter 2 for more information about research on reading instruction.)

   - *Make it practical!* Stress the practical nature of the new approach or instructional strategy. Help teachers understand that learning this new strategy will make their teaching more effective rather than just making more work for them!

2. Provide modeling and demonstration of instructional strategies.

   - *Model any new or unfamiliar procedures.*

   - *Have successful teachers demonstrate strategies to each other.*

3. Be sure to plan for active involvement. Here are some suggestions:

   - *Include time for discussion with other teachers.* For example, you might ask for a one-sentence reaction to a question or statement printed on a chart or integrated into your presentation. Have each teacher write only one sentence in response. Then provide three minutes for teachers to discuss their responses in pairs.

   - *Have teachers role-play to practice new activities and strategies.* Model strategies for providing feedback and scaffolding, then have teachers practice in pairs or small groups, with one teacher role-playing the part of a teacher and others role-playing students; practice conducting oral reading fluency assessments.

   - *Have teachers put objectives and teaching activities in order by difficulty level or developmental sequence.* For example, provide teachers with a list of objectives related to phonological awareness—such as syllable segmentation, blending onsets and rimes, and first sound identification. Demonstrate each task, and then ask teachers to work in groups of three to try to put the objectives in order of difficulty for most students (Learning First Alliance, 2000).

   - *Have teachers practice developing strategies for providing their students with many opportunities to practice skills.* For example, teachers may think of ways that students could have repeated encounters with and opportunities to use new vocabulary words (Learning First Alliance, 2000).

   - *Have teachers practice grouping students based on assessment results.* Have teachers bring the results of one or two key assessments they have administered to their students. Discuss the interpretation of the results and assist teachers in using the results to create small groups of students who have similar instructional needs. Encourage teachers to work together on this activity.

   - *Have teachers create sample lessons or lesson plans.* Assist teachers in creating lessons based on the results of assessments of their own students, or provide a scenario for a fictitious group of students, including assessment data, and guide the teachers in using the data to plan instruction for these students.

4. Encourage self-reflection and help teachers become problem solvers.

- *Observe and discuss live or videotaped lessons.*

- *Ask teachers to share what has worked well in their classrooms, or strategies they have used to identify and solve student problems.*

- *Provide a format for self-reflection.* This may consist of a simple form teachers complete after a lesson and bring to team meetings or study groups: What was supposed to happen? What happened? What worked well? What would I do differently next time? See the Appendix for a sample Lesson Reflection form.

STUDY GROUPS

Study groups are groups of teachers who meet on a regular basis to improve their instructional practices and collaborate to solve problems related to student learning. Murphy (1992) suggests that there are three main functions for teacher study groups: learning to implement instructional practices, collaboratively planning for school improvement, and studying research on best practices. Another very important component of a teacher study group is examining their students' work and responding to the results of students' assessments. Teachers in many successful schools meet regularly to examine the progress of their students and to discuss ways to support students who do not make adequate progress. In the challenged, but successful schools described by Denton, Foorman, and Mathes (2003), an instructional leader or facilitator met with each group of teachers.

In her report of her experience organizing teacher study groups in 54 schools over a period of years, Murphy (1992) says she has found that the groups should contain no more than six teachers. In her experience, when groups are larger, some teachers don't get actively involved, and small groups of two or three teachers may split off into cliques. The groups can be organized by grade level or across grade levels. In some schools, study groups meet during the school day. One school described in Murphy's paper extended the school day slightly on four days of the week so that students could be released early once a week to provide time for study groups. In other schools,

teachers meet after school or during one planning period each week. Teachers in two very successful high schools said that block scheduling enabled them to have the time they needed for study groups and collaboration (Wallace, Anderson, & Bartholomay, 2002).

Murphy (1992) also stresses the importance of keeping a regular schedule. She recommends that teachers meet once a week for about an hour. In the study groups she describes, teachers rotate the job of group leader. Murphy also suggests that participation in groups should not be voluntary, because the improvement of student outcomes is not optional. In one school district she describes, once a school has decided to adopt a study group model, all certified staff, including administrators, are expected to participate in study groups.

One group of researchers described lessons they learned from conducting small-group professional development with teachers in elementary, middle, and high schools (Schumm & Vaughn, 1995). The goal of this project was to have teachers participate in "professional dialogues" (p. 347) in which teachers examined the professional knowledge base on a topic with input from university experts, talked about their own personal knowledge of the topic, and synthesized the two.

As they began the professional development effort, they found that teachers seemed to value the professional knowledge but that discussions tended to focus more on their personal knowledge and experiences. The teachers seemed to appreciate the chance to share their challenges and knowledge with their colleagues. Although a university facilitator was present, that person did not take a large role in determining the direction or content of the meetings. Over time, some groups of teachers seemed to begin to trust the researchers more, and they tended to have the researchers take over more of the responsibility for making decisions about the groups' activities.

Interestingly, during the second phase of this professional development initiative, the researchers decided to include more information on key topics. The sessions were more organized than in the first phase and included a lot of current information. Although they had intended to maintain the professional dialogues, teachers' active participation decreased noticeably. The teachers were satisfied with the sessions and appreciated the chance to learn from "experts," but they did not make the same kinds of personal connections with what they were learning as the teachers in the first phase had made. The experiences of Schumm and Vaughn (1995) illustrate the important balance that must be achieved in teacher study groups between teacher discussion and sharing of research-based content.

Guskey (2003) has a wise warning about teacher collaboration: "… Individuals can collaborate to block change or inhibit progress just as easily as they can to enhance the process" (p. 2). Study groups must be purposeful and focused on improving student learning. Three things are very important in planning and organizing study groups: (1) Keep the focus on the students and use assessment data to guide the topics; (2) don't let the groups become forums for teachers to compare stories or vent frustrations without focusing on *solutions* to problems; and (3) keep the focus on research-based instructional strategies for which there is evidence of effectiveness.

IN-CLASS COACHING AND MODELING

Coaching in teachers' classrooms can take several different forms. We described in detail a collaborative problem-solving format in Chapters 5–7. Other activities can include modeling, observation and feedback, co-planning, and co-teaching. The coach also has the important role of supporting teachers as they make changes in their classrooms. This support may include listening to teachers and empathizing with the frustrations they face, but the focus should always be skillfully directed to the impact of new techniques on student improvement that include:

- *Modeling instruction.* The reading coach may demonstrate an instructional strategy in a teacher's classroom with the teacher's own students.

- *Observation and feedback.* (See Chapter 6 for a full discussion of issues related to classroom observations). One of the most common practices of coaching is observing teachers and providing feedback. This can also be one of the most difficult for the teacher. As much as possible, link your feedback to student participation and learning. It is helpful to make notes during an observation about things like the level of student participation in discussions or how successful students were during the lesson. When you give the teacher feedback, be sure to include specific comments about these aspects of the lesson. In any case, remember to emphasize the positive things you observed, especially

any implementation of strategies from the professional development. Don't present more than one or two suggestions to the teacher, and break these down into manageable steps (Gersten, Morvant, & Brengelman, 1995). Later in this chapter we will suggest a method of peer coaching (teachers coaching each other) that can be preferable in many cases to "expert" coaching delivered directly by the reading coach. Above all, the reading coach can *never* evaluate a colleague; that is one of the differences that exists between supervision and coaching.

DISCUSSING ASSESSMENT RESULTS

It's particularly important to give teachers feedback that relates to the effects of new strategies and approaches they have used. For example, if teachers implement a new strategy for teaching oral reading fluency, point out results from assessments that show improved fluency. We can't emphasize enough the power of feedback based on continually monitoring student growth through repeated assessments. If teachers see that their efforts are resulting in their students becoming better readers, they are much more likely to continue to implement new ideas in their classrooms.

CO-PLANNING

Coaching includes working collaboratively with teachers to integrate new instructional approaches and strategies into daily lessons (Joyce & Showers, 1981). It can be very helpful to meet with individual teachers or small groups of teachers to plan instruction, especially when they provide different instruction to small groups of students targeted at their strengths and needs. Some teachers may need quite a lot of support until they begin to understand the process of using student assessment data to form groups and plan instruction.

CO-TEACHING

In some cases a reading coach may take on the task of co-teaching. This can be a powerful way to provide professional development and build collaborative relationships. Although there are several ways to co-teach, we suggest a model in which one teacher provides instruction while the other circulates, monitoring and supporting students, with the two teachers trading roles at different points. Although co-teaching may provide valuable support for a teacher and for struggling readers, we caution the coach *not* to adopt this as a permanent strategy. The coach must have time to be available to *all* of the teachers in the school rather than being scheduled to assist in particular classrooms on a regular basis. Perhaps a better implementation of co-teaching might be having the coach cover one teacher's class for a few sessions while that teacher engages in co-teaching with a second teacher. This can be useful if at least one of the teachers is very proficient at implementing research-based reading practices. (We discuss models of co-teaching in greater depth in Chapter 9.)

PEER COACHING

Peer coaching can be an important way to encourage teachers to reflect on their own practices (Daniels, 2002). Peer coaches observe each other, model for each other, and provide feedback and support to each other. Peer coaches can give teachers three kinds of support: *practical support* (such as answering questions, emphasizing important teaching points, participating in problem solving, and helping choose materials); *emotional support* (reassuring teachers, confirming what they had learned, encouraging teachers to take risks and not give up); and *reflective support* (helping teachers reflect on their own teaching) (Swafford, 1998).

Peer coaching without feedback.

Peer coaching is often characterized as having one teacher observe another and then give the observed teacher feedback on the lesson taught. In Chapter 6, we briefly discussed an approach to observation that does not include providing feedback. We will elaborate on it here. Showers and Joyce (1996) found that when teachers gave each other feedback, their collaborative relationships tended to be weakened. Instead, they implemented a model of peer coaching that did *not* include having one teacher provide feedback to another. They had pairs of teachers observe each other, but they called *the one doing the teaching* the "coach" and said that the one observing was being coached. The one who is teaching the lesson is providing modeling, and the observing teacher is learning from the one who is teaching. Rather than giving feedback, the observer merely thanks the coach for the opportunity to observe and to pick up some good ideas for the classroom.

Showers and Joyce (1996) found that the *real* power of these pairs of teachers working together came from what they learned from each other as they planned lessons together, developed materials for the lessons, watched each other work with students, and reflected together about the impact of their behaviors on what their students learned. They found that taking out the step of having teachers give each other verbal feedback on their lessons did not make the outcomes for students or teachers any less successful—but it *did* make it easier for pairs of teachers to trust each other and continue to work together.

As a reading coach, you may find this a very useful model of peer coaching to enhance the learning of teachers and students. But use caution in pairing the teachers. At least one of the teachers in each pair must be fairly proficient in the instructional strategies the reading coach is emphasizing in professional development and individual coaching. If two teachers who are resistant to change are paired, there is little likelihood that the result will be growth for either one.

Peer coaching with feedback.

Another type of peer coaching that *does* include feedback is based on a model called cognitive coaching. The success of this type of peer coaching depends on the teachers having a trusting relationship, a desire to learn and grow, and the ability to work both independently and collaboratively (Daniels, 2002). In this model, teachers meet in a preplanning session. The teacher who is going to be observed tells the peer coach what to look for in the lesson and identifies specific areas where feedback is desired. The two teachers also plan what kind of observation approach or tool will be used. (See Chapter 6 for some suggestions.) After this kind of observation, the teachers meet again, and the coach shares the data collected using the observation tool. We suggest that the two teachers use a form to help them summarize their reflections on what was supposed to happen in the lesson, what happened, what should be kept the same, and what should be changed in the future. A Lesson Reflection Form for this kind of self-evaluation is included in the Appendix of this book.

A UNIFIED APPROACH

Just having teachers meet regularly *doesn't mean they will automatically make changes in their classrooms.*

Poglinco & Bach (2004), who spent a year researching coaching as a kind of professional development, concluded that the key is to have a clear link between the professional development group activities and individual coaching. The reading coach needs to have clear objectives in planning each phase of professional development in the school, and the different facets of professional development must be coordinated to address those objectives. Teachers work together in study groups, engage in peer coaching, participate in workshops, have individual coaching and modeling, and collaborate to solve problems, all in a unified, purposeful way.

The Content of Professional Development

Professional development in reading instruction can be organized in two ways: around the research-based characteristics of effective instruction or around the critical components of the reading program. These are described in Chapter 2, but we include a list in Tables 8.1 and 8. 2 as a reference to assist you in planning workshops, study groups, and individual coaching sessions.

In Table 8.1, we list some of the characteristics of effective instruction. For each characteristic, we also provide

Table 8.1 Some Research-Based Characteristics of Effective Reading Instruction

Characteristic	Professional Development Activity
Targeted instruction based on assessments	Administer various assessments, and use the results to form instructional groups, list objectives for lessons based on the assessment results, and plan lessons to address the objectives.
Appropriate text selection	Determine students' instructional reading levels using the "90% rule" (see Chapter 2), and select text appropriate to teach different objectives.
Explicit instruction	Observe and practice a teaching approach based on modeling skills and strategies, clearly explaining concepts and providing examples, providing guided practice, providing prompts and scaffolding, providing specific praise related to reading, providing specific corrective feedback, providing for and monitoring independent practice, and reteaching or clarifying instruction, as needed.
Effective instructional delivery, including instruction in which teachers: • Communicate enthusiasm and warmth. • Use effective eye contact, vocal tone, and proximity. • Deliver lessons with effective pacing and use of time. • Ensure that students are actively involved in learning. • Elicit responses from all students. • Communicate expectations that all students will learn.	Observe models of effective instructional delivery (may include videotapes). Evaluate videotaped lessons for these characteristics. (Use tapes of lessons that are *not* from your school, unless teachers have agreed to self-evaluate tapes of their own teaching. Viewing tapes of your own teaching can be a valuable learning experience, but take great care not to embarrass teachers in this activity.)
Continuous monitoring of student progress	Conduct one-minute assessments of oral reading fluency, graph student progress, and use the graphs to determine whether students are achieving adequate growth or whether instruction should be changed to promote quicker growth.
Effective classroom management	Observe and practice strategies to increase positive student behavior, including clearly communicating expectations to students, reinforcing positive behavior through praise and positive statements (making three positive statements for every negative statement or correction), and teaching students classroom routines to provide support for student independence and efficient use of time.

suggestions for activities for professional development. This list is not complete, but it is designed to give you some examples to use in planning. (Please review Chapter 2 for a detailed discussion of research-based reading instruction.)

Table 8.2 lists the key components of reading instruction and the grade levels at which they should be addressed. Professional development can be organized around the knowledge and skills teachers need in these areas. The Learning First Alliance's *Every Child Reading: A Professional Development Guide* is an excellent resource for planning professional development focused on these components of research-supported reading instruction. We highly recommend it and provide information about it in our Resources section. We have adapted Table 8.2 from this publication, and the original guide provides more complete information. The *Every Child Reading* professional development guide was developed by a committee chaired by Louisa Moats, who is also the author of the series of professional development called *Language Essentials for Teachers of Reading and Spelling* (LETRS) (Moats, 2004). The LETRS series is aligned with the Every Child Reading guide, and LETRS training can prepare the reading coach to offer effective professional development to teachers. We include information about LETRS in the Resources section of this book.

Strategic Coaching Professional Development Planning Guide

As we have noted, the reading coach performs several important roles within a school. The coach facilitates collaboration between professionals in the school and works with teachers to solve problems when students do not make sufficient progress in learning to read. A central role of the reading coach is to plan and help deliver effective professional development with the goal of improving the quality of reading instruction in a school. We believe that a reading coach with a game plan is much more likely to be successful in this role. Simply put, if you know where you want to go, you are much more likely to get there! On the other hand, as a reading coach at one of our workshops once said, "If you aim at nothing, you'll hit it every time!"

We developed the *Strategic Coaching Professional Development Planning Guide (SCPDP Guide)* to enable a reading coach to assess the needs in a school and plan coaching activities that address these needs. Our approach includes five steps:

1. Assess the needs for professional development in the school.

2. Prioritize the needs.

3. Write objectives to address the needs.

4. Plan activities to address the objectives.

5. Evaluate the effectiveness of the plan.

You will find a copy of the *Strategic Coaching Professional Development Planning Guide* in the Appendix.

Conclusion

Professional development takes many forms—large-group workshops, small study groups, collaborative sharing of ideas among teachers, and individual coaching. The reading coach must keep the needs of the teachers—and the students—in mind when planning both the format and the content of the professional development. Just as we ask teachers to be flexible in their instruction of students with different needs, the reading coach must be flexible in supporting the growth of the reading teachers in the school. And above all, the reading coach must keep the real goal in mind at all times. Remember—*it's all about the students!*

Table 8.2 Critical Components of the Reading Program

Component	Possible Professional Development Activities
Concepts of print (pre-K–3)	• Model and practice explicit lessons to teach children in kindergarten and early 1st grade print-related vocabulary such as *letter*, *word*, *first letter of a word*, *sentence*.
Phonemic awareness (pre-K–1)	• Understand the important role of phonemic awareness in learning to read. • Practice skills such as onset-rime segmentation, phoneme segmentation, and phoneme blending. • Model and practice providing instruction in phonemic awareness skills. • Design lessons that link phonemic awareness activities with phonics and spelling.
Phonics and decoding (K–3)	• Select words that contain various letter patterns (*ae*, *ow*, *ee*) or syllable patterns (open, closed, silent *e*). • Practice techniques such as sound blending, word analysis, and word sorting. • Use student assessments to identify objectives for phonics and decoding instruction. • Observe models of explicit phonics instruction and practice instructional techniques.
Fluent text reading (K–12)	• Practice assessing oral reading fluency. • Compare the fluency rates of students to established norms for fluency to determine which students need fluency instruction. • Observe and practice instructional techniques for promoting fluency, including repeated reading and partner reading.
Vocabulary (pre-K–12)	• Select books to read aloud that will support students' vocabulary growth. • Select words from text that should be directly taught before reading and tell the reasons for these choices. • Observe and practice strategies for explicitly teaching the use of context to determine word meanings.
Reading comprehension (pre-K–12)	• Understand the role of comprehension strategy instruction. • Observe and practice instruction designed to teach students to use comprehension strategies before, during, and after reading (such as prediction, questioning, summarizing). • Discuss the importance of teaching comprehension of both narrative and expository text and comprehension strategies that apply to each.
Spelling and word analysis (K–12)	• Examine students' work to estimate their levels of spelling development. • Develop a sequence of spelling instruction that coordinates with instruction in phonics and decoding. • Design lessons to explicitly teach spelling of various word types. • Practice techniques such as word sorts and categorizing words according to morphemes such as prefixes, suffixes, and Latin and Greek roots.
Written expression (K–12)	• Examine student work to identify strengths and weaknesses. • Discuss strategies for making writing part of the daily classroom routine. • Work together to generate rubrics that can be used to evaluate student writing and to apply the rubrics consistently. • Observe and practice instructional strategies for teaching students to proofread and self-correct their writing.
Motivating students to read (K–12)	• Collaboratively develop a format for evaluating text for readability, quality, and usefulness in reading instruction. • Collaboratively identify strategies to promote students' independent reading.

9

SUPPORTING SUSTAINED
SCHOOLWIDE COMMITMENT

In most schools, teaching is a solitary task. Teachers work in their own classrooms and often have little interaction with each other about professional matters. Although they may sometimes talk about their frustrations to colleagues (too often in the teachers' lounge), they seldom have the experience of working as a team to solve problems or plan for student success. Their principals may observe them once or twice a year, but for the most part many teachers are left alone to work through challenges in their classrooms. In recent years, teachers have been given mandates about the kind of curriculum to use and the importance of their students meeting standards on statewide or districtwide tests. However, many teachers receive little in the way of professional development on the materials they are asked to implement or on strategies for making sure their students are successful.

An unfortunate result of teachers' professional isolation is the notion that only one teacher is really responsible for any individual student (in elementary schools) or any specific subject area (at the secondary level). If statewide assessment scores for students in an elementary classroom are low, one teacher is often held responsible. And if students qualify for special education and receive instruction in a resource room, their classroom teachers may give up responsibility for their progress, assuming that these students are now "someone else's kids."

A Schoolwide Approach for Reading Excellence

Researchers have found a different pattern in schools that are able to overcome challenges so that most of their students are successful readers. These schools have a *schoolwide approach to working for reading excellence*. At these schools, there is a sense of belonging to a team of educators who are *all* responsible for the success of *each*

student in the school. Some examples of a schoolwide approach follow.

- The schools exhibit a "sense of urgency" about *working toward schoolwide literacy*. Everyone in the school is included in the goal of having all students read on grade level. Teachers recognize their key role as professional educators and are respected and supported in their efforts (Adler & Fisher, 2001; Denton, Foorman, & Mathes, 2003; Lein, Johnson, & Ragland, 1997).

- There is a strong instructional leader, either the principal or another person (such as a literacy specialist), who has *clear goals for schoolwide literacy*. Everyone in the school knows about these goals, and there is the sense of an *organized effort* to improve reading outcomes (Adler & Fisher, 2001; Denton, Foorman et al., 2003; Parker, O'Neill, Hall, & Hasbrouck, 2004).

- *Teachers meet regularly to look at the results of assessments* of student progress, which are administered on a regular basis. They work together to discuss steps to be taken for students who are not making adequate progress.

In many schools, the principal or another instructional leader meets with these teams of teachers to monitor and plan for student success (Denton, Foorman et al., 2003; Lein et al., 1997; Parker et al., 2004).

- *Teachers and administrators receive the professional development and support they need* to be able to meet the needs of their students. Teachers know that expectations for student success are high, but they also know that they are not working alone (Denton, Foorman et al., 2003). Support may include bringing in experts to provide professional development, but teachers are given opportunities to learn in many formats, including study groups and individual coaching. Each teacher expects to participate in some form of professional development activity. In one school district we visited recently, teachers develop personal goals at the beginning of each semester and are given a choice of three formats of professional development activities to help them meet their goals. They may choose to attend three half-day workshops, participate in a weekly study group with other teachers, or participate in individual coaching sessions. Teachers select their options, review them with their principals, and sign contracts agreeing to participate actively in the form of professional development they selected (Sherri White, personal communication, April 20, 2004).

- *Teachers are given adequate time to plan and collaborate* for effective reading instruction (Caron & McLaughlin, 2002; Parker et al., 2004). Schedules are supportive of teachers meeting within grade levels or subject areas, or in more heterogeneous groups. In some schools, substitute teachers are hired to cover classes for half-day periods at regular intervals so that teachers can collaborate to set goals and plan for their own professional growth.

- *Decisions in the school are made based on the likelihood that academic excellence will be enhanced* (Lein et al., 1997). When budgets are developed, priority is given to hiring or keeping reading intervention teachers and to purchasing books and materials for the reading program.

- *Results of statewide tests are used to evaluate the reading program as a whole* rather than individual teachers (Parker et al., 2004).

- *Intervention is provided to all students who need it.* Reading intervention teachers, special educators, and classroom teachers work as a team to ensure that each student gets the kind and amount of instruction needed for success. When assessments identify students who are struggling in reading, a safety net of intervention is available. Many successful schools offer intervention in more than one format (Denton, Foorman et al., 2003). Students who are struggling tend to read more than other children in these schools. They may have as much as three hours of reading instruction every day! Denton, Foorman et al. (2003) described this as a "relentless effort" to bring students up to grade level (p. 261). In these schools, special education is seen as a last resort—after students have been given ample opportunities to learn.

- *Reading instruction and intervention are given priority when schedules are developed.* In the elementary grades, the schedule includes 90 minutes of uninterrupted time for classroom reading instruction. There is a provision for having some struggling readers leave the classroom to receive supplemental intervention. At the middle and high school levels, students who have not yet learned to read adequately may be enrolled in classes with names like "Linguistics," where they learn the basics of the English language and apply this knowledge in reading and writing (Tollestrup, 2002).

- In one school district, a student's classroom teacher (in elementary schools) or homeroom teacher (in middle and high schools) is considered the student's caseworker. In other words, even though that student may receive instruction or services from other people in the school (including special educators, counselors, or therapists), *the classroom or homeroom teacher is the coordinator of the services and has the primary responsibility for the student* (Tollestrup, 2002).

- Teachers, administrators, and other professionals in the school adopt a *no-excuses attitude with high expectations for all students.* Although it may be easy to find reasons why some students don't learn to read—poverty, problems at home, attention difficulties—teachers in schools with a schoolwide commitment to literacy recognize that it is their job to teach *all* of their students to read. If students are not making enough progress, the educators examine their own instruction

and determine what changes can be made to help their students achieve success. Teachers in successful schools have high expectations for themselves and believe they can solve problems and overcome barriers (Denton, Foorman et al., 2003; Lein et al., 1997; Ragland, Clubine, Constable, & Smith, 2001).

- *Parents are seen as important participants* in their student's learning. Schools that succeeded with even highly challenged populations placed on parent communication, involvement, and support. Parents were also encouraged to work with the school to continue practice of their child's reading skills (Parker et al., 2004).

THE READING COACH AS A FACILITATOR

The reading coach has an important role in facilitating this kind of schoolwide team approach in which everyone in the school and the wider community is committed to the success of each student. So along with the reading coach's tasks of Collaborative Problem Solver and Teacher/Learner, the coach is also a Facilitator. The dictionary defines the word *facilitate* as a verb meaning "to make a process easier or less difficult." The task of the reading coach is to make it easier for professionals in the school to work together with a commitment to student success. That's not quite the same as having full responsibility for wholesale change in the climate and practices of the school (thank goodness!). The goal of the reading coach is to help bring down the barriers to change and to provide opportunities and encouragement for professional educators to work together with a sense of shared responsibility.

Still, the task of facilitating schoolwide commitment may seem a bit overwhelming. But in many ways it is a natural outgrowth of the problem-solving and professional development tasks we have already described. Working with teachers individually to implement Systematic Problem Solving (SPS) can lead naturally to having groups of teachers work together to implement SPS. Coaching teachers by observing them and providing feedback or by modeling effective instructional strategies can lead to groups of teachers observing each other, modeling effective instruction for each other, and sharing their good ideas. Teaching teachers how to regularly monitor student progress can lead to having groups of teachers

work together to examine the results and discuss how to help students become more successful.

Even though facilitating schoolwide commitment may stem from your efforts in problem solving and professional development, change is more likely to happen if you have a blueprint to follow. We're going to briefly revisit a topic from Chapter 2 now, where we told you about a five-part model that may help administrators, teachers, and others follow the lead of schools with successful reading programs to improve students' reading outcomes. This model can be the blueprint for the reading coach in facilitating a schoolwide focus on success for all students.

REVISITING SAILS

Our model is known as SAILS: adopting **s**tandards to focus and guide instruction; using **a**ssessments to screen, diagnose, monitor, and evaluate the progress of student learning; delivering **i**nstruction and **i**nterventions designed to meet the needs of each student at all levels of reading development; providing **l**eadership to assist with the implementation, evaluation, and improvement of each of the three previous components of the model; and finally making a **s**ustained **s**choolwide commitment to help every student achieve success in reading by adopting a no-excuses attitude (Hasbrouck & Denton, 2004).

The reading coach focuses efforts of teachers and other school professionals to (1) support every student's progress towards *standards;* (2) use *assessments* to find out what students need; (3) plan instruction to address students' needs and monitor progress; and (4) develop expertise in designing and delivering *instruction and intervention* to meet the needs of all students. At the same time, the coach *makes it easier* (facilitates) for the school to adopt a committed attitude toward excellence in reading instruction.

As a Facilitator, the reading coach works with administrators to support their *leadership* for schoolwide success in reading instruction. For too long, teachers have been left to experiment with or develop instructional approaches with very little guidance. The fact that we now have quality research about what is most effective in teaching all students to read means that leaders have the responsibility for providing guidance based on these research results. The reading coach can have an important role in advising building or district administrators about how research in

effective reading can be applied in the school and how it can be used to guide their policy decisions.

The reading coach can be a source of instructional leadership, too. By applying the fine art of both supporting and "nudging" teachers, a process Dole (2004) calls "balancing on a fine, thin line between supporting the status quo and placing too much stress on teachers" (p. 19), the reading coach can be an instructional leader providing guidance in research-supported reading instruction. In one school district we visited, an administrator had high praise for the two reading coaches who worked in the elementary schools. When we asked what made them strong coaches, the administrator replied that the coaches had both the people skills to work effectively with teachers *and* the backbone to stand up to those who were resistant to adopting effective practices or who tried to manipulate the coaches. This is a good illustration of the role of the coach as an instructional leader.

The final *S* in SAILS stands for a **s**ustained **s**choolwide commitment, which is the focus of this chapter. We can't overstate the importance of schoolwide commitment in reading success. As we said in Chapter 8, lasting change takes place on both the individual and organizational levels. Change must happen not only in the individual classrooms of a school but in the school as a whole. It must be evident in the school's priorities in scheduling and appropriation of resources. The focus on standards, use of assessments, provision of quality instruction and supplemental intervention, and leadership will not result in *lasting* excellence in a reading program unless there is an understanding among everyone in the school that the reading success of each child is the responsibility of everyone—not just the child's teacher, the reading specialist, the reading coach, the special education teacher, or the parents.

A LOOK AT COLLABORATION IN SUCCESSFUL SCHOOLS

Researchers examined the collaborative practices in four elementary schools and two middle schools that have high student outcomes (Caron & McLaughlin, 2002). These schools are known as the "Beacons of Excellence Schools." Four Beacons of Excellence high schools were the subject of scrutiny by Wallace, Anderson, and Bartholomay (2002). The researchers identified several collaborative practices in the Beacons schools. All of the information in this section comes from the reports by these two sets of researchers, unless otherwise noted.

Collaborative planning.

In the Beacons schools, groups of teachers worked together to plan for student success. Teachers in some of these schools said that they frequently had joint planning sessions that included discussions of the curriculum standards and expectations for their students. In particular, they met at the beginning of each semester or grading period or before beginning a unit of instruction. During these meetings, teachers focused on clarifying the critical concepts and skills that all students were expected to master, selecting materials to use in the instruction, and identifying accommodations and adaptations that might be needed by some students. In one school, teachers coordinated their planning across grade levels so that students would receive a coordinated instructional program as they progressed through school. Collaborative planning was evident in the Beacons high schools as well as the elementary and middle schools. Teachers had common times when they were free to plan, to talk about what was working and what was not working, and what changes they might make to support student success. One school district had one day per month in which students were released early to allow for collaborative planning.

Collaborative teaching.

Several of the teachers in the Beacons schools engaged in co-teaching and met frequently to plan lessons and instructional strategies. There are six basic approaches to co-teaching (Morocco & Aguilar, 2002):

1. One teacher provides the primary instruction to the class while another circulates among students, monitoring and helping them as needed. The teachers change roles frequently.

2. Teachers instruct students at different stations set up around the room. Students rotate through these two "teaching stations" and other stations in the room.

3. Two teachers plan a lesson together, divide the class in half, and each teach the same lesson to half of the class, sometimes using different instructional strategies.

4. Teachers in the same classroom provide instruction to students in small, flexible groups based on their assessment results and the need for re-teaching.

5. One teacher teaches the class while another provides instruction or re-teaching to small groups of students who need further support. The teachers change roles.

6. Two teachers instruct the whole class together. They take turns taking the lead for different activities or topics.

Co-teaching approaches might help to promote collaboration and shared responsibility for student success, but the research on the effectiveness of co-teaching is limited, and merely participating in co-teaching does not ensure good student outcomes (Zigmond & Magiera, 2001). What matters more is the kind of instruction students receive and whether it is targeted to help them learn the essential reading skills they need.

Support for collaboration.

Teachers in the Beacons schools were given enough time to work together to plan for student success. Teachers need to have enough time to spend in each other's classrooms, teach together, reflect on and discuss their teaching practices, and attend professional development together (provided within the school or outside of the school).

In three of the Beacons schools, teachers were given formally scheduled time for regular collaboration. Teachers most often used this time to plan together for a particular lesson or unit or to problem-solve about a particular student's progress. In one school, teams made up of four general education and two special education teachers met at least once a week to plan and problem-solve. In another school, where there was little formal time set aside for collaboration, teachers tried to meet informally during recess, at lunch, or before or after school, but the amount of effort this took led many of the teachers to stop trying to collaborate. In two of the Beacons high schools, teachers said that block scheduling helped provide time for joint planning and collaboration.

The authors of the study of the Beacons elementary and middle schools caution that just providing time for collaboration doesn't mean teachers will collaborate. In one school, time was provided for joint planning sessions, but many teachers still used that time for individual activities rather than collaborative planning.

Another way that collaboration among teachers in the Beacons schools was supported was through opportunities for professional development that were purposefully planned to foster collaboration. At two Beacons elementary schools, teams of teachers and other professionals all attended the same workshops that focused on an area of need of a student they all worked with. They all heard the same information and could work together with a unified approach. At one of the Beacons high schools, the school district paid expenses for teachers who attended conferences *only* if a regular education teacher and a special education teacher attended together, attended all of the same sessions, and reported back about what they had learned that would benefit their students.

Technology-based communication.

Several teachers in the Beacons schools said that their collaboration was supported by their use of voice mail and e-mail. Teachers considered these tools valuable because they gave the teachers the chance to share ideas and information quickly and efficiently. In some schools, there was an internal e-mail system that could be used by teachers without concerns about outside intrusion. Still, teachers must be careful not to share confidential information about their students on e-mail.

Shared leadership and decision making.

In most of the Beacons schools, there was some form of shared leadership. Some principals involved teachers in setting goals but kept the responsibility for determining how these goals would be pursued. In other schools, principals and teachers had a highly collaborative model in which they jointly set goals and then made use of the expertise of different people to work toward the goals.

Principals in the Beacons schools had different leadership styles. In one school, the principal was very directive and had limited shared decision making. The principal's main focus was on improving student scores on the statewide assessment. Teachers in this school were described as frustrated and resistant to the principal's demands. Even though the principal invited them to participate in some shared decision making, they resisted, not believing that the effort at collaboration was sincere. The principal reported feeling isolated and forced to make hard decisions without faculty input.

In another Beacons school, the principal had a strong leadership style but also shared many important decisions with the staff. Teachers in this school reported feeling that they could share their opinions, collaborate, and even compromise on decisions.

In other schools, there was a genuine model of shared leadership. Teams of teachers were responsible for goal formation, curriculum and instruction, school improvement, and professional development. The principals had clear expectations for student outcomes but saw their role as supporting their faculties with necessary resources rather than controlling teacher behavior.

One of the Beacons high schools was divided into seven academies, each with teams that had important decision-making roles. Teachers and administrators said that these teams were very important for the success of the school. In several of the Beacons schools, someone other than the principal had an important role in building a collaborative community. In one, an experienced teacher led a group of teachers who worked closely together and helped promote a feeling of professionalism and shared responsibility.

Collaborative culture.

Two elements of a collaborative culture that were evident in the Beacon's schools were *trust* and a having a *shared set of expectations for all students*. For teachers to form a collaborative community, they must have a feeling of trust and comfort with their peers. If teachers feel that they will be criticized because of their practices or suggestions, or if they think that other teachers will gossip about them, they are unlikely to be able to share ideas openly. A collaborative school is one where the doors of the classrooms are open and teachers are respectful of each other.

In several of the Beacons schools, the teachers had common goals and expectations for students that were based on the state standards for outcomes at each grade level. Individual teachers at these schools said they were willing to work with any student to help the student meet the standards. A teacher in one of the Beacons high schools said, "Where they [students] need it [support], they get it. Even though the expectations are [to be maintained], there's a lot of support to reach goals. There's this whole safety net . . . to support the kids and to work directly with their academic and vocational teachers. I think it works well. . . . But it's a support, not a crutch" (Wallace et al., 2002, pp. 364–365). Another high school teacher said, "We don't care what category they're in [or what

label they have]. We don't excuse them from succeeding" (Wallace et al., 2002, p. 363).

Professional community. The final important element in the collaborative Beacons schools was the feeling of teachers that they had the support of their peers and belonged to a community of professionals. Teachers in elementary, middle, and high schools said that they relied on each other for help and support. They reported a feeling of being "all in this together." Teachers were kept informed and felt that they were "in the loop" as far as what was being done to improve student outcomes. One principal said that peer pressure was an important factor and that everyone felt that it was important that they "pulled their weight."

A WARNING

Merely having teachers collaborate doesn't mean that student learning will improve. As we stated in Chapter 8, people can collaborate to block change just as much as to facilitate change. Clearly, just giving teachers time to collaborate isn't enough. Guskey (2003), who synthesized literature on effective professional development, noted that in some studies, spending more time in professional development activities did not result in better student outcomes. What is important is how that time is spent. The process has to be well organized and purposeful and always focused on research-based instructional practices and on improving student outcomes. Remember that the goal is to *facilitate a schoolwide commitment to helping every student achieve success in reading.*

SUSTAINING THE COMMITMENT

The research on factors that are related to sustaining educational innovations offers guidance for facilitating (or *making easier*) this kind of long-term focus. One of the factors most often cited as key to making lasting changes is ongoing mentoring and support of classroom teachers (Gersten, Chard, & Baker, 2000). In other words, being an effective reading coach can go a long way toward making a good reading program last. Teachers who have the time, resources, and support needed to develop real competence in the implementation of instructional practices are more likely to continue to use these practices in spite of obstacles such as demands on their time or changing administrations (Gersten et al., 2000).

Teachers are more likely to keep using effective practices when they feel empowered to take ownership and responsibility for the process of school change (Cooper, 1998). They should feel like collaborators in pursuit of important goals rather than victims of someone else's agenda for them. "People skills," like effective communication and collaboration, are absolutely essential (see Chapters 4 and 5). But above all, teachers are more likely to adopt this attitude of ownership if they get enough training and support to develop a real mastery of the new practices (Gersten et al., 2000). A good facilitator not only helps individual teachers implement the program successfully but is also able to deal with problems and overcome obstacles that come up along the way (Slavin, 2004). Slavin suggests that an effective facilitator can help protect a school from changes in administrators or district policies.

STEPS FOR SUPPORTING SCHOOLWIDE COMMITMENT AND PARTICIPATION

The Learning First Alliance (2000) offered suggestions for establishing a context that supports making changes in schools to improve student reading. The five concrete steps we list here are based on their suggestions:

1. *Have a plan.* Develop both short-term and long-range plans for facilitating excellence in reading instruction in the school. The Learning First Alliance (2000) points out that "short-term solutions to long-range challenges will not work" (p. 10). There must be a long-term plan—with funding—that is linked directly to the expectation that student reading outcomes will improve. This plan should allow for three to five years of growth. In the meantime, the coach must also develop a cohesive, short-term plan. To make your plan, begin by *writing down* your goals. Then decide which priorities you want to address first. Think of all the roles and tasks of the reading coach that we have described in this book and decide how they will be coordinated to address those priorities.

2. *Get everyone involved.* Developing long- and short-term plans in collaboration with administrators, teachers, and others can foster joint ownership of the process. You can coordinate your plan with a needs assessment like the one we described in Chapter 8. Don't forget to include professionals such as counselors and librarians. You may not provide coaching directly to some of the professionals in the school, but include them in the schoolwide team with the goal of successful reading outcomes for all students. Be sure to also include the special education teachers in your activities. If all of the students in the school are to succeed, the students who have disabilities are included.

3. *Align standards, curriculum, textbooks, instructional programs, and assessments.* There should be a direct connection between the standards for student outcomes, the curriculum that describes what will be taught at each grade level, the materials and programs used to teach the standards, and the assessments used to measure student progress and outcomes. If these elements are not coordinated across each grade level, the result will be a fragmented reading program rather than a concentrated, schoolwide effort.

4. *Organize your time.* Make sure that you have enough time for all the tasks of the reading coach, including all the phases of professional development. (See Chapter 4 for more information about managing time.)

5. *Use the expertise of colleagues, mentors, and outside experts.* You don't have to do it all alone. Reenergize by taking advantage of opportunities for professional development outside of school or conversing with mentors who can support you as you work toward the very ambitious, but very important, goal of making sure all students can become successful readers.

10

A NOTE TO ADMINISTRATORS WHO WORK WITH READING COACHES

Dear Administrator,

Thank you for taking time from your busy schedule to read this chapter in *The Reading Coach: A How-to Manual for Success*. We hope you will eventually find time to read through the entire book. However, given the critical role administrators have in determining the success or failure of reading coaches, we wanted to be sure that you were given an opportunity to get an overview of the role of reading coach and to consider how coaches can work most effectively in a school with support from their primary supervisor.

You may have noticed that the topic of reading coaches is currently very newsworthy. In fact, the International Reading Association has identified coaching as "the hot trend in professional development" ("Coaches," 2004). Unfortunately, even though it seems everyone is talking about reading coaches, and many schools across the nation have hired teachers to be reading coaches, we know there is a big gap in knowledge about the role and expectations for reading coaches, and as well, about the role and expectations for the people who supervise reading coaches (Poglinco & Bach, 2004).

Unfortunately, few teachers who are given the demanding job of reading coach receive sufficient support or training to perform this role adequately ("Coaches," 2004; Hall, O'Neill, Hasbrouck, & Parker, 2003; Poglinco & Bach, 2004). Teachers who have been tapped to be coaches are often very talented, knowledgeable, and experienced professionals who are expected to learn how to coach their colleagues while they are performing this new and unfamiliar role. However, as Poglinco and Bach (2004) state so clearly: "Being an effective classroom teacher is no guarantee that one will also be an effective coach" (p. 400). This situation is complicated by the fact that very few administrators have received any preparation themselves to support or guide the reading coaches with whom they work (Hall et al., 2003).

With these challenges in mind, we decided to write this how-to manual for reading coaches as a way to bridge this gap. Our goal was to provide a guide for reading coaches—and their supervisors—to explain what exactly a reading coach is supposed to do and some suggestions for how to do it well. Topics covered include:

- How to introduce the new role of coach into a school;

- How a coach can provide advice to peer colleagues without insulting them;

- How a coach can work with teachers who are resistant to working with a coach;

- How to address schoolwide issues (i.e., curriculum; assessments; scheduling; and interfacing among Title I, special education, and the general classrooms); and, perhaps of key importance to you . . .

- How to work with the principal.

What Is a Reading Coach?

We have defined a reading coach in this way: An *experienced* teacher who has a *strong knowledge base in reading* and *experience* providing effective reading instruction to students, especially struggling readers. In addition, we suggested that a reading coach has received *training in how to work effectively with peer colleagues* to help them improve their students' reading outcomes and *receives support* in the school for providing coaching to other teachers, instructional assistants, parents, or administrators. We have presented a model of coaching that we call "Student-Focused Coaching" in which we see a coach performing three different kinds of roles: (1) *Facilitator*, helping effective and skillful teachers continue their success and helping professionals in the school work together toward the goal of schoolwide success; (2) *Collaborative Problem Solver*, using a structured systematic problem-solving process to work with teachers in addressing students' reading problems; and (3) *Teacher/Learner*, sharing effective, proven strategies, methods, and techniques with groups of teachers through high-quality and sustained professional development. In Student-Focused Coaching, these three roles are all used to target the real purpose of coaching: to help our students be the best they can be!

PROVIDING SUPPORT TO A READING COACH

Having a reading coach in your building can go a long way toward helping every student in your school achieve at the highest level possible. Coaches can provide many services, which may include some or all of the following:

- *Observing* teachers' reading lessons and *providing feedback* for instructional improvement

- Helping teachers with the *organization and management* of their literacy programs

- *Developing intervention plans* for struggling readers

- *Meeting with parents* who have concerns about their children's reading skills

- Helping to *identify and address schoolwide concerns* related to reading

- *Facilitating collaboration* among teaching teams

- *Presenting workshops* to introduce teachers to effective new strategies

- *Providing follow-up support* for professional development

- *Reviewing curriculum* materials

- *Making suggestions for adopting* or supplementing instructional resources

- *Organizing and facilitating teacher study* groups to explore relevant topics of interest

- *Advising administrators* on how reading research applies to program policy decisions

It's quite a list, isn't it? The idea of having a person on your staff available to provide these kinds of services is truly an exciting possibility for any administrator. But there is a catch. A coach *must* be given sufficient *training, time,* and *sustained support* to pull this off. Success is simply not possible without those resources. This is where you come in! An administrator plays an essential role in helping provide the foundation for a coach's success. This foundation is built by working collaboratively with your coach to *define the role of reading coach, schedule* the coach for success, and ensure that the coach is working within a *sustained, schoolwide model* for reading success.

DEFINING THE ROLE OF READING COACH

In Chapter 3 of this book, "Getting Started," we suggest that reading coaches work closely with their supervisors to define their new roles. Our suggestions include having a coach and supervisor engage in a series of conversations to discuss and reach some agreement about the following topics: agreeing upon the *rationale* for this new role within your school, describing the *coaching process*, determining what *tasks* the coach will undertake and which services the coach can provide (as well *limits* to those tasks and services), and setting *priorities* for the coach's *time*.

As the supervisor, you will eventually have to evaluate the performance of your reading coach. Because this role is so new, guidelines are rarely available for how to accomplish this important task. It is often unclear what standards of practice and performance should be used for evaluating a reading coach. Taking the time to carefully define a role for the coach will make this process far easier to accomplish. We also developed a form you may find helpful in evaluating the performance of a reading coach. You will find the *Evaluation Checklist for SFC Coaches/Consultants* (Hasbrouck & Denton, 2004) in the Appendix.

Using data to define the role of coach.

We suggest to the coaches in Chapter 4, "Time Management and Communication," that they consider occasionally using some kind of time-tracking or other data-collection system to monitor the way they are spending their professional time. Another valuable source of information about the role of the reading coach that we mentioned in Chapter 3 is a survey of the teachers, parents, or others who may have worked with the reading coach. This kind of information can be invaluable to you, as a supervisor, for working with your coach to analyze how that role is developing in your school.

Coaching versus supervision.

One of the most challenging aspects of defining the coaching role is the similarity of coaching to the role of supervisor. We discuss this topic in Chapter 3 in a section entitled "Confidentiality and Professional Ethics." Coaching certainly can involve observing a teacher conducting a lesson and then providing feedback to that teacher. On the surface, this looks much like an evaluation of a teacher's classroom performance. It is critical for you as supervisor, as well as for the coach and the teachers who work with the coach, to understand the subtle, yet significant differences between coaching and supervision.

A key difference between these two roles is their purpose. The primary purpose of supervision is to provide information so a supervisor can make evaluative judgments: Is this teacher performing in a professionally competent manner or not? Of course, a good supervisor also works with teachers to help them improve their professional skills, but a key point is evaluation. Coaching, in contrast, is *never* about making evaluative decisions about professional competence.

Another critical difference between coaching and supervision is the element of cooperation. A coach *must be invited* to work with a teacher, whether that work involves observing a lesson and providing feedback, discussing a student's progress, or participating in a study group. If a teacher is not willing to work with a coach, coaching cannot occur. Period. Obviously, this is not the case when you observe a teacher. While a teacher may have some control and input about when to be supervised, the option of not permitting the principal to watch a lesson being taught does not exist.

Confidentiality and trust.

It is also essential for you to understand that a coach cannot share any information about a teacher's performance that may be obtained during the process of coaching. This may not seem to make much sense at first glance. You may be thinking that coaching is all about helping students become the best readers they can be: "If my coach happened to work with teachers who

are having difficulty providing adequate instruction to their students, isn't that important information for me to know about?"

The problem is, trust and confidentiality are cornerstones of coaching. Coaching can occur *only* within a cooperative professional relationship. These professional relationships must be built on trust and mutual respect. If a coach is perceived by teachers as working as a "spy for the principal" or as a gossip who talks about one teacher to another, that coach will soon be unable to provide any coaching services at all. Few, if any, teachers will work with a coach if they don't believe the coach will maintain their privacy and keep all communication strictly confidential.

Of course, there are certain areas where this level of complete confidentiality must be breeched. Those would be the same areas where any professional educator would be ethically and even legally obligated to report evidence of cruelty, abuse, or neglect. If a coach witnesses a teacher being emotionally or physically abusive to any student at any time, you should be notified of this. The issue becomes a bit less clear in other situations. A coach may observe a teacher who is simply a low-skilled teacher with low expectations for students, or one who provides little, if any, meaningful instruction in the classroom. What should a coach do about this? Does this fall into a category that could reasonably be called "neglect" or "abuse" of students? Some may argue that it does. However, the line is less obvious. How "poorly" does a teacher have to teach before a coach is justified in reporting this to a supervisor? How will this level of "poor instruction" be defined? This may be one other agenda item to add to your ongoing conversations with your coach.

As enticing as the possibility may seem of having the reading coach serve as your "assistant evaluator," this plan won't work in the long run. You cannot send the coach in to "fix" a teacher's poor reading instruction. That same teacher must willingly invite the coach to help or coaching, by definition, cannot be provided.

We also noted that some coaches may have duties and responsibilities that require them to work with teachers in a way that mirrors supervision. We consider that coaches in these situations are providing coaching *plus* supervision. We maintain that the coaching role itself should be defined as a voluntary peer-to-peer process.

Having periodic conversations with your coach to analyze and discuss any available data, as well as listening to how the coach is feeling about this new and demanding role, can go a long way toward developing a clear, workable, mutually understood and accepted definition of the roles and responsibilities for a reading coach. This will certainly make that eventual evaluation process go much more smoothly and go a long way toward ensuring that your coach can be successful in this role.

Scheduling a coach for success.

The list of possible tasks and services a reading coach can provide to your school can be tantalizing. That same list can also appear overwhelming to the coach, who may feel pressured to do too much with too little time available, and perhaps with insufficient expertise. We don't want this to happen. As a supervisor, you know full well how important it is to retain our best professional educators, not burn them out or scare them away!

We would like to suggest that the same information that can be used to develop a definition of the coach's role could also facilitate the collaborative development of a plan for using your coach's limited and valuable time. Data collected by the coach from some kind of time-tracking system, along with results from a survey or questionnaire of peer colleagues and parents, can be invaluable in this effort. Matching the *time available* against the list of *priorities for the tasks and services* that can be provided by the coach will help you both develop some clear and workable guidelines for professional time management.

We also want to underscore once again the importance of revisiting these issues periodically with the reading coach. A coach's role tends to expand and refine itself over time. This can lead to frustration on the part of the coach who may need some guidance from you about how to reprioritize how the time for coaching is being spent.

DEVELOPING A MODEL FOR READING SUCCESS: SAILS

In our work with schools across the country, we have found that more and more principals and district administrators are focusing their attention on students' reading skills. We often hear from these administrators that they are ready to take the next step, to help their school move forward, from being a school that meets the needs of most of the students to a school that seriously tackles the challenge of helping *every* student become a skillful and competent reader. Perhaps you are in that same category and you see the reading coach as your partner in this effort. We certainly commend you for this! Coaches working in partnership with a visionary and supportive administrator can help a school achieve great things for students. We also want to suggest a framework for helping you take the next steps toward instructional excellence that we developed to assist school administrators such as yourself.

SAILS is a five-part model designed specifically to guide efforts for improving students' reading skills and outcomes. The components of SAILS consist of: adopting **s**tandards to focus and guide instruction; using **a**ssessments to screen, diagnose, and evaluate the progress of student learning; delivering **i**nstruction and **i**nterventions designed to meet the needs of each student at all ability and skill levels; providing **l**eadership to assist with the implementation, evaluation, and improvement of each of the three previous components of the model; and finally making a **s**ustained **s**choolwide commitment to help *every* student achieve success in reading by having the school adopt a no-excuses attitude. We acknowledge that this model for instructional improvements must also be implemented in a school environment that is safe, orderly, and positive (Hasbrouck & Denton, 2004).

In Chapter 2, "Foundational Knowledge for the Reading Coach," we present SAILS as a way for a reading coach to focus efforts for instructional improvement in classrooms and across an entire school or district. We all know that many school-improvement efforts fail in the long run, in part because they tend to focus only on a piece of the problem rather than taking a systemic view of the interrelated complexities of academic concerns. You cannot fix things by simply going out and buying a new reading curriculum. School change is far more complicated than that.

Working in partnership with a supervisor, a reading coach can help guide the efforts of teachers and other school professionals to:

1. Support every student's progress towards *standards* by:
   - Ensuring that every teacher is aware of the curriculum standards being used in that state, district, and school

- Working toward alignment of all instructional materials to these standards

- Providing professional development in teaching to standards

2. Use *assessments* to determine which students need assistance (*screening*), what instruction should be provided to each student (*diagnosis*), how to plan instruction or intervention to address the identified instructional needs, and whether progress is being made (*progress monitoring*) by:

- Making sure every teacher knows about the three types of assessments, their purpose, and how to use them effectively to improve instruction and learning

3. Develop expertise in designing and delivering *instruction and intervention* to meet the needs of all students by:

- Providing 1:1 assistance to teachers who want to make improvements in their instructional skills by observing, modeling, and providing feedback and support

- Presenting workshops to teachers about effective and proven instructional strategies

- Reviewing current curriculum materials and evaluating new materials to make sure teachers have adequate tools for teaching the standards to students

4. Support *leadership* efforts for schoolwide success in reading instruction by:

- Helping keep the building leaders informed of results from a convergence of high-quality research about reading tools and practices

- Working with administrators to plan and implement relevant, sustained, and high-quality professional development focused on reading outcomes

- Providing frequent and up-to-date data for making informed decisions about the reading program in the school or district

- Facilitating collaboration of school professionals across grades, subject areas, or specializations

5. Support efforts toward developing a *sustained schoolwide commitment* attitude across all faculty, staff, and parents with a no-excuses attitude about student success by:

- Supporting the use of frequently collected reading data from individual classrooms to guide schoolwide decisions about providing services to students

- Helping teachers work together for student success by having a unified plan and getting all the teachers involved

- Finding ways to involve and inform parents about the reading program, efforts being made at school, and ideas for supporting reading at home

- Publicizing and celebrating the successes of hardworking teachers and parents

Conclusion

We have watched many skillful, resourceful, and dedicated reading coaches work hard to help students who are struggling by sharing their knowledge and expertise with other teachers. Too often we have watched these efforts fail. This failure is frequently due, at least in part, to a lack of support from an administrator. In order to succeed, coaches must have sufficient training, sufficient time, and sufficient support. Poglinco and Bach (2004) make this point clear in their summary of research on reading coaches: "We found there is a strong need for principals to enter into a partnership with coaches if the coaching model is going to succeed in their schools (p. 399)." We hope this chapter will assist you in forming this partnership with your reading coach, and we wish you, your reading coach, your faculty, all of your students and their families the best of luck in achieving the vital goal *of teaching all of our students to read.*

REFERENCES

Chapter 1

Clark, K. F. (2004). What can I say besides "sound it out"? Coaching word recognition in beginning reading. *The Reading Teacher, 57*(5), 440–449.

Coaches, controversy, consensus. (2004, April/May). *Reading Today, 21*(5), 1, 18.

Dole, J. (2004). The changing role of the reading specialist in school reform. *The Reading Teacher, 57*(5), 462–471.

Hall, L. D., O'Neill, K. J., Hasbrouck, J. E., & Parker, R. I. (2003, May). *The best of both worlds: Texas Master Reading Teachers as teachers and mentors*. Research poster session presented at the meeting of the International Reading Association, Orlando, FL.

Kampwirth, T. J. (1999). *Collaborative consultation in the schools: Effective practices for students with learning and behavior problems*. Merrill: Upper Saddle River, NJ.

Kroth, R. L., & Edge, D. (1997). *Strategies for communicating with parents and families of exceptional children* (3rd ed.). Denver: Love Publications.

Morrow, L. M. (2003, August/September). Make professional development a reality. *Reading Today*, 6–7.

Poglinco, S. M., & Bach, A. J. (2004, January). The heart of the matter: Coaching as a vehicle for professional development. *Phi Delta Kappan*, 398–400.

Sugai, G. M., & Tindal, G. A. (1993). *Effective school consultation: An interactive approach*. Brookes/Cole: Pacific Grove, CA.

Chapter 2

Adler, M. A., & Fisher, C. W. (2001). Early reading programs in high-poverty schools: A case study of beating the odds. *Reading Teacher, 54*, 616–619.

Baker, S. K., & Good, R. (1995). Curriculum-based measurement of English reading with bilingual Hispanic students: A validation study with second-grade students. *School Psychology Review, 24*, 561–578.

Clay, M. M. (1987). Learning to be learning disabled. *New Zealand Journal of Educational Studies, 22*, 155–173.

Curtis, M. E., & Longo, A. M. (1999). *When adolescents can't read: Materials and methods that work*. Cambridge, MA: Brookline Books: Cambridge.

Deno, S. L., Mirkin, P .K., & Chiang, B. (1992). Identifying valid measures of reading. *Exceptional Children, 49*, 36–45.

Denton, C. A., Foorman, B. R., & Mathes, P. M. (2003). Schools that "beat the odds": Implications for reading instruction. *Remedial and Special Education, 24*, 258–261.

Denton, C. A., & Hasbrouck, J. E. (1999). Teaching students with disabilities to read: A parent information brief. Parents Engaged in Educational Reform (PEER) Project/Federation for Children with Special Needs. Boston.

Denton, C. A., Vaughn, S., & Fletcher, J. M (2003). Bringing research-based practice to scale. *Learning Disabilities Research and Practice, 18*, 201–211.

Dickson, S., & Bryant, D. P. (2002). *A framework for developing secondary remedial reading programs*. Unpublished document, University of Texas Center for Reading and Language Arts, University of Texas at Austin.

Ellis, A. K. (2001). *Research on educational innovations* (3rd ed.). Larchmont, NY: Eye on Education.

Foorman, B. R., Fletcher, J. M., & Francis, D. (1997). A scientific approach to reading instruction. Retrieved December 28, 2004, from LD OnLine, http://ldonline.org

Foorman, B. R., & Moats, L. C. (2004). Conditions for sustaining research-based practices in early reading instruction. *Remedial and Special Education, 25,* 51–60.

Foorman, B. R., & Torgesen, J. (2001). Critical elements of classroom and small-group instruction promote reading success in all children. *Learning Disabilities Research and Practice, 16,* 203–212.

Francis, D. J., Shaywitz, S. E., Stuebing, K. K., Shaywitz, B. A., & Fletcher, J. M. (1996). Developmental lag versus deficit models of reading disability: A longitudinal individual growth curves analysis. *Journal of Educational Psychology, 88,* 3–17.

Fuchs, L. S., & Fuchs, D. (1986). Effects of systematic formative evaluation: A meta-analysis. *Exceptional Children, 53,* 199–208.

Fuchs, L. S., Fuchs, D., Hosp, M. K., & Jenkins, J., (2001). Oral reading fluency as an indicator of reading competence: A theoretical, empirical, and historical analysis. *Scientific Studies of Reading,* (5)3, 239–256.

Fuchs, L. S., Fuchs, D., & Stecker, P. M. (1989). Effects of curriculum-based measurement on teachers' instructional planning. *Journal of Learning Disabilities, 22,* 51–59.

Good, R. H, & Kaminski, R. (2003). *Dynamic indicators of basic early literacy skills* (6th ed.). Longmont, CO: Sopris West.

Good, R. H., Wallin, J. U., Simmons, D. C., Kame'enui, E. J., & Kaminski, R. A. (2002). *System-wide percentile ranks for DIBELS benchmark assessment* (Tech. Rep. No. 9). Eugene, OR: University of Oregon. Retrieved August 24, 2004, from http://dibels.uoregon.edu

Graves, M. F., & Braaten, S. (1996). *Scaffolded reading experiences: Bridges to success* [Electronic version]. Preventing School Failure, 40 (4), 169–173.

Hasbrouck, J. E., & Denton, C. A. (2004). *SAILS: A comprehensive systemic model for improving students' reading outcomes.* Seattle: JH Consulting.

Hasbrouck, J., Ihnot, C., Parker, R. I., and Woldbeck, T. (1999). One teacher's use of curriculum-based measurement: A changed opinion. *Learning Disabilities, Research & Practice, 14*(2), 118–126.

Hasbrouck, J. E., & Tindal, G. (1992). Curriculum-based oral reading fluency norms for students in grades 2 through 5. *Teaching Exceptional Children, 24*(3), 41–44.

Haycock, K. (2001, March). Closing the achievement gap. *Educational Leadership, 58*(6), 6–11.

Juel, C. (1988). Learning to read and write: A longitudinal study of children in first and second grade. *Journal of Educational Psychology, 80,* 437–447.

Kame'enui, E. (2002). *An analysis of reading assessment instruments for K–3: Final report.* Eugene, OR: University of Oregon, Institute for the Development of Educational Achievement. Retrieved January 12, 2004, from http://idea.uoregon.edu/assessment/index.html

Kraus, R. (1998). *Leo the late bloomer.* NY: HarperCollins.

Lein, L., Johnson, J. F., & Ragland, M. (1997, February). *Successful Texas schoolwide programs: Research study results.* Austin, TX: The Charles A. Dana Center. Retrieved April 29, 2004, from http://www.starcenter.org/products/resources/nationalawards/research.html

Lyon, G. R. (1995). Toward a definition of dyslexia. *Annals of Dyslexia, 45,* 3–27.

Mathes, P. G., & Denton, C.A. (2002). The prevention and identification of reading disability. *Seminars in Pediatric Neurology, 9*(3), 185–191.

Mathes, P.G., Denton, C.A., Fletcher, J.M., Anthony, J.L., Francis, D.J., & Schatschneider, C. (2005). The effects of theoretically different instruction and student characteristics on the skills of struggling readers. *Reading Research Quarterly, 40,* 148-182.

Moats, L. C. (2004). *LETRS: Language essentials for teachers of reading and spelling.* Longmont, CO: Sopris West.

National Center for Education Statistics (2003). *A report card for the nation and the states.*

National Reading Panel (2000). *Teaching children to read: An evidence-based assessment of the scientific research literature on reading and its implications for reading instruction.* Washington, DC: National Institute of Child Health and Human Development.

Parker, R. I., O'Neill, K., Hall, L., & Hasbrouck, J. E. (2004, April). *Preventing reading failure with effective instructional practice: Results from the Texas Special Education/Reading Interface Study.* A paper presented at the annual meeting of the American Educational Research Association Conference. San Diego, CA.

Pressley, M., Rankin, J., & Yokoi, L. (1996). A survey of instructional practices of outstanding primary-level literacy teachers. *Elementary School Journal* 96, 363–384.

Ragland, M., Clubine, B., Constable, D., & Smith, P. (2001, August). *Making education special: Achieving exemplary performance with minimal special education exemptions.* Austin, TX: The Charles A. Dana Center.

Rayner, K., Foorman, B. R., Perfetti, C. A., Pesetsky, D. & Seidenberg, M. S. (2001). How psychological science informs the teaching of reading. *Psychological Science in the Public Interest, 2*(2). Retrieved April 16, 2004, from http://www.psychologicalscience.org//journals/pspi/2_2.html

Scarborough, H. S. (1998). Early identification of children at risk for reading disabilities: Phonological awareness and some other promising predictors. In P. Accardo, A. Capute, & B. Shapiro (Eds.), *Specific reading disability: A view of the spectrum.* Timonium, MD: York Press.

Shaywitz, S. (2003). *Overcoming dyslexia.* NY: Knopf.

Shinn, M. R. (Ed.) (1989). *Curriculum-based measurement: Assessing special children.* NY: Guilford.

Shinn, M. R. (Ed.) (1998). *Advanced applications of curriculum-based measurement.* NY: Guilford.

Simos, P. G., Breier, J. I., Fletcher, J. M., Bergman, E., & Papanicolaou, A. C. (2000). Cerebral mechanisms involved in word reading in dyslexia children: A magnetic source imaging approach. *Cerebral Cortex, 10,* 809–816.

Simos, P. G., Breier, J. I., Fletcher, J. M., Foorman, B. R., Bergman, E., Fishbeck, K., & Papanicolaou, A. C. (2000). Brain activation profiles in dyslexic children during nonword reading: A magnetic source imaging study. *Neuroscience Reports, 290,* 61–65.

Snow, C. E., Burns, M. S. & Griffin, P. (1998). *Preventing reading difficulties in young children.* Washington, DC: National Academy Press.

Stanovich, K. (1986). Matthew effects in reading: Some consequences of individual differences in the acquisition of literacy. *Reading Research Quarterly, 21,* 360–407.

Torgesen, J. K. (1998, Spring/Summer). Catch them before they fail: Identification and assessment to prevent reading failure in young children. *American Educator,* 1–12.

Torgesen, J. K. (2000). Individual differences in response to early interventions in reading: The lingering problem of treatment resisters. *Learning Disabilities Research & Practice, 15,* 55–64.

Torgesen, J. K., & Burgess, S. R. (1998). Consistency of reading-related phonological processes throughout early childhood: Evidence from longitudinal-correlational and instructional studies. In J. Metsala, & L. Ehri (Eds.), *Word recognition in beginning reading.* Hillsdale, NJ: Lawrence Erlbaum Associates.

Vaughn, S., & Linan-Thompson, S. (2003). Group size and time allotted to intervention: Effects for students with reading difficulties. In B. R. Foorman (Ed.), *Preventing and remediating reading difficulties: Bringing science to scale* (pp. 445–463). Timonium, MD: York Press.

Wolf, M., O'Brien, B., Adams, K. D., Joffe, T., Jeffery, J., Lovett, M., & Morris, R. (2003). Working for time: Reflections on naming speed, reading fluency, and intervention. In B. R. Foorman (Ed.), *Preventing and remediating reading difficulties: Bringing science to scale* (pp. 355–379). Timonium, MD: York Press.

Wolf, M. A., & Bowers, P. G. (1999). The double-deficit hypothesis for the developmental dyslexias. *Journal of Educational Psychology, 91,* 415–438.

Ysseldyke, J. (2001). Reflections on a research career: Generalizations from 25 years of research on assessment and instructional decision making. *Exceptional Children, 67,* 295–309.

Chapter 3

Anderson, D., Major, R. L., & Mitchell, R. R. (1992). *Teacher supervision that works.* Westport, CT: Greenwood Publishing.

Carey, K. T. (1995). Consultation in the real world. *Journal of Educational and Psychological Consultation, 6*(4), 397–400.

Changing role of reading specialists outlined in recent *RT* article. (2002, August/September). *Reading Today*, 3.

Corey, G., Corey, M. S., & Callanan, P. (1993). *Issues and ethics in the helping professions* (2nd ed.). Pacific Grove, CA: Brookes/Cole.

Dole, J. (2004). The changing role of the reading specialist in school reform. *The Reading Teacher, 57*(5), 462–471.

Greenspan, S., & Negron, E. (1994). Ethical obligations of special services personnel. *Special Service in the Schools, 8*(2), 185–209.

Hasbrouck, J., & Denton, C. (2004). *Evaluation Checklist for School-based Coaches/Consultants.* (in Appendix)

Heron, T. E., Martz, S. A., & Margolis, H. (1996). Ethical and legal issues in consultation. *Remedial and Special Education, 17*(6), 377–385.

Lefever-Davis, S., Wilson, C., Moore, E., Kent, A., Hopkins, S. (2003). Teacher study groups: A strategic approach to promoting student literacy development. *The Reading Teacher, 56*(8), 728–784.

Pipes, R. B. (1981). Consulting in organizations: The entry problem. In J. C. Conoley (Ed.), *Consultation in the schools: Theory, research, procedures* (pp. 11–33). NY: Academic Press.

Chapter 4

Bolton, R. (1979). *People skills: How to assert yourself, listen to others, and resolve conflicts.* NY: Simon & Schuster.

Corey, G., Corey, M. S., & Callanan, P. (1993). *Issues and ethics in the helping professions* (2nd ed.), Pacific Grove, CA: Brookes/Cole.

Egan, (G). (1994). *The skilled helper: A problem-management approach to helping.* Pacific Grove, CA: Brooks/Cole.

Harris, K. C. (1991). An expanded view on consultation competencies for educators serving culturally and linguistically diverse exceptional students. *Teacher Education and Special Education, 14*(1), 25–29.

Hasbrouck, J. E., Parker, R. I., & Denton, C. A. (2003). *3T-SR: Teacher time-tracking in special programs for reading teachers & specialists.* Department of Educational Psychology, Texas A&M University: College Station, TX. (in Appendix)

Heron, T. E., Martz, S. A., & Margolis, H. (1996). Ethical and legal issues in consultation. *Remedial and Special Education, 17*(6), 377–385.

Kroth, R. L., & Edge, D. (1997). *Strategies for communicating with parents and families of exceptional children* (3rd ed.). Denver: Love Publications.

Westra, M. (1996). *Active communication.* Pacific Grove, CA: Brooks/Cole.

Chapter 5

Carey, K. T. (1995). Consultation in the real world. *Journal of Educational and Psychological Consultation, 6*(4), 397–400.

Denton, C.A., Foorman, B. R., & Mathes, P. M. (2003). Schools that "beat the odds": Implications for reading instruction. *Remedial and Special Education, 24*, 258–3261.

D'Zurilla, T. J., & Goldfried, M. R. (1971). Problem-solving and behavior modification. *Journal of Abnormal Psychology, 78*(1), 107–126.

Egan, G. (1994). *The skilled helper: A problem-management approach to helping* (5th ed.). Pacific Grove, CA: Brooks/Cole.

Fuchs, L. S., Fuchs, D., Hosp, M. K., & Jenkins, J. R. (2001). Oral reading fluency as an indicator of reading competence: A theoretical, empirical, and historical analysis. *Scientific Studies of Reading, 5*(3), 239–256.

Gick, M. L. (1986). *Problem-solving strategies. Educational Psychologist, 21* (1&2), 99–120.

Hayes, J. R. (1989). *The complete problem solver* (2nd ed.). Hillsdale, NJ: Lawrence Erlbaum Associates.

Hughes, J. A., & Hasbrouck, J. E. (1997). *Consultant evaluation rating form (CERF) training manual.* Unpublished manuscript. Texas A&M University, College Station, TX.

Hughes, J. A., Hasbrouck, J. E., Serdahl, E., Heidgerken, A., & McHaney, L. (2001). Responsive systems consultation: A preliminary evaluation of implementation and outcomes. *Educational & Psychological Consultation, 12*(3), 179–202.

Kampwirth, T. J. (1999). *Collaborative consultation in the schools.* Upper Saddle River, NJ: Merrill.

Krulik, S. & Rudnick, J. A. (1984). *Sourcebook for teaching problem-solving.* Boston: Allyn & Bacon, Inc.

Nolet, V., Tindal, G., & Hasbrouck, J. (1991). School-wide alternative program (SWAP) teams. In Tindal, G. & Marr, J. (Eds.), In *Search of a new model: Three essays on staff development* (Monograph No. 4) (pp. 1–13). Eugene, OR: University of Oregon, Resource Consultant Training Program.

Parker, R. I., O'Neill, K., Hall, L., & Hasbrouck, J. E. (2004). *Overview of special education/reading interface study*. Unpublished manuscript. Texas A&M University.

Sprick, R. S., Sprick, M., & Garrison, M. (1993). *Interventions*. Longmont, CO: Sopris West.

Sugai, G. M., & Tindal, G.A. (1993). *Effective school consultation: An interactive approach*. Brookes/Cole: Pacific Grove, CA.

Swanson, H. L., O'Connor, J. E., & Cooney, J. B. (1990). An information processing analysis of expert and novice teachers' problem solving. *American Educational Research Journal, 27*(3), 533–556.

VanGundy, A. B. (1987). *Creative problem solving: A guide for trainers and management*. New York: Quorum Books.

Voss, J. F., Tyler, S. W., & Yengo, L. A. (1983). Individual differences in the solving of social science problems. In R. F. Dillon & R. R. Schmeck (Eds.), *Individual differences in cognition* (Vol. 1) (pp. 205–232). New York: Academic Press.

Witt, J. C. (1986). Teachers' resistance to the use of school-based interventions. *Journal of School Psychology, 24*, 37–44.

Chapter 6

Cohen, L.G., & Spenciner, L. J. (2003). *Assessment of children and youth with special needs* (2nd ed). Boston: Allyn & Bacon.

Denton, C. A. (2004a). *Literacy instruction feedback template*. Unpublished manuscript. (in Appendix)

Denton, C. A. (2004b). *Student success—teacher strategy observation*. Unpublished manuscript. (in Appendix)

Denton, C. A., Parker, R. I., Hasbrouck, J. E. (2004). *Activity structures observation system—revised*. Unpublished document. (in Appendix)

Good, R. H, & Kaminski, R. (2003). *Dynamic indicators of basic early literacy skills* (DIBELS) (6th ed.). Longmont, CO: Sopris West.

Harris, K. C. (1991). An expanded view on consultation competencies for educators serving culturally and linguistically diverse exceptional students. *Teacher Education and Special Education, 14*(1), 25–29.

Hasbrouck, J. E. (1997). "Mediated" peer coaching for training preservice teachers. *Journal of Special Education, 31*, 251–271.

Hasbrouck, J. E. (2005). Quick Phonics Screener (QPS). St. Paul, MN: Read Naturally.

Hasbrouck, J. E., & Christen, M. (1996). Providing peer coaching in inclusive settings: A tool for consulting teachers. *Intervention in School and Clinic, 32*(3), 141–148.

Hasbrouck, J. E., & Parker, R. (1995). *Scale for coaching instruction effectiveness (SCIE)*. Texas A&M University: College Station, TX. (in Appendix)

Reading Fluency Monitor. (2003). Read Naturally: St. Paul, MN.

Showers, B. & Joyce, B. (1996). The evolution of peer coaching. *Educational Leadership, 53*, 12–16.

Sugai, G. M., & Tindal, G. A. (1993). *Effective school consultation: An interactive approach*. Pacific Grove, CA: Brooks/Cole.

Chapter 7

Gutkin, T. G., & Conoley, J.C. (1990). Reconceptualizing school psychology from a service delivery perspective. *Journal of School Psychology, 28*, 203-224.

Witt, J. C. (1986). Teachers' resistance to the use of school-based interventions. *Journal of School Psychology, 24*, 37–44.

Chapter 8

Baker, S., Gersten, R., Dimino, J. A., & Griffiths, R. (2004). The sustained use of research-based instructional practice: A case study of peer-assisted learning strategies in mathematics. *Remedial and Special Education, 25*, 5–24.

Birman, B. F., Desimone, L., Porter, A. C., & Garet, M. S. (2000, May). Designing professional development that works. *Educational Leadership, 57*, 28–33.

Borman, G. D., Rachuba, L., Datnow, A., Alberg, M., MacIver, M., Stringfield, S., & Ross, S. (2000). *Four models of school improvement: Successes and challenges in reforming low-performing, high-poverty Title 1 schools* (Tech. Rep. No. 48). Ann Arbor, MI: University of Michigan, Center for the Improvement of Early Reading Achievement.

Daniels, D. C. (2002). Becoming a reflective practitioner. *Middle School Journal*, 33, 52–56.

Denton, C. A., Foorman, B. R., & Mathes, P. M. (2003). Schools that "beat the odds": Implications for reading instruction. *Remedial and Special Education*, 24, 258–261.

Gersten, R., Chard, D., & Baker, S. (2000). Factors enhancing sustained use of research-based instructional practices. *Journal of Learning Disabilities*, 33, 445–457.

Gersten, R. Morvant, M., & Brengelman, S. (1995). Close to the classroom is close to the bone: Coaching as a means to translate research into classroom practice. *Exceptional Children*, 62, 414–429.

Gersten, R., & Woodward, J. (1990). Rethinking the regular education initiative: Focus on the classroom teacher. *Remedial and Special Education*, 11 (3), 7–16.

Guskey, T. R. (1995). Results-oriented professional development: In search of an optimal mix of effective practices. North Central Regional Educational Laboratory. Retrieved April 7, 2004, from http://www.ncrel.org/sdrs/areas/rpl_esys/pdlitrev.htm

Guskey, T. R. (2003). What makes professional development effective? [Electronic version] *Phi Delta Kappan*, 84, 748–s750.

Joyce, B. R., & Showers, B. (1981). Transfer of training: The contribution of "coaching." *Journal of Education*, 163, 163–172.

Klingner, J. K., Vaughn, S., Hughes, M. T., & Arguelles, M. E. (1999). Sustaining research-based practices in reading: A three-year follow-up. *Remedial and Special Education*, 20, 263–274, 287.

Learning First Alliance (2000). Every child reading: A professional development guide. Baltimore, MD: author. Retrieved April 28, 2004, from http://www.nasbe.org/Educational_Issues/Reports/Reading_Prof_Develop.pdf

LeFevre, D., & Richardson, V. (2000). *Staff development in early reading intervention programs: The facilitator* (Tech. Rep. No. 3-011). Ann Arbor, MI: University of Michigan, Center for the Improvement of Early Reading Achievement.

Maslow, A. (1987). Motivation and personality (3rd ed.). NY: Harper Collins.

Moats, L. C. (2004). *LETRS: Language essentials for teachers of reading and spelling.* Longmont, CO: Sopris West.

Murphy, C. (1992). Study groups foster schoolwide learning. *Educational Leadership*, 50, 71–74.

Poglinco, S. M., & Bach, A. J. (2004). The heart of the matter: Coaching as a vehicle for professional development. *Phi Delta Kappan*, 85, 398–400.

Schumm, J. S., & Vaughn, S. (1995). Meaningful professional development in accommodating students with disabilities. *Remedial and Special Education*, 6, 344–353.

Showers, B. & Joyce, B. (1996). The evolution of peer coaching. *Educational Leadership*, 53, 12–16.

Showers, B., Joyce, B., & Bennett, B. (1987). Synthesis of research on staff development: A framework for future study and a state-of-the-art analysis. *Educational Leadership*, 45, 77–87.

Stanovich, P. J., & Stanovich, K. E. (1997). Research into practice in special education. *Journal of Learning Disabilities*, 30, 477–481.

Swafford, J. (1998). Teachers supporting teachers through peer coaching. *Support for Learning*, 13 (2), 54–58.

Wallace, T., Anderson, A. R., & Bartholomay, T. (2002). Collaboration: An element associated with the success of four inclusive high schools. *Journal of Educational and Psychological Consultation*, 13, 349–381.

Chapter 9

Adler, M. A., & Fisher, C. W. (2001). Early reading programs in high-poverty schools: A case study of beating the odds. *Reading Teacher*, 54, 616–619.

Caron, E. A., & McLaughlin, M. J. (2002). Indicators of Beacons of Excellence schools: What do they tell us about collaborative practices? *Journal of Educational and Psychological Consultation*, 13, 285–313.

Cooper, R. (1998). *Socio-cultural and within-school factors that affect the quality of implementation of school-wide programs* (Tech. Rep. No. 28). Baltimore, MD: Johns Hopkins University, Center for Research on the Education of Students Placed At-Risk.

Denton, C. A., Foorman, B. R., & Mathes, P. M. (2003). Schools that "beat the odds": Implications for reading instruction. *Remedial and Special Education, 24,* 258–261.

Dole, J. (2004). The changing role of the reading specialist in school reform. *Reading Teacher, 57*(5), 462–471.

Gersten, R., Chard, D., & Baker, S. (2000). Factors enhancing sustained use of research-based instructional practices. *Journal of Learning Disabilities, 33,* 445–457.

Guskey, T. R. (2003). What makes professional development effective? [Electronic version] *Phi Delta Kappan,* 84, 748–750.

Hasbrouck, J. E., & Denton, C. A. (2004). *SAILS: A comprehensive systemic model for improving students' reading outcomes.* Seattle: JH Consulting.

Learning First Alliance (2000). Every child reading: A professional development guide. Baltimore, MD: Author. Retrieved April 28, 2004, from http://www.nasbe.org/Educational_Issues/Reports/Reading_Prof_Develop.pdf

Lein, L., Johnson, J. F., & Ragland, M. (1997, February). *Successful Texas schoolwide programs: Research study results.* Austin, TX: The Charles A. Dana Center. Retrieved April 29, 2004, from http://www.starcenter.org/products/resources/nationalawards/research.html

Morocco, C. C., & Aguilar, C. M. (2002). Coteaching for content understanding: A schoolwide model. *Journal of Educational and Psychological Consultation, 13,* 315–347.

Parker, R. I., O'Neill, K., Hall, L., & Hasbrouck, J. E. (2004, April). *Preventing reading failure with effective instructional practice: Results from the Texas Special Education/Reading Interface Study.* A paper presented at the annual meeting of the American Educational Research Association Conference. San Diego: CA.

Ragland, M., Clubine, B., Constable, D., & Smith, P. (2001, August). *Making education special: Achieving exemplary performance with minimal special education exemptions.* Austin, TX: The Charles A. Dana Center.

Slavin, R. E. (2004). Built to last: Long-term maintenance of success for all. *Remedial & Special Education, 25*(1), 61–66.

Tollestrup, B. (2002, June). *Neverstreaming: Collaborative academic support teams.* Presentation at the Vancouver School District Redesign Special Services Conference, Vancouver, WA.

Wallace, T., Anderson, A. R., & Bartholomay, T. (2002). Collaboration: An element associated with the success of four inclusive high schools. *Journal of Educational and Psychological Consultation, 13,* 349–381.

Zigmond, N., & Magiera, K. (2001, Autumn). *Current practice alerts: A focus on co-teaching.* [Electronic version]. Division for Learning Disabilities and Division for Research of the Council for Exceptional Children.

Chapter 10

Coaches, controversy, consensus. (2004, April/May). *Reading Today, 21*(5), 1, 18.

Hasbrouck, J., & Denton, C. (2004). *Evaluation checklist for school-based coaches/consultants.* (in Appendix)

Hasbrouck, J. E., & Denton, C. A. (2004). *SAILS: A comprehensive systemic model for improving students' reading outcomes.* Seattle: JH Consulting.

Hall, L. D., O'Neill, K. J., Hasbrouck, J. E., & Parker, R. I. (2003, May). *The best of both worlds: Texas Master Reading Teachers as teachers and mentors.* Research poster presented at the meeting of the International Reading Association, Orlando, FL.

Poglinco, S. M., & Bach, A. J. (2004, January). The heart of the matter: Coaching as a vehicle for professional development. *Phi Delta Kappan,* 398–400.

RESOURCES FOR THE READING COACH

Assessments

SCREENING MEASURES

Good, R. H, & Kaminski, R. (2003). *Dynamic Indicators of Basic Early Literacy Skills* (6th ed.). Longmont, CO: Sopris West. (Grades K-3) www.sopriswest.com; http://dibels.uoregon.edu/.

Reading Fluency Monitor (2003). St. Paul, MN: Read Naturally. www.readnaturally.com; info@readnaturally.com. 1-800-788-4085 or (651) 452-4085.

Texas Primary Reading Inventory (TPRI). (2004). (Grades K-3) www.tpri.org.

DIAGNOSTIC MEASURES

Phonemic Awareness

Auditory Analysis Test, by Rosner & Simon, described in: Rosner, J., & Simon, D. P. (1971). Auditory Analysis Test: An Initial Report. *Journal of Learning Disabilities*, 4(7), 41–48. (For use with students in K-6.)

Good, R. H, & Kaminski, R. (2003). *Dynamic Indicators of Basic Early Literacy Skills (DIBELS)* (6th ed.). Longmont, CO: Sopris West. (Grades K–3) www.sopriswest.com; http://dibels.uoregon.edu/.

Lindamood, C. H., & Lindamood, P. C. (1979). *Lindamood Auditory Conceptualization Test*. AGS Publishing. http://www.agsnet.com/.

Riccio, C. A., Davis, G. N., Imhoff, B., Hasbrouck, J. E. (2004). *Test of Phonological Awareness in Spanish (TOPAS)*. Austin, TX: Pro-Ed, Inc. www.proedinc.com.

Torgeson, J. K., & Bryant, B. (1993). *Test of Phonological Awareness (TOPA)*. Austin, TX: Pro-Ed, Inc. www.proedinc.com. 1-800-897-3202.

Wagner, R. K., Torgeson, J. K., & Rashotte, C. A. (2000). *Comprehensive Test of Phonological Awareness*. Austin, TX: Pro-Ed, Inc. www.proedinc.com. 1-800-897-3202.

Yopp-Singer Test of Phoneme Segmentation. Described in: Yopp, H. K. (1995). A Test for Assessing Phonemic Awareness in Young Children. *The Reading Teacher*, 49(1), 20–29. Available at http://teams.lacoe.edu/reading/assessments/yopp.html.

Phonics/Decoding and Spelling

Duffelmeyer, F. A., Kruse, A. E., Merkley, D. J., & Fyfe, S. A. (1994). Further Validation and Enhancement of the Names Test. *Reading Teacher*, 48, 118–128.

Hasbrouck, J. E. (1998). *Quick Phonics Screener-Revised (QPS)*. Seattle: JH Consulting.

Names Test. Described in: Cunningham, P. M. (1990). Names Test: A Quick Assessment of Decoding Ability. *Reading Teacher*, 44, 124–129.

Roswell-Chall Diagnostic Reading Test of Word Analysis Skills. (1997). Cambridge, MA: Educators Publishing Service. www.epsbooks.com. 1-800-225-5750.

Fluency

AIMSweb Assessment System. (2004). http://www.edformation.com/aimsweb.htm; Info@edformation.com. 1-888-944-1882 or (320) 245-2401.

Good, R. H., & Kaminski, R. (2003). *Dynamic Indicators of Basic Early Literacy Skills (DIBELS)* (6th ed.). Longmont, CO: Sopris West. (Grades K–3) www.sopriswest.com. Grades 4–6 and Grades K–3 Spanish available at http://dibels.uoregon.edu/.

Reading Fluency Monitor (2005). St. Paul, MN: Read Naturally. www.readnaturally.com; info@readnaturally.com. 1-800-788-4085 or (651) 452-4085.

Comprehension

Burns, P. C., & Roe, B. D. (2002). *Informal Reading Inventory Preprimer to 12th Grade* (6th ed.). Boston: Houghton Mifflin.

Leslie, L. & Caldwell, J. (2002). *Qualitative Reading Inventory (QRI-3)* (3rd ed.). Pearson Allyn & Bacon.

Woods, M. L., & Moe, A. J. (2002). *Analytical Reading Inventory* (7th ed.) Englewood Cliff, NJ: Merrill Hall.

PROGRESS MONITORING MEASURES

AIMSweb Assessment System. (2004). http://www.edformation.com/aimsweb.htm; Info@edformation.com.1-888-944-1882 or (320) 245-2401.

Dynamic Indicators of Basic Early Literacy Skills (DIBELS) (2003). (6th ed.). Sopris West. (Grades K–3) Grades 4–6 and Grades K–3 Spanish available at http://dibels.uoregon.edu/.

Fuchs, L., Hamlett, C., & Fuchs, D. *Monitoring Basic Skills Progress (MBSP)* (1997). (Computer tool for progress monitoring in reading and math) Austin, TX: Pro-Ed, Inc. www.proedinc.com.

Reading Fluency Monitor (2005). St. Paul, MN: Read Naturally. www.readnaturally.com; info@readnaturally.com. 1-800-788-4085 or (651) 452-4085.

Texas Primary Reading Inventory (TPRI). (1998). (Grades K–3) www.tpri.org.

Other Helpful Tools

OBSERVATION INSTRUMENTS

Hasbrouck, J., & Parker, R. (1995). *Scale for Coaching Instructional Effectiveness (SCIE).* Department of Educational Psychology, Texas A&M University: College Station, TX. (See Appendix.)

TIME MONITORING/TRACKING

Hasbrouck, J. E., Parker, R. I., & Denton, C. A. (2000). *3T-SR. Teacher Time-Tracking in Special Programs for Reading Teachers & Specialists.* Department of Educational Psychology, Texas A&M University: College Station, TX. (See Appendix.)

EVERY CHILD READING: A PROFESSIONAL DEVELOPMENT GUIDE

http://shop.ascd.org/productdisplay.cfm?productid=300303.

http://www.nasbe.org/Educational_Issues/Reports/Reading_Prof_Develop.pdf.

FREE MATERIALS FROM THE NATIONAL READING PANEL (FOR TEACHERS AND PARENTS)

http://www.nationalreadingpanel.org/Publications/publications.htm.

EVALUATING COACHES/CONSULTANTS

Hughes, J. A. & Hasbrouck, J. E. (1996). *Consultant Evaluation Rating Form (CERF) Scoring Manual.* Department of Educational Psychology. Texas A&M University: College Station, TX.

Books

* Adams, Marilyn J. (1991). *Beginning to Read: Thinking & Learning About Print.* Cambridge, MA: MIT Press.

Baumann, J. F., & Kame'enui, E. J. (2003). *Vocabulary Instruction: Research to Practice.* NY: Guilford Press.

Bearn, D. R., Invernizzi, M., Templeton, S., & Johnston, F. (2004). *Words Their Way: Word Study for Phonics, Vocabulary, and Spelling Instruction.* Upper Saddle River, NJ: Pearson.

Beck, I. L., & McKeown, M. G. (2002). *Bringing Words to Life: Robust Vocabulary Instruction.* Guilford Press.

Bender, W. N., & Larkin, M. J. *Reading Strategies for Elementary Students with Learning Difficulties* (includes a facilitator guide for professional development). Thousand Oaks, CA: Corwin Press.

Bos, C. S., & Vaughn, S. (2002). *Strategies for Teaching Students with Learning and Behavior Problems.* Boston: Allyn & Bacon.

Carnine, D., Silbert, J., & Kameenui, E. J. (1997). *Direct Instruction Reading* (3rd ed.). Columbus, OH: Merrill.

Cowen, J. E. (2003). *A Balanced Approach to Beginning Reading Instruction: A Synthesis of Six Major U.S. Research Studies.* Newark, DE: International Reading Association.

* Curtis, Mary E., & Longo, Ann Marie (1999). *When Adolescents Can't Read*. Cambridge, MA: Brookline.

Egan, G. (1994). *The Skilled Helper: A Problem-Management Approach to Helping*. Pacific Grove, CA: Brooks/Cole.

* Ellis, A. K. (2001). *Research on Educational Innovations* (3rd ed.). Larchmont, NY: Eye on Education.

Fry, E. B., Kress, J. E., & Foutoukidis, D. L. (2000). *The Reading Teacher's Book of Lists* (4th ed.). San Francisco: Jossey-Bass.

Gambrell, L. B., Morrow, L. M., Neuman, S. B., & Pressley, M. (1999). *Best practices in literacy instruction*. NY: Guildford.

Hall, S. L., & Moats, L. C. (1999). *Straight Talk about Reading*. Lincolnwood, IL: Contemporary Books.

Kampwirth, T. J. (1999). *Collaborative Consultation in the Schools*. Upper Saddle River, NJ: Merrill.

Idol, L., Nevin, A., & Paolucci-Whitcomb, P. (1999). *Models of Curriculum-Based Assessment* (3rd ed.). Austin, TX: Pro-Ed, Inc.

McEwan, E. K. (2001). *Raising Reading Achievement in Middle and High Schools*. Thousand Oaks, CA: Corwin.

McEwan, E. K. (1998). The Principal's Guide to Raising Reading Achievement. Thousand Oaks, CA: Corwin.

McGuinness, C., & McGuinness, G. (1999). *Reading Reflex: The Foolproof Phono-Graphix Method for Teaching Your Child to Read*. NY: Simon & Schuster.

* Moats, L. C. (2000). *Speech to Print*. NY: Brooks.

Moats, L. C. (2004). *LETRS: Language Essentials for Teachers of Reading and Spelling*. Longmont, CO: Sopris West.

National Reading Council (1999). *Starting Out Right: A Guide to Promoting Children's Reading Success*. Washington, DC: National Academy Press.

O'Neill, R. E., Horner, R. H., Albin, R. W., Sprague, J. R., Storey, K., & Newton, J. S. (1997). *Functional Assessment and Program Development for Problem Behavior: A Practical Handbook*. Pacific Grove, CA: Brooks/Cole.

Pressley, M. (1998). *Reading Instruction That Works*. NY: Guilford.

Rosenfield, S. A. (1987). *Instructional Consultation*. Hillsdale, NJ: Lawrence Erlbaum.

* Shaywitz, S. (2004). *Overcoming Dyslexia*. NY: Alfred Knopf.

Shinn, M. R. (Ed.) (1998). *Advanced Applications of Curriculum-Based Measurement*. NY: Guilford.

Shinn, M. R. (Ed.). (1989). *Curriculum-Based Measurement: Assessing Special Children*. NY: Guilford.

Simmons, D. C., & Kameenui, E. J. (1998). *What Reading Research Tells Us About Children With Diverse Learning Needs: Bases and Basics*. Mahwah, NJ: Erlbaum.

* Snow, C. E., Burns, S. M., & Griffin, P. (1998). *Preventing Reading Difficulties in Young Children*. National Research Council. Washington, DC: National Academy Press.

Sprick, R., Sprick, M., & Garrison, M. (1993). *Interventions: Collaborative Planning for Students At Risk*. Longmont, CO: Sopris West.

Sugai, G. & Tindal, G. A. (1993). *Effective School Consultation: An Interactive Approach*. Pacific Grove, CA: Brookes/Cole.

Tinajero, J. V., & DeVillar, R. A. (2000). *The Power of Two Languages 2000: Effective Dual-Language Use Across the Curriculum*. NY: McGraw-Hill.

University of Texas Center for Reading and Language Arts. *Three-Tier Reading Model*. http://www.texasreading.org/utcrla/products/3tier_materials.asp.

Vaughn, S. & Briggs, K. L. (Eds.) *Reading in the Classroom*. Baltimore: Brookes.

Westra, M. (1996). *Active Communication*. Pacific Grove, CA: Brooks/Cole.

Instructional Materials

PHONEMIC AWARENESS

Adams, M. J., Foorman, B. J., Lundberg, I., & Beeler, T. (1998). *Phonemic Awareness in Young Children*. Baltimore: Brookes.

---

* We suggest these books for use in teacher study groups.

Blachman, B. A., Ball, E. W., Black, R., & Tangel, D. M. (2000). *Road to the Code*. Baltimore: Brookes.

FLUENCY

Adams, G. N., & Brown, S. (2003). *The Six-Minute Solution*. Longmont, CO: Sopris West.

Rasinski, T. V. (2003). *The Fluent Reader: Oral Reading Strategies for Building Word Recognition, Fluency, and Comprehension*. New York: Scholastic Professional Books.

Read Naturally (a fluency building program). (2001; 2004). www.readnaturally.com; info@readnaturally.com. 1-800-788-4085 or (651) 452-4085.

SPELLING AND PHONICS

Bear, D. R., Invernizzi, M., Templeton, S., & Johnston, F. (1996). Words Their Way: Word Study For Phonics, Vocabulary, and Spelling Instruction. Upper Saddle River, NY: Prentice-Hall.

COMPREHENSION

Klingner, J. K., Vaughn, S., Dimino, J., Schumm, J. S., & Bryant, D. (2001). *Collaborative Strategic Reading*. Longmont, CO: Sopris West.

EARLY READING PROGRAMS

Denton, C., & Hocker, J. *Responsive Reading Instruction*: A supplemental early reading intervention program forthcoming from Sopris West. www.sopriswest.com.

Mathes, P. G., Allor, J. H., Torgesen, J. K., & Allen, S. H. (2001). *Teacher-Directed PALS: Paths to Achieving Literacy Success*. Longmont, CO: Sopris West.

McGuinnes, C., & McGuinness, G. (1999). *Phono-Graphix*. www.readamerica.net.

Proactive Beginning Reading: A supplemental early reading intervention program forthcoming from SRA/McGraw-Hill. www.sra4kids.com.

Sprick, M. M., Howard, L .M., & Fidanque, A. (1998). *Read Well: Critical Foundations in Primary Reading*. Longmont, CO: Sopris West.

PEER-ASSISTED LEARNING

Mathes, P. G., Clancy-Menchetti, J., & Torgesen, J. K. (2001). *K-PALS:. Kindergarten Peer-Assisted Literacy Strategies*. Longmont, CO: Sopris West.

Mathes, P. G., Torgesen, J. K., Allen, S. H., & Allor, J. H. (2001). *First Grade PALS: Peer-Assisted Literacy Strategies*. Longmont, CO: Sopris West.

INTERVENTION PROGRAMS FOR OLDER STRUGGLING READERS

Archer, A. L., Gleason, M. M., & Vachon, V. (2004). *REWARDS Plus: Application to Social Studies*. Longmont, CO: Sopris West. www.sopriswest.com.

Archer, A. L., Gleason, M. M., & Vachon, V. (2000). *REWARDS*. Longmont, CO: Sopris West. www.sopriswest.com.

Corrective Reading. (2001). New York: SRA/McGraw-Hill www.sra4kids.com.

Language! (2001). Longmont, CO: Sopris West. www.sopriswest.com.

Wilson, B., (1996). *Wilson Reading System*. Austin, TX: Pro-Ed, Inc. www.proedinc.com. For a review, see: http://www.ecs.org/clearinghouse/19/01/1901.htm.

Web Sites

Analysis of Reading Assessment Instruments for K–3. http://idea.uoregon.edu/assessment/.

Big Ideas in Beginning Reading. http://reading.uoregon.edu/.

Center for Academic and Reading Skills (CARS) at the University of Texas Health Science Center, Houston. http://cars.uth.tmc.edu/.

Center for Applied Linguistics. Improving communication through better understanding of language and culture. http://www.cal.org/.

Center for Early Intervention in Reading and Behavior to Improve the Performance of Young Children. http://www.lsi.ku.edu/jgprojects/r&b/.

Center for the Improvement of Early Reading Achievement. http://www.ciera.org/.

Consortium on Reading Excellence (CORE). http://www.corelearn.com/.

DIBELS Home Page. http://dibels.uoregon.edu/.

Education Commission of the States. www.esc.org.

Every Child Reading: An Action Plan of the Learning First Alliance. http://shop.ascd.org/productdisplay.cfm?productid=300303; http://www.readbygrade3.com/readbygrade3co/lfa.htm.

Oral Reading Fluency Norms Table

Grades 1–8

Grade	Percentile	Fall WCPM	Winter WCPM	Spring WCPM	Grade	Percentile	Fall WCPM	Winter WCPM	Spring WCPM
1	90		81	111	5	90	166	182	194
	75		47	82		75	139	156	168
	50		23	53		50	110	127	139
	25		12	28		25	85	99	109
	10		6	15		10	61	74	83
	SD		32	39		SD	45	44	45
	Count		16950	19434		Count	16212	13331	15292
2	90	106	125	142	6	90	177	195	204
	75	79	100	117		75	153	167	177
	50	51	72	89		50	127	140	150
	25	25	42	61		25	98	111	122
	10	11	18	31		10	68	82	93
	SD	37	41	42		SD	42	45	44
	Count	15896	18229	20128		Count	10520	9218	11290
3	90	128	146	162	7	90	180	192	202
	75	99	120	137		75	156	165	177
	50	71	92	107		50	128	136	150
	25	44	62	78		25	102	109	123
	10	21	36	48		10	79	88	98
	SD	40	43	44		SD	40	43	41
	Count	16988	17383	18372		Count	6482	4058	5998
4	90	145	166	180	8	90	185	199	199
	75	119	139	152		75	161	173	177
	50	94	112	123		50	133	146	151
	25	68	87	98		25	106	115	124
	10	45	61	72		10	77	84	97
	SD	40	41	43		SD	43	45	41
	Count	16523	14572	16269		Count	5546	3496	5335

WCPM: Words correct per minute

Adapted from Hasbrouck, J. & Tindal, G. A. (2006). Oral reading fluency norms: a valuable assessment tool for reading teachers. The Reading Teacher.

Coach/Consultant _____ Date _____ Supervisor _____

Evaluation Checklist for SFC Coaches/Consultants

E = *Exceptional*   S = *Satisfactory/Good*   I = *Improvement Needed*

● **Comments ●**

COACHING/CONSULTING COMPETENCIES

____ 1. Actively continues to EXPAND KNOWLEDGE BASE in SBRR for coaching reading.

____ 2. Works effectively with colleagues/parents across COACHING ROLES in Student-Focused Coaching: (a) *Facilitator*, (b) *Collaborative Problem Solver*, (c) *Teacher/Learner*.

____ 3. Collects and uses DATA to guide decisions (student assessments; observations; interviews; time management; etc.).

____ 4. Actively works to IMPROVE STUDENTS' READING OUTCOMES at individual, classroom, and school levels.

GENERAL PROFESSIONAL COMPETENCIES

____ a. Works COOPERATIVELY and COLLEGIALLY with others (supervisors, colleagues, other staff, parents).

____ b. COMMUNICATES EFFECTIVELY with students, colleagues, and families.

____ c. Exhibits FLEXIBILITY in dealing with students, colleagues, and families.

____ d. Demonstrates SENSITIVITY to, and ACCEPTANCE of, diverse cultural backgrounds of colleagues, students, and families.

____ e. ACCEPTS constructive critiques/feedback; USES the information for growth and improvement.

____ f. Demonstrates appropriate TIME MANAGEMENT for planning and completing all tasks and duties.

____ g. Uses APPROPRIATE and PROFESSIONAL written and spoken LANGUAGE and DEMEANOR.

____ h. Promptly uses APPROPRIATE CHANNELS for solving interpersonal or professional conflicts or concerns, as necessary.

____ i. Maintains and respects CONFIDENTIALITY and RIGHTS to PRIVACY of students, families, and colleagues, in all professional interactions.

Coach/Consultant Signature/Date: _____

Supervisor Signature/Date: _____

3T-SR

TEACHER TIME TRACKING IN SPECIAL PROGRAMS FOR READING TEACHERS & SPECIALISTS

**An instrument for monitoring a reading teacher
or specialist's time in professional activities**

Jan Hasbrouck, Ph.D.

Richard I. Parker, Ph.D.

Carolyn A. Denton, Ph.D.

INTRODUCTION

The *3T-SR Teacher Time Tracking in Special Programs for Reading Teachers and Specialists* was developed for use by reading coaches, reading specialists, reading teachers, consulting teachers, and others working in literacy interaction in special settings, particularly those working with students who have reading difficulties/disabilities. Teachers and specialists who spend a significant portion of their day in a variety of settings often have difficulty managing their time or explaining to others how their time is being spent. The *3T-SR* can help with (a) accountability (How is time being spent by our teachers/specialists? Is enough time being allocated to cover essential services?), (b) program planning and evaluation (Are teachers and specialists spending their time as productively as possible? Are there overlaps or gaps in services? Can we streamline schedules to maximize time spent with students?), and (c) self-monitoring to develop an effective personal time-management system.

You may find that using the *3T-SR* for only a week or two will give you sufficient information to answer your time-management questions. Some teachers and specialists use the *3T-SR* one or two days per month for general monitoring; others use it on a daily basis because their need for careful record keeping is more stringent.

HOW TO USE THE 3T-SR

DAILY TIME-TRACKING FORM

Begin by reading through the code definitions so you can be consistent in your record keeping. Putting your daily copy of the *3T-SR* form on a clipboard to carry with you throughout the day is the easiest way to use it. It is helpful to code your activities and make brief notes on your *3T-SR* form as *activities end*. It is very hard, if not impossible, to accurately reconstruct your day at 4:30 in the afternoon! Often several different activities occur within a single time block or activities run over from one time block to another. Use your best judgement to estimate how the MAJORITY of time was spent within each block of time and use that code.

SUMMARY SHEET

The results of your daily record keeping can be summarized on the *3T-SR Summary Sheet,* which functions as an easily interpreted bar graph. Each 15 minutes spent in an activity is marked as one small square on the *Summary Sheet*. A coach or specialist can use the *3T-SR* either as an overall tracking system (summarizing time spent each day in all activities on one form) or for case-by-case tracking (keeping an individual sheet for each "case," which can be work being done with a single student, a group of students or teachers, a curriculum-related concern, a district planning committee, etc.).

3T-SR CODE DEFINITIONS

1. Tch-Reg (Direct Teaching: In Regular Class)

Use this code for all teaching conducted *within regular classroom settings* where students are taught (a) with their age/grade peers or (b) in small, homogeneous groups but still in the regular classroom. Activities may be coded by whether teaching was conducted individually (1:1), in small groups (2–10 students), or in large groups (over 10 students). Use this code for time spent monitoring cooperative learning groups or peer- or cross-age tutoring groups if these activities are taking place in *regular class settings*. This code includes times when small groups or individuals from a regular class may be taught for short periods in the hall outside the classroom, in an adjacent workroom or office, etc.

2. Tch-S (Direct Teaching: In Special Class)

Code all teachings conducted in *special settings* (Title 1 classroom, tutoring settings, reading clinic or labs, special education classrooms, etc.). Activities may be coded by whether teaching was conducted individually (1:1), in small groups (2–5) students, or in large groups (over 5 students). Use this code for time spent monitoring cooperative learning groups or peer- or cross-age tutoring groups if these activities are taking place in *special classroom settings*.

3. Data (Data: Active Data Collection)

Time spent conducting individual or group assessments of students including formal and informal tests, diagnostic teaching, student interviews, etc. Also, conducting problem identification/intervention development interviews with teachers or parents. Activities may be coded by whether assessment was conducted individually or in groups.

4. Obs (Observation: Passive Data Collection)

Time spent conducting observations of students or teachers. Observations for collecting information about classroom ecololgy/activity patterns, etc., is coded as student observation. This code includes other forms of passive information gathering such as reviewing student records or work samples.

5. Coach (Coaching: Direct/Phone/E-mail)

General coaching and consultation activities such as demonstrating or modeling procedures, idea sharing, exchanging current information/data, providing sources, materials, etc., or listening/encouraging, etc. If desired, you may separately code coaching activities with classroom teachers (5a Coach-Reg), other professionals (5b Coach-Pro), aides or instructional assistants (5c Coach-Asst), or parents (5d Coach-Prnt).

6. Sprv (Supervise)

Activities related to the supervision of others (e.g., supervising instructional assistants or student teachers, etc.). This would include time spent observing instructional assistants or student teachers for supervision. If desired, you may separately code supervision activities with other professionals, including student teachers (6a Sprb-Pro), aides, paraprofessionals, or instructional assistants (6b Sprv-Asst).

7. ProD (Provide Inservice/Pro Development)

Activities related to the preparation for and delivery of inservice trainings, including professional study groups. If desired, you may separately code training or inservice activities with regular classroom teachers (7a ProD-Reg), other professionals, including student teachers (7b ProD-Pro), aides or instructional assistants (7c ProD-Asst), or parents (7d ProD-Prnt).

8. Plan-Self (Planning/Preparation for own teaching)

General planning and materials preparation for lessons that primarily <u>you</u> will be directly teaching or co-teaching.

9. Plan-Oth (Planning/Preparation for others)

General planning and materials preparation for lessons that primarily <u>others</u> will teach, including materials for peer- or cross-age tutors to use.

10. Grd (Grading/Scoring/Correcting)

Time spent correcting student papers, calculating grades, writing reports, reviewing student work portfolios, etc.

11. Admin (Administrative tasks related to student academic progress)

All general administrative tasks related to student progress (including academics and behavioral/social skills) such as setting up/putting away equipment needed for a lesson, attending meetings with parents, ARD/IEP or MDT meetings, meetings with problem-solving teams (Student Study Teams, Academic Improvement Teams), etc. Includes phone calls, e-mails, or reading/writing letters or reports relating to a specific student or group of students.

12. Ad-Not (Administrative tasks not related to student academic progress)

Time spent on miscellaneous management tasks such as ordering materials, creating bulletin boards, scheduling field trips, general housekeeping or paperwork, etc.

13. Tran (Transitions between activities)

Time spent between instructional or supervisory activities including time spent traveling between classrooms or buildings.

14. Mon (Monitoring/Supervison of students)

Time spent in monitoring hallways, study areas, cafeterias, playgrounds, bus loading areas, etc. *If you do other tasks during your supervision, record BOTH codes on your record sheet.*

15. Brk (Breaks)

Lunch, coffee breaks, etc. *If you do other tasks during your break, record BOTH codes on your record sheet.*

Note: Professionals often find themselves doing multiple tasks within any given time period. You should only record what you were doing for the MAJORITY of the time. Except for codes 14 (Mon) and 15 (Brk), *code only ONE activity type for each time block.*

3T-SR: Teacher Time Tracking in Special Programs for Reading Teachers and Specialists

Daily Time-Tracking Form: **15-Minute Blocks**

Date: _____ Teacher: _____ School: _____

Direct Teaching: In Regular Class

1. Tch-Reg
   1a. 1:1
   1b. small grp (2–10)
   1c. large grp (>10)

Direct Teaching: In Special Class

2. Tch-S
   2a. 1:1
   2b. small grp (2–5)
   2c. large grp (>5)

Data (Active)

3. Data
   3a. 1:1
   3b. group

Observation (Passive)

4. Obs
   4a. Obs-St
   4b. Obs-Tchr
   4c. Obs-Othr

Coaching (Direct/Phone)

5. Coach
   5a. Coach-Reg
   5b. Coach-Pro
   5c. Coach-Asst
   5d. Coach-Prnt

Supervise

6. Sprv
   6a. Sprv-Pro
   6b. Sprv-Asst

Professional Development

7. ProD
   7a. ProD-Reg
   7b. ProD-Pro
   7c. ProD-Asst
   7d. ProD-Prnt

Plan/Prepare

8. Plan-Self
9. Plan-Other

Grading/Scoring/Correcting

10. Grd

Admin. (Student Progress)

11. Admin

Admin. (Not St. Progress)

12. Ad-Not

Transition

13. Tran

Monitoring/Supervision

14. Mon

Breaks

15. Brk

Time	Code(s)	Describe
7:00		
7:15		
7:30		
7:45		
8:00		
8:15		
8:30		
8:45		
9:00		
9:15		
9:30		
9:45		
10:00		
10:15		
10:30		
10:45		
11:00		
11:15		
11:30		
11:45		
12:00		

Time	Code(s)	Describe
12:15		
12:30		
12:45		
1:00		
1:15		
1:30		
1:45		
2:00		
2:15		
2:30		
2:45		
3:00		
3:15		
3:30		
3:45		
4:00		
4:15		
4:30		
4:45		
5:00		

Evenings:

3T-SR: Teacher Time Tracking in Special Programs for Reading Teachers and Specialists SUMMARY SHEET

Each block equals 15 minutes.

Dates:

Instruction/Counseling/Assessment

1. Tch-Reg = Direct Teaching Regular TOTAL
- 1a. 1:1
- 1b. Small Group (2–10)
- 1c. Large Group (>10)

2. Tch-S = Direct Teaching Special TOTAL
- 2a. 1:1
- 2b. Small Group (2–5)
- 2c. Large Group (>5)

3. Data = Active Student Assessment TOTAL
- 3a. 1:1
- 3b. Group

4. Obs = Passive Assessment/Observation TOTAL
- 4a. Student
- 4b. Teacher
- 4c. Other

Professional Contacts

5. Coach = Coaching (Direct/Phone/E-mail) TOTAL
- 5a. Regular Teacher
- 5b. Other Professional
- 5c. Aide/Assistant
- 5d. Parent

6. Sprv = Supervise TOTAL
- 6a. Professional
- 6b. Aide/Assistant

7. Professional Development TOTAL
- 7a. Regular Teacher
- 7b. Other Professional
- 7c. Aide/Assistant
- 7d. Parent

Preparation/ Management

8. Plan-Self = Plan/Prepare for Self
9. Plan–Other = Plan/Prepare for Other
10. Grd = Grading, Scoring, Correcting
11. Admin = Admin. Tasks (Student Progress)
12. Ad-Not = Admin. Tasks (NOT Student Progress)

Other

13. Transition
14. Monitor
15. Break

Communication Skills Practice Form

Coach: _____ Colleague/Parent: _____ Observer: _____

	Comments
Listening without unnecessary interruptions; using minimal encouragers	
Reflecting, responding to feelings	
Paraphrasing	
Asking questions to clarify, check perceptions, seek elaboration; closed and open questions	
Avoiding jargon	
Summarizing	

SOLER and minimal encouragers
  – Sit squarely
  – Open posture
  – Lean forward
  – Eye contact
  – Relaxed	

DEBRIEFING:

(1) *Observer* asks the *Colleague/Parent*: How well did you feel the *Coach* listened and responded to your concerns? What communication skill did the *Coach* use most effectively in communicating with you? Do you have any suggestions for the *Coach*?

(2) The *Observer* shares the notes from the observation and makes comments about what the Coach did well. The *Observer* also makes suggestions for improvement.

(3) The *Coach* shares his/her impressions about the conversation.

ACTIVITY STRUCTURES OBSERVATION SYSTEM–REVISED (ASOS-R)

Carolyn A. Denton, Richard Parker, & Jan Hasbrouck (2004)

Preparation

1. Read and understand the definitions of the Teacher Behaviors, Grouping Formats, and Student Behaviors.

2. Practice the observation procedure.

3. Have a pre-observation conference with the teacher.

4. Materials: Observation form, stopwatch or watch with second hand, clipboard.

Directions

1. Choose a Comparison Student (or a small group of students) who is a classmate or a member of the same instructional group as the Target Student, and is as similar to the Target Student as possible. You will observe this Comparison Student (or a group of Comparison Students) along with the Target Student, at the same time, engaged in the same activities, so that you can compare their on-task behaviors. Complete the top of the observation form.

2. Observe informally for a minute or two to determine the subject area (probably reading or language arts).

3. Observe to determine the teacher behavior and grouping format (described below), and enter this information at the beginning of the first coding strip.

4. At the *end of 10 seconds*, look quickly at *both* the Target and Comparison Students and *for that moment* quickly code on task, off task, or disruptive behavior by putting a dot in the appropriate square on the coding strip.

5. After 10 more seconds, glance again at the Target and Comparison Students, decide on the behavior of each *at that moment*, and code it quickly.

6. If the teacher behavior or grouping format changes, start a new coding strip.

7. If the teacher goes back to the original teacher behavior and grouping format, resume coding on the first coding strip.

8. Continue until the end of the observation period. The ASOS-R observation normally lasts about 20 minutes.

Note: See the completed sample on the following page.

Teacher Behaviors

- **Lecture**: Teacher speaks to or directly instructs students about content or skills; includes use of audiovisuals.

- **Directions**: Teacher gives directions related to academic work. (Does not include discipline.)

- **Demonstrate**: Teacher models or demonstrates a skill, strategy, or procedure (something students will later do themselves).

- **Ask**: Teacher verbally asks questions related to content or skills; teacher-led discussion.

- **Evaluate**: Teacher evaluates correctness or quality of student responses or work. Includes teacher listening to students read with no feedback in order to evaluate or assess their performance.

- **Answer**: Teacher answers questions related to subject matter or skills, makes clarifications.

Activity Structures Observation System–Revised

(Completed Sample of Part of an ASOS-R Observation)

Carolyn A. Denton, Richard Parker, & Jan Hasbrouck (2004)

Start time: __9:00__   End time: __9:20__

Subject: __Reading__

Observer __Cindy Scott__

Student __Michael M.__

Teacher __Melinda R.__

School __Summerside__

Date __4/29/04__

Directions

1. Write in teacher behavior and grouping format.
2. Observe *both* students at 10-second intervals and record behavior for *both* at that moment.
3. Start a new section if teacher behavior or grouping changes or if you come to the end of the line.

Teacher	Grouping
• Lecture	• Whole Class
• Directions	• Large
• Demonstrate	• Small (2–5)
• Ask	• Individual (1:1)
• Evaluate	
• Answer	
• Observe	
• Non-Academic Activities	

Section 1

	1				5					10					15	...	20	25	30	35	40	45
Target																						
On Task	X	X	X	X	X	X	X	X	X	X												
Off Task	X	X	X	X	X	X	X	X	X	X	X	X	X	X	X							
Disruptive	X	X	X	X	X																	
Comparison																						
Grouping: Whole Class																						
On Task	X	X	X	X	X	X	X	X	X	X	X	X	X	X	X							
Off Task	X	X	X	X	X	X	X	X	X	X	X	X										
Disruptive	X	X																				

Section 2

	1				5					10					15			20	...	25	30	35	40	45
Target																								
On Task	X	X	X	X	X	X	X	X	X	X	X	X	X	X	X	X	X	X	X	X				
Off Task	X	X	X	X	X	X	X																	
Disruptive	X																							
Comparison																								
Grouping: Small Group Including T & C																								
On Task	X	X	X	X	X	X	X	X	X	X	X	X	X	X	X	X	X							
Off Task	X	X	X	X	X	X	X	X	X	X														
Disruptive	X	X																						

- **Observe**: Teacher observes or supervises students during academic activities. This may include the teacher giving feedback, praise, or scaffolding. Includes teacher listening to students read and providing feedback and support.

- **Non-Academic Activities**:
  - **Non-Academic Feedback** (*including discipline*)
  - **Free time**
  - **Transitions or Housekeeping** (taking attendance, lunch count, setting up an activity, putting away materials, passing out papers)
  - **Interruptions** (intercom, visitor, sick student)
  - Any other activity not related to instruction or practice (grading papers, working on computer, etc.)

Grouping Formats

- **Whole Class**: All students in the class (includes times when teacher works with whole class but briefly helps or answers questions for individual students)

- **Large Group**: A subset of the class with 6 or more students in it

- **Small Group**: Group of 2–5 students. Note whether the Target and Comparison Students are included in the small group.

- **Individual**: Teacher works with 1 student individually (does not include briefly helping or answering questions)

Student Behaviors

- **On task**: Active engagement in a learning activity OR passive engagement in learning by listening or watching

- **Off task**: Behavior that would reasonably interfere with taking in the information or performing the required behaviors OR that is different from the teacher-directed behavior

- **Disruptive**: Behavior that does, or could reasonably be expected to, move the focus of other students' attention from the teacher's intended activity to the disruptive activity

Notes

- If the teacher behavior or grouping format changes only for a short time but quickly returns to the original behavior or format, you do not need to start a new coding strip.

- If you need to, take a 20–30 second rest every few minutes.

Completing the Summary Reports

- Select the format(s) of the *Summary Report* that you want to use to share the results with the teacher.
  - **Behavior of Student Within Classroom Instructional Formats**: to report the percentage of time the Target Student was on task, off task, and disruptive *during different instructional formats* (different teacher behaviors: e.g., Lecture, Demonstrate, Ask questions, etc.)
  - **Behavior of Student Within Classroom Grouping Formats**: to report the percentage of time the Target Student was on task, off task, and disruptive *during different grouping formats*
  - **Classroom Instructional Formats Observed**: to report the percentage of time the teacher was observed using different instructional formats (different teacher behaviors: e.g., Lecture, Demonstrate, Ask questions, etc.)
  - **Behavior of Student Compared to Peers**: to report the percentage of time the Target Student was on task, off task, and disruptive compared to the percentage of time the Comparison Student (or small groups of students) was on task, off task, and disruptive

- Add up the number of 10-second intervals that were coded as on task, off task, and disruptive during each teaching format for the Target Student and for the Comparison Student. Convert the number of *intervals* to the number of *seconds* by multiplying by 10.

- Divide the number of seconds each student was on task, off task, and disruptive during each format by the *total number of seconds* you observed the student during that format. This will result in the percentage of time the Target Student and the Comparison Student were on task, off task, and disruptive during *each* of the different instructional formats the teacher used.

- Complete the *Summary Report* Form(s).

  - **Behavior of Student within Classroom Instructional Formats**: Complete this form *for the Target Student only*. Fill in each teacher behavior you observed in the boxes under *Format*. Fill in the total number of seconds (or convert to minutes and seconds by dividing by 60) you observed the student being on task, off task, and disruptive during each instructional format. Color in the bar graphs to indicate the percentage of the total observed time the student was on task, off task, and disruptive.

  - **Behavior of Student Within Classroom Grouping Formats**: Complete this form *for the Target Student only*. Fill in each grouping format you observed in the boxes under *Grouping*. Fill in the total number of seconds (or convert to minutes and seconds by dividing by 60) you observed the student being on task, off task, and disruptive during each grouping format. Color in the bar graphs to indicate the percentage of the total observed time the student was on task, off task, and disruptive.

  - **Classroom Instructional Formats Observed**: This form simply summarizes the total percentage of time the teacher was engaged in different instructional formats (teacher behaviors) during the observed period without including the student behaviors. Under *Format*, list each instructional format (teacher behavior) you observed. Under *Frequency*, put the total number of seconds (or convert to minutes and seconds by dividing by 60) that you observed the teacher in each format. Color in the graphs to show the percentage of total time the teacher used each instructional format.

  - **Behavior of Student Compared to Peers**: Fill in the total number of minutes (or convert to minutes and seconds by dividing by 60) you observed the Target Student and the Comparison Student being on task, off task, and disruptive. Color in the graphs to show the percentage of total time the two students were on task, off task, and disruptive during the lesson.

Adapted from Parker, R. I., Hasbrouck, J. E., & Tindal, G. A. (1992). *Activity Structures Observation System (ASOS)*. Unpublished document. Texas A&M University: College Station, TX.

Activity Structures Observation System–Revised

Carolyn A. Denton, Richard Parker, & Jan Hasbrouck (2004)

Teacher
- Lecture
- Directions
- Demonstrate
- Ask
- Evaluate
- Answer
- Observe
- Non-Academic Activities

Grouping
- Whole Class
- Large
- Small (2–5)
- Individual (1:1)

Observer _____

Student _____

Teacher _____

School _____

Date _____

Start time: _____ End time: _____

Subject: _____

Directions
1. Write in teacher behavior and grouping format.
2. Observe *both* students at 10-second intervals and record behavior for *both* at that moment.
3. Start a new section if teacher behavior or grouping changes or if you come to the end of the line.

Target — 1 5 10 15 20 25 30 35 40 45

Teacher: On Task / Off Task / Disruptive

Grouping — *Comparison*: On Task / Off Task / Disruptive

Target — 1 5 10 15 20 25 30 35 40 45

Teacher: On Task / Off Task / Disruptive

Grouping — *Comparison*: On Task / Off Task / Disruptive

Chart 1

		1	5	10	15	20	25	30	35	40	45
Teacher	*Target*										
	On Task										
	Off Task										
	Disruptive										
Grouping	*Comparison*										
	On Task										
	Off Task										
	Disruptive										

Chart 2

		1	5	10	15	20	25	30	35	40	45
Teacher	*Target*										
	On Task										
	Off Task										
	Disruptive										
Grouping	*Comparison*										
	On Task										
	Off Task										
	Disruptive										

Chart 3

		1	5	10	15	20	25	30	35	40	45
Teacher	*Target*										
	On Task										
	Off Task										
	Disruptive										
Grouping	*Comparison*										
	On Task										
	Off Task										
	Disruptive										

Adapted from Parker, R. I., Hasbrouck, J. E., & Tindal, G. A. (1992). *Activity Structures Observation System (ASOS)*. Unpublished document. Texas A&M University: College Station, TX.

APPENDIX

ASOS-R
Summary Report

Behavior of Student Within Classroom Instructional Formats

Student _____ Observer _____

Date(s) of Observation(s) _____ Teacher _____

Format		Total	Percent of Total Time																		
			5	10	15	20	25	30	35	40	45	50	55	60	65	70	75	80	85	90	95	100
	On Task																					
	Off Task																					
	Disruptive																					
	On Task																					
	Off Task																					
	Disruptive																					
	On Task																					
	Off Task																					
	Disruptive																					
	On Task																					
	Off Task																					
	Disruptive																					
	On Task																					
	Off Task																					
	Disruptive																					
	On Task																					
	Off Task																					
	Disruptive																					
	On Task																					
	Off Task																					
	Disruptive																					
	On Task																					
	Off Task																					
	Disruptive																					
	On Task																					
	Off Task																					
	Disruptive																					
	On Task																					
	Off Task																					
	Disruptive																					

Adapted from Parker, R. I., Hasbrouck, J. E., & Tindal, G. A. (1992). *Activity Structures Observation System (ASOS)*. Unpublished document. Texas A&M University: College Station, TX.

© Sopris West Educational Services. Permission is granted to photocopy this page.   THE READING COACH **131**

ASOS-R
Summary Report

Behavior of Student Within Classroom Grouping Formats

Student _____ Observer _____

Date(s) of Observation(s) _____ Teacher _____

Grouping		Total	Percent of Total Time																		
			5	10	15	20	25	30	35	40	45	50	55	60	65	70	75	80	85	90	95	100
	On Task																					
	Off Task																					
	Disruptive																					
	On Task																					
	Off Task																					
	Disruptive																					
	On Task																					
	Off Task																					
	Disruptive																					
	On Task																					
	Off Task																					
	Disruptive																					
	On Task																					
	Off Task																					
	Disruptive																					
	On Task																					
	Off Task																					
	Disruptive																					
	On Task																					
	Off Task																					
	Disruptive																					
	On Task																					
	Off Task																					
	Disruptive																					
	On Task																					
	Off Task																					
	Disruptive																					
	On Task																					
	Off Task																					
	Disruptive																					

Adapted from Parker, R. I., Hasbrouck, J. E., & Tindal, G. A. (1992). *Activity Structures Observation System (ASOS)*. Unpublished document. Texas A&M University: College Station, TX.

ASOS-R
Summary Report

Classroom Instructional Formats Observed

Student _____   Observer _____

Date(s) of Observation(s) _____   Teacher _____

Format	Frequency	Percent of Total Time																		
		5	10	15	20	25	30	35	40	45	50	55	60	65	70	75	80	85	90	95	100

Adapted from Parker, R. I., Hasbrouck, J. E., & Tindal, G. A. (1992). *Activity Structures Observation System (ASOS)*. Unpublished document. Texas A&M University: College Station, TX.

ASOS-R
Summary Report

Behavior of Student Compared to Peers

Student _____   Observer _____

Date(s) of Observation(s) _____   Teacher _____

		Total	Percent of Total Time																		
			5	10	15	20	25	30	35	40	45	50	55	60	65	70	75	80	85	90	95	100
Target	On Task																						
	Off Task																						
	Disruptive																						
Peers	On Task																						
	Off Task																						
	Disruptive																						

Adapted from Parker, R. I., Hasbrouck, J. E., & Tindal, G. A. (1992). *Activity Structures Observation System (ASOS).* Unpublished document. Texas A&M University: College Station, TX.

ABC Observation Form
Antecedent (Before), Behavior, Consequence (After)

Student _____ Teacher _____

Observer _____ Date _____

Class _____ Start Time _____ End Time _____

Antecedent	Behavior	Consequence

Literacy Instruction Feedback Template (LIFT)

Teacher _____   Coach _____

Date _____   Start time: _____   Stop time: _____

Lesson focus: ❑ PA/Phonics/Words   ❑ Fluency   ❑ Vocabulary   ❑ Comprehension

❑ Writing   ❑ Unclear   ❑ Other _____

Grouping Formats: ❑ Whole class ❑ Large group (≥ 6) ❑ Small group (2–5) ❑ Individualized (1:1)

Very Much　　　　　*Not Observed*	**Notes about student behaviors:**

Organization and planning:

Lesson is purposeful/focused on objectives
　　5　　4　　3　　2　　1

Modeling and Instruction:

Models skills and strategies
　　5　　4　　3　　2　　1

Clearly explains concepts
　　5　　4　　3　　2　　1

Practice, support, and feedback:

Provides guided practice
　　5　　4　　3　　2　　1

Provides scaffolding to enable success
　　5　　4　　3　　2　　1

Provides specific corrective feedback
　　5　　4　　3　　2　　1

Provides specific praise
　　5　　4　　3　　2　　1

Provides for and monitors independent practice
　　5　　4　　3　　2　　1

Reteaches/clarifies instruction as needed
　　5　　4　　3　　2　　1

Student involvement and success:

Secures and maintains student attention
　　5　　4　　3　　2　　1

Provides for active student involvement
　　5　　4　　3　　2　　1

Elicits responses from all students
　　5　　4　　3　　2　　1

Achieves successful/accurate student responses
　　5　　4　　3　　2　　1

Adapted from Haagar, D., Gersten, R., Baker, S., & Graves, A. (2003). The English-language learner classroom observation instrument for beginning readers. In Vaughn, S., & Briggs, K. L. (Eds.) *Reading in the Classroom*. Baltimore: Brookes.

Administering the LIFT Observation

The *Literacy Instruction Feedback Template* (LIFT; Denton, 2004) is a brief observation form that is directed specifically at the implementation of explicit instruction in the reading classroom (see Chapter 2). The LIFT form provides space to record the areas of focus of the reading lesson and the grouping formats the teacher uses. As the reading coach observes the lesson, the coach rates the extent to which the teacher employed various aspects of explicit instruction. Next to the rating scales on the form, there is space for taking notes about specific examples of explicit instruction you have observed.

THE STEPS FOR USING THE LIFT TOOL ARE:

1. Complete the information at the top of the form. Record the time when the observation begins.

2. Check *all* examples of lesson focus that you observe during the observation period using the following definitions:

   a. *PA/Phonics/Words:* Any instruction that is focused on phonological awareness, phonemic awareness, letter-sound correspondences, using phonics to read or spell words, or identifying or spelling words as units; any practice activities in manipulating the sounds of English, identifying letter-sound correspondences, spelling words, or reading words.

   b. *Fluency:* Any instruction designed to promote *quick* and *accurate* reading of *connected text*; instruction focused on reading text with expression or interpreting punctuation while reading text.

   c. *Vocabulary:* Any instruction that is focused on meanings of individual words.

   d. *Comprehension:* Any instruction that is focused directly on understanding, summarizing, synthesizing, evaluating, or interpreting text, answering questions related to text, or making inferences about text. This includes writing answers to comprehension questions or oral or written retelling of text.

   e. *Writing:* Any instruction focused specifically on writing, including the writing process—planning, composing, editing, revising, and publishing text.

This does *not* include writing answers to comprehension questions or the written retelling of text.

   f. *Unclear:* Check this if you cannot determine the focus or objectives for a substantial part of the lesson.

   g. *Other:* If you observe instruction focused on other objectives, record these.

3. Check *all* grouping formats you observe during the lesson, using the guidelines for numbers of students in each format listed on the LIFT form. Record the size of the groups with which the teacher directly interacts. In other words, if students are working independently, but the teacher does not interact with them, do not note this as individualized instruction. Likewise, if an instructional assistant or another person works with a small group of students within the classroom, but the regular reading teacher is instructing the rest of the class as a whole, record this as "whole group" instruction.

4. During the lesson, take notes about the aspects of explicit instruction you observe during the lesson. Also, note any clear relationships you observe among these aspects of instruction and student behaviors, involvement, and success. Use the categories listed on the form to guide your observation:

   a. *Lesson is purposeful and focused on objectives:* Can you clearly determine the objective of each part of the lesson, and are these objectives related to the essential elements of reading instruction?

   b. *Teacher models skills and strategies:* Does the teacher demonstrate or model new or difficult skills and strategies?

   c. *Teacher clearly explains concepts:* If the objective of the lesson is to teach a concept rather than a skill or strategy, does the teacher clearly explain the concept? Does the teacher provide clear examples to clarify the concept?

   d. *Teacher provides guided practice:* Does the teacher provide opportunities for students to practice new skills and strategies or apply new concepts with guidance, support, and feedback?

   e. *Teacher provides scaffolding to enable success:* Does the teacher respond to student errors, hesitations, and uncertainty with hints and prompts, or provide another form of support, such as breaking tasks into smaller steps?

f. *Teacher provides specific corrective feedback:* Does the teacher promptly and clearly provide feedback when students make errors?

g. *Teacher provides specific praise:* Does the teacher provide praise that clearly identifies to students the aspects of skills, strategies, or application of knowledge that they do well?

h. *Teacher provides for and monitors independent practice:* Does the teacher provide opportunities for students to independently practice skills and strategies, and does the teacher monitor this practice to provide feedback and support when it is needed?

i. *Teacher reteaches and clarifies instruction as needed:* If students experience difficulty when practicing a skill or strategy, or while applying a concept, does the teacher provide additional instruction and clarification?

j. *Teacher secures and maintains student attention and involvement:* Does the teacher skillfully obtain and keep the attention of students during modeling, instruction, and provision of feedback? Are most of the students on-task for most of the class, or does the teacher effectively re-direct off-task behavior?

k. *Teacher provides for active student involvement:* Does the lesson provide many opportunities for students to be actively involved in learning rather than be passive listeners or observers?

l. *Teacher elicits responses from all students:* Does the teacher direct questions and ensure the participation of all students in the instructional group?

m. *Teacher achieves successful and accurate student responses:* Do most of the students appear to have a high rate of success?

5. Immediately after the lesson, rate the lesson on a scale of 1–5 for each aspect of explicit instruction. Use the following scale:

5: Very much, to a large degree for nearly all of the lesson

4: Yes, to a large degree for much of the lesson

3: Occasionally

2: Minimally, to a small degree for a small amount of the lesson

1: Not observed during this lesson

Student Success–Teacher Strategy Observation (SS-TS)

Teacher _____

Coach _____

Focus Student _____

Date _____ School _____

Focus of Lesson Component: ❑ Phonological Awareness/Phonics/Words ❑ Fluency ❑ Vocabulary ❑ Comprehension ❑ Writing ❑ Unclear
❑ Other

Grouping Format: ❑ Whole class ❑ Large group (≥6) ❑ Small group (2–5) ❑ Individualized (1:1)

Student Observation

What is the student expected to do?

❑ Listen ❑ Answer questions/discuss ❑ Write

❑ Worksheets ❑ Hands-on activity/project

❑ Oral practice of skills (PA/word reading/Letter-Sounds, etc.)

❑ Read orally ❑ Read silently ❑ Round robin reading ❑ Unclear

❑ Other

Observed student behaviors:

Teacher Observation

Organization and planning:

❑ Lesson is purposeful/focused on objectives

❑ Teacher appears organized with materials ready

Instructional elements:

❑ Effective lesson delivery: eye-contact/position(s) in room/enthusiasm/warmth

❑ Models skills and strategies/Clearly explains concepts

❑ Provides specific corrective feedback

❑ Provides scaffolding and specific praise

❑ Provides opportunities for practice

Student involvement and success:

❑ Secures and maintains student attention

❑ Provides for active student involvement

❑ Has appropriate pacing and smooth transitions between activities

❑ Achieves successful/accurate student responses

Administering the SS-TS Observation

The *Student Success–Teacher Strategy Observation* (SS-TS; Denton, 2004) is similar to the LIFT in some ways, but it places more emphasis on the interaction between student and teacher behaviors.

TO COMPLETE THIS OBSERVATION:

1. Complete the information at the top of the form.

2. Check *all* examples of lesson focus that you observe during the observation period using the same definitions used for the LIFT.

3. Check *all* grouping formats you observe during the lesson, using the guidelines for numbers of students in each format listed on the SS-TS form. Record the size of the groups *in which the target student is included.* (This is different from the LIFT directions.)

4. Observe to find out what the student is expected to do during this lesson segment. Check all that apply. For example, if the teacher is teaching a phonics lesson and the student is expected to listen, practice skills orally, and complete a worksheet, check all three. Use the following guidelines:

   - *Listen:* Student is expected to listen to the teacher or to some other person. Includes times when the student is expected to listen and "follow along" while someone else is reading.

   - *Answer Questions/Discuss:* Student is expected to answer questions orally or participate in an oral discussion.

   - *Write:* Student is expected to write words, sentences, or text. Does not include completing worksheets.

   - *Worksheets:* Student is expected to complete a worksheet.

   - *Hands-on activity/project:* Student is expected to participate in an activity or project, either individually or in a group.

   - *Oral practice of skills:* Student is expected to orally practice skills associated with phonemic awareness/phonological awareness, word reading, decoding, letter-sound correspondences, etc. This includes flash card activities.

   - *Read orally:* Student is expected to participate in oral reading that is *not* in the round-robin format (students "going around the small group/room" and taking turns reading while others follow along). Partner-reading activities *are* included in *read orally.*

   - *Read silently:* Student is expected to engage in independent silent reading.

   - *Round robin reading:* Student is expected to participate in oral reading that is in the round-robin format (students "going around the small group/room" and taking turns reading while others follow along).

   - *Unclear:* Expected student activity is unclear.

   - *Other:* Student is expected to engage in some other activity (please list).

5. Check the items under Teacher Observation if they apply during the time you observe. It may be easier for you to take running notes on paper and complete this checklist just after you leave the room following the observation.

6. Take notes about specific student behaviors you observe, especially if they seem to be related to the teacher behaviors or the expected student action (listening, writing, etc.). Add an extra sheet for your notes, if needed.

SCIE

SCALE FOR COACHING INSTRUCTIONAL EFFECTIVENESS

Training Manual

Jan Hasbrouck, Ph.D.
Jan Hasbrouck Consulting, Inc.
2100 3rd Ave. #2003 Seattle, WA 98121
reading@jhasbrouck.net

Richard I. Parker, Ph.D.
Department of Educational Psychology
Texas A&M University
College Station, TX 77843-4225
rparker@tamu.edu

Background and Description

The Scale for Coaching Effective Instruction (SCIE) was developed for use by teachers to observe colleagues in classroom settings and provide feedback in the form of professional and collegial critiquing for instructional improvement. The SCIE was developed from three sources: (a) a review of effective schools research (NWREL, 1990); (b) an examination of published teacher and classroom evaluation scales; and (c) feedback from field-based experts. The current version of the SCIE has evolved from several preliminary versions, some of which were field-tested in informal pilot studies conducted at Texas A&M University within the *Consulting Teacher M.Ed. Program* of the Department of Educational Psychology/Special Education Area. The SCIE has 16 items divided into 51 sub-items. Items are grouped into three categories: (a) planning and organization (2 items; 5 sub-items); (b) instruction (9 items; 32 sub-items); and (c) classroom management (4 items; 14 sub-items).

Scoring

Each item on the SCIE contains a description and examples of specific effective teaching behaviors. On 24 of the 51 sub-items the observer rates a teacher's performance on a 2-point scale; the remaining 28 sub-items use a 3-point scale. The options for ratings on the 2-point scale are (a) "NI" (Needs Improvement: the desired behavior was not implemented and should have been, or was implemented with low quality/skill, or was used with only a small portion of the students, or for only a small part of the lesson); or (b) "Yes: √" (the desired behavior was implemented with at least fair/moderate quality or fair/moderate skill for most of the lesson with most of the students). On the 27 sub-items with a 3-point scale, the observer can also rate the teacher's performance as "Yes: +" (the desired behavior was implemented with good or excellent quality or high skill for all or almost all of the lesson with all or almost all of the students). Each item can also be coded as "NtOb: not observed in this lesson" (the described behavior was not observed, or was not applicable, or the observer could not judge the quality. This is a neutral, rather than a negative rating).

Procedure

Because coaches often have very limited time to work with their colleagues, the SCIE was designed to (a) assess a teacher's performance within only a single observed lesson of at least 20 minutes duration; and (b) be usable and effective with minimal training. To use the SCIE, a "coach/observer" first observes a colleague teaching a complete lesson (at *least* 20 minutes long), making detailed anecdotal notes about the teacher's behaviors (e.g., pacing, responsiveness to students' performance, use of corrections, positive or negative comments, etc.) and student reactions (e.g., attentiveness, correct or incorrect responses, opportunities to respond, general understanding of directions, etc.). Following the lesson, the coach codes the lesson on the SCIE protocol, using the descriptors for each of the 51 sub-items to guide the ratings. The coach refers back to the anecdotal notes as needed to help maintain consistent coding. Note: if agreeable to the observed teacher, the lesson may also be video- or audio-taped. The coach can then review the tape while completing the SCIE protocol to confirm his/her recollections and provide more specific feedback. The teacher can also watch/listen to the tape before meeting with the coach to debrief.

Items are to be scored based *only* on what has been observed and addressing *only* what the behavior described in the item. For example, Item A1b: T. PREPARES & ORGANIZES materials for lesson parts. If the teacher has pulled together some poor quality, irrelevant materials but has prepared and organized them so that they are readily available during the lesson, then the score for A1B should be at least a √, or perhaps even a +. The quality and appropriateness of the materials would be rated in A2: Quality/Match of Curriculum Materials/Media.

DEBRIEFING.

After coding is completed, and as soon after the completion of the lesson as possible, the coach/observer debriefs the lesson and the ratings with the observed teacher. The purpose of this debriefing is for *critiquing, not criticizing*. The observer *must* base comments on observed teacher performance, providing feedback as specifically as possible. Referring back to the anecdotal notes can help maintain a specific focus. If the lesson was audio- or video-taped, the coach and teacher may want to review the tape together during the debriefing. Based on the ratings of the SCIE items, the comments and feedback from the coach, and the teacher's own personal reflection, the teacher then identifies a goal or goals for improving lesson planning and organization, instruction or classroom management. The coach and teacher can then engage in brainstorming possible resources for helping the teacher reach these improvement goals, which may include attending training workshops, reading relevant materials, having the coach or another person visit the teacher's classroom to model instructional techniques or for further observation, visiting other teachers' classrooms to observe, etc.

Following the debriefing process, the coach is encouraged to complete the *Debriefing Checklist* at the end of the SCIE protocol to reflect on his/her performance as a coach. The observed teacher may also be asked to independently complete a *Debriefing Checklist* to provide additional feedback to the coach.

TEACHER TRAINING.

One possible use of the SCIE is to enhance the training of novice teachers (either preservice or inservice). A novice teacher who observes a colleague's teaching and completes the SCIE process becomes familiar with research-based "best practice" in instructional delivery and has an early opportunity to engage in collegial collaboration through the coaching process.

The SCIE procedure varies slightly for use in teacher training. In this case, the novice teacher/coach *simultaneously* observes a colleague teaching (either an experienced or novice teacher) alongside an experienced teacher/coach. Both observers *independently* take anecdotal notes and *independently* complete separate SCIE protocols. Before meeting to debrief with the observed teacher, the two observers meet to complete a third SCIE protocol. This protocol is completed item-by-item with the two observers discussing their independent ratings and their rationales for these scores. (If a video- or audio-tape was made, both observers may want to watch the tape together to enhance the accuracy and specificity of their ratings and coaching feedback.) Consensus is reached on each item and this consensus rating is recorded on a third SCIE protocol (the *Consensus Form*). Following completion of the *Consensus Form*, the two observers meet with the observed teacher to debrief and brainstorm suggestions for improvement as outlined above as the standard SCIE procedure.

Definitions of Items and Scoring Guidelines

A. Planning & Organization

A1. LESSON PLANNING/PREPARATION

a. T. selects APPROPRIATE objective(s)/purpose for lesson (amount and quality). (MATCHES students' instructional needs, ages, background, developmental and skill levels; IMPORTANT/VALUABLE skill/ knowledge for future learning or "real life"; REASONABLE number of objectives for students, topic, and time available).

Students should have the background skill or knowledge needed for learning the new content of this lesson, and the lesson content should have high utility for school success (academic, behavior or social) and/or important real life application. If students have difficulty with a foundation skill (i.e., reading, spelling, writing, math computation) necessary for mastering or accomplishing the objective or lacks key vocabulary or conceptual understanding, then the objective/purpose is NOT appropriate and the item should be rated "NI."

b. T. PREPARES AND ORGANIZES materials for all lesson parts.

Materials needed for the lesson are obtained or prepared in advance and readily available without breaking logical flow of lesson or causing delays.

c. T. LOGICALLY ORGANIZES lesson presentation (sequence/order of lesson parts are logically linked and enhance understanding).

The parts of the lesson follow each other in a logical, easily understood pattern. Lesson does not skip around, start with one idea, move to another, and then return to the first idea. Order of presentation helps students understand. There is an overall cohesiveness to the lesson.

A2. QUALITY/MATCH OF CURRICULUM MATERIALS/MEDIA

a. T. uses GOOD QUALITY materials/media.

Instructional materials/media used in the lesson should be easily read, heard, and used. Torn, broken, faded, or damaged materials are not considered good quality.

b. T. uses materials necessary or beneficial to learning; materials ENHANCE learning.

If the lesson objectives/content would be enhanced by use of materials/media, they should be used by the teacher. (*Example*: a science lesson on the songs whales use for communication would be enhanced by having students listen to recordings of whale songs. A math lesson on making change should likely include opportunities for students to see and use money (real or "pretend").

B. Instruction

B1. STARTING LESSON

a. T. starts lesson PROMPTLY and PURPOSEFULLY (focused on objectives/purpose).

Lesson starts in a business-like manner, setting tone of seriousness of purpose (importance of lesson; importance of learning). Teacher begins immediately and starts with lesson content without discussing or referring to unrelated matters (e.g., previous or future lessons, administrative tasks, behavior issues) unless DIRECTLY related to lesson, such as a review or a logical "link." Any distractions handled quickly.

b. T. skillfully gains students' attention before beginning. (+ = ALL or ALMOST ALL students attending before starting; √ = MOST students' attention gained)

Teacher ensures students are ready to begin lesson (physically positioned, mentally focused). Teacher gains this attention quickly by an attention signal and does not begin until all or almost all students are ready. Teacher QUICKLY and SMOOTHLY provides assistance to those students needing help to become ready (proximity, removing distracters, quick verbal or nonverbal reminders, etc.). If students are attending but the teacher did not overtly work to gain their attention, score + if ALL or ALMOST ALL students are attending before the teacher starts the lesson; score √ if MOST of the students are attending. However, even if all or most students are attending, if the teacher gained the students' attention in an UNSKILLFUL way (yelling, flashing the lights repeatedly, etc.), the item should be scored as NI.

c. T. helps students understand PURPOSE of lesson.

Teacher communicates to students WHY this lesson is being taught in a way that is appropriate to age, skill levels, etc. Short, clear descriptions of objectives or purpose: How will this lesson help them? What is their advantage in learning this particular content? If purpose is general knowledge, teacher can set a MOTIVATIONAL purpose appropriate to age/skills of students.

d. T. LINKS prior knowledge, previously learned skills to current lesson (at least some mention made of how this lesson relates to previous learning, if appropriate).

When lesson is part of a related set of lessons, teacher helps students understand the relationship of this lesson to others by linking the information or skill to previous lessons (verbally/visually). If the lesson is the first in a new unit or topic and there is no logical need to link it to previous learning, the item should be scored as NtOb. The amount of time spent in linking can vary from a brief mention to a continued comparison throughout the lesson.

B2. COMMUNICATION

a. T. uses ACCURATE and APPROPRIATE language in speaking and writing (syntax/grammar, vocabulary, handwriting, and spelling).

Some use of regional dialects or phrases (e.g., "y'all" or "you guys") in more informal parts of lessons are acceptable but overuse (more than 3 times) or use within a more formal, serious part of a lesson should be rated as NI.

b. T. uses voice at an APPROPRIATE VOLUME/TONE for communication and instruction.

Teacher's voice is sufficiently loud for all to hear. Tone and volume is matched to needs of lesson. Overly negative, angry, sarcastic voice tone is not appropriate. (**Note**: this is a different rating from using voice tones/volume for group management. See item C2a.)

B3. ACTIVE LEARNING

a. T. provides students with opportunities to ACTIVELY PARTICIPATE in learning tasks (talking, answering/asking questions, reading, writing, etc.; minimal time spent just listening).

b. T. DISTRIBUTES opportunities to participate among students.

If the lesson is being taught to only one student, score NtOb for not observed.

c. T. keeps students FOCUSED and ENGAGED in activity; ON TASK. (+ = ALL or ALMOST ALL students for ALL or ALMOST ALL of lesson with skillful redirecting as necessary.)

If students begin to get off task the teacher should respond quickly and help the students return to their work, using the least intrusive method possible, reflecting the skills and ages of the students. This would include moving toward the student, making eye contact, using a non-verbal signal, a quiet and short verbal reminder, or a combination of these.

B4. LESSON PACING/FOCUS

a. T. uses REASONABLE pace (not rushed or dragging).
(+ = During ALL or ALMOST ALL of lesson; √ = MOST of lesson)

b. T. MAINTAINS FOCUS on objectives/purpose; stays "on track."
(+ = During ALL or ALMOST ALL of lesson; √ = MOST of lesson)

c. T. spends reasonable and appropriate AMOUNT OF TIME on all lesson parts (long enough for students to learn; short enough to keep up momentum given students' ages, skill, and developmental levels).
(+ = ALL or ALMOST ALL lesson parts; √ = MOST lesson parts of reasonable length)

B5. GIVING DIRECTIONS

a. T. skillfully GAINS STUDENTS' ATTENTION before giving directions.
(+ = ALL or ALMOST ALL students attending; √ = most students attending)

Teacher ensures students are ready to attend to directions (physically positioned, mentally focused). Teacher gains this attention quickly by an attention signal and does not begin giving directions until all or almost all students are ready. Teacher QUICKLY and SMOOTHLY provides assistance to those students needing help to become ready (proximity, removing distracters, quick verbal or nonverbal reminders, etc.). If students listen to directions but the teacher did not overtly work to gain their attention, score + if ALL or ALMOST ALL students are attending before the teacher starts giving directions; score √ if MOST of the students attend. However, even if all or most students are attending, if the teacher gained the students' attention in an UNSKILLFUL way (yelling, flashing the lights repeatedly, etc.), the item should be scored as NI.

b. T. skillfully MAINTAINS STUDENTS' ATTENTION while giving directions.
(+ = ALL or ALMOST ALL students' attention maintained; √ = most students' attention maintained)

Teacher prompts/reminds students to listen and attend to directions verbally or non-verbally (with pauses, waiting for attention, attention signals, etc.).

c. T. gives directions CLEARLY (appropriate difficulty/length to ages and skill levels) and COMPLETELY (essential parts of the directions given BEFORE task started).

To be given a + a teacher does not excuse students to begin their task until ALL directions have been given and are clear and understood by students. If the teacher needs to add to the directions after the students have begun the task, she should have them stop and listen to the new directions before restarting. This would be scored as √ or NI depending on the frequency and skill level.

d. T. CHECKS FOR UNDERSTANDING before beginning task.

Checking may include unison, choral responses to questions ("Everyone, what are you supposed to do FIRST?"), signals from students (e.g., thumbs up if directions understood); having student partners checking understanding, teacher checking with individual students, etc.

B6. PRESENTING NEW INFORMATION/SKILL/STRATEGY; REVIEW, PRACTICE

a. T. skillfully PRESENTS a sufficient amount of relevant and helpful EXAMPLES or EXPLANATIONS of new information such as concepts, rules, facts, principles, operations (appropriate to lesson objectives and students' ages, developmental and skill levels).

b. T. MODELS or DEMONSTRATES as necessary new or unmastered skill/strategy (well-timed, well-paced, of reasonable duration to ensure learning).

Teacher SHOWS students how to do a new or unmastered skill (how to use a new piece of equipment, how to say a word, how a study strategy can be used). Makes sure students understand how to do the new task before they begin practicing. A demonstration can be a single presentation ("This is how to say this new vocabulary word") or a longer and repeated demonstration ("Watch carefully how I pour the liquid into the beaker. Watch again.").

c. T. provides GUIDED practice as necessary to help students learn skill/strategy (well-timed, well-paced, of reasonable duration to ensure learning).

Students practice a new skill or strategy while teacher guides, models, and corrects, stopping the group of students as necessary to clarify or explain. Guided practice is more "teacher controlled" than monitored independent practice (see B6d below).

d. T. MONITORS and PROVIDES FEEDBACK during independent practice.

Students independently practice a new skill or strategy while teacher only infrequently clarifies or explains, usually to individual students. Independent practice is less "teacher controlled" than guided practice (B6c above).

e. T. presents ACCURATE information (e.g., word definitions, statements of facts, explanations of concepts, etc.).

If a teacher presents information that confuses the students or presents inaccurate information related to a central or key part of the lesson, score NI. If the teacher makes other, more minor errors, one error is scored as √, more than 2 is scored as NI.

f. T. uses a VARIETY of presentation and response modes and activities (appropriate to lesson objectives and students' ages, developmental and skill levels).

B7. MONITORING LEARNING/RESPONSIVE LESSON ADJUSTMENT

a. T. PROMPTLY CORRECTS or CLARIFIES errors with patience and encouragement.

b. T. PROMPTLY and APPROPRIATELY ACKNOWLEDGES correct responses.

c. T. encourages students to MONITOR accuracy and quality of their own work.

Teacher may provide answer keys in some cases or simply remind students to check their own work (or the work of a classmate) and attends to/reinforces serious self-monitoring efforts.

d. T. ADJUSTS lesson based on student responses (provides extra practice or examples; slows or speeds pace; modifies task/lesson).

B8. QUESTIONING TECHNIQUES

a. T. uses questions that FOCUS on KEY ELEMENTS in lesson (appropriate to content [fact/recall or open-ended/interpretive] and to students).

A teacher does not need to always use questions in the lesson, but when questioning techniques are used as part of instruction, questions should be appropriate and focused on key aspects of the lesson.

b. T. allows appropriate WAIT TIME after asking a question (varying for type of question, student ability/skill level).

c. T. "STAYS WITH" or RETURNS TO student when initial response incorrect (prompting/probing for correct response; providing correct fact then returning later to repeat question).

B9. LESSON CLOSURE

a. T. uses appropriate closure activities (may include SUMMARIZING/SYNTHESIZING key points; commenting on students' ACCOMPLISHMENTS; PREVIEWING upcoming learning; etc.).

b. T. spends reasonable AMOUNT of TIME in closure.

c. T. INVOLVES STUDENTS in closure activities when appropriate (given ages, skill levels, lesson subject, and time available).

C. Classroom Management

C1. RULES: UNDERSTOOD; CONSISTENTLY & FAIRLY APPLIED

   a. T. USES rules in teaching; reminds students of rules as necessary.

   b. T. ENFORCES rules APPROPRIATELY, consistently & fairly.

C2. MANAGEMENT ROUTINES/PROCEDURES

   a. T. uses PROACTIVE, PREVENTATIVE TECHNIQUES to minimize lesson interference (voice tones/ volume; continual scanning of students; purposeful movement among students; effective use of proximity control; non-verbal signaling; changes in pacing; removing distractions).

   b. T. has effective ROUTINES/PROCEDURES to MINIMIZE DISRUPTIONS TO LEARNING in place and uses them (handling student questions during work time; administrative tasks; tasks for those finishing work early; distributing/collecting papers/materials, etc.).

   c. T. ensures SHORT, SMOOTH TRANSITIONS between tasks and lessons minimizing, confusion, off task behavior, and lost instructional time (students know what to do; function independently).

   d. T. PHYSICALLY ARRANGES CLASSROOM to minimize distractions and focus on learning.

      Students face T. and can see presented materials easily; seating allows T. to move about and monitor effectively; low-acheiving students/those with special needs given preferential seating, etc.).

C3. POSITIVE REINFORCEMENT/MOTIVATION

   a. T. is POSITIVE, ENCOURAGING (tries to "catch students in the act of being good").

   b. T. uses SPECIFIC, DESCRIPTIVE age/developmentally appropriate praise; CONTINGENT on good/correct behavior.

   c. T. demonstrates VALUE OF and/or SINCERE INTEREST in lesson content.

   d. T. uses mostly SOCIAL REINFORCERS (smiles, pats/handshakes, encouraging remarks, non-verbal signals, etc.) appropriate to age/developmental levels of students; token/tangible reinforcements (stickers, candy, etc.) used appropriately and only as necessary.

C4. OFF-TASK, NEGATIVE BEHAVIORS ADDRESSED

   a. T. REDIRECTS OFF-TASK behavior to on-task focus.

   b. T. effectively and appropriately IGNORES minor behaviors (paired with praise/appropriate attention).

   c. T. PROMPTLY STOPS DISRUPTIVE BEHAVIOR with minimum interruption of lesson.

   d. T. administers consequences FAIRLY, CONSISTENTLY, and NON-EMOTIONALLY.

Scale for Coaching Instructional Effectiveness (SCIE)

Date: ____/____/____   Start Time: _____   Stop Time: _____   Code: _____

Teacher: _____   Observer/Rater: _____

Grade/Class: _____   Number of students in instructional group: _____

Lesson Content: _____

KEY

- **YES+** = Good/excellent quality; high skill; occurs ALL or ALMOST ALL of lesson; with ALL/ALMOST ALL students.
- **YES √** = At least fair/moderate quality; fair/moderate skill; MOST of lesson; with MOST of students.
- **NI** = Needs Improvement: Not implemented and should have been; low quality/skill; SMALL part of lesson; only FEW students.
- **NtOb** = Not observed; not applicable; cannot judge. Not implemented but not necessary. A NEUTRAL rating.

A. Planning and Organization

A1. LESSON PLANNING/PREPARATION

	Yes	NI	NtOb
a. T. selects APPROPRIATE objective(s)/purpose for lesson (amount and quality). (MATCHES students' instructional needs, ages, background, developmental and skill levels; IMPORTANT/VALUABLE skill/knowledge for future learning or "real life"; REASONABLE number of objectives for students, topic, and time available).	√	√ −	
b. T. PREPARES AND ORGANIZES materials for all lesson parts.	+ √	√ −	
c. T. LOGICALLY ORGANIZES lesson presentation (sequence/order of lesson parts are logically linked and enhance understanding).	√	√ −	

A2. QUALITY/MATCH OF CURRICULUM MATERIALS/MEDIA

	Yes	NI	NtOb
a. T. uses GOOD QUALITY materials/media.	√	√ −	
b. T. USES materials necessary or beneficial to learning; materials ENHANCE learning.	+ √	√ −	

B. Instruction

B1. STARTING LESSON

	Yes	NI	NtOb
a. T. starts lesson PROMPTLY and PURPOSEFULLY (focused on objectives/purpose).	+ √	√ −	
b. T. skillfully GAINS STUDENTS' ATTENTION before beginning. (+ = ALL or ALMOST ALL students attending before starting; √ = MOST students' attention gained)	+ √	√ −	
c. T. helps students UNDERSTAND PURPOSE of lesson.	√	√ −	
d. T. LINKS prior knowledge, previously learned skills to current lesson (at least some mention made of how this lesson relates to previous learning, if appropriate).	√	√ −	

B2. COMMUNICATION

	Yes	NI	NtOb
a. T. uses ACCURATE and APPROPRIATE language in speaking and writing (syntax/grammar, vocabulary, handwriting, and spelling).	√	√ −	
b. T. uses voice at an APPROPRIATE VOLUME/TONE for communication and instruction.	√	√ −	

Scale for Coaching Instructional Effectiveness (SCIE) — continued

B3. ACTIVE LEARNING

	Yes		NI		NtOb
a. T. provides students with opportunities to ACTIVELY PARTICIPATE in learning tasks (talking, answering/asking questions, reading, writing, etc.; minimal time spent just listening).	+	√	√	−	
b. T. DISTRIBUTES opportunities to participate among students.	+	√	√	−	
c. T. keeps students FOCUSED and ENGAGED in activity; ON TASK. (+ = ALL or ALMOST ALL students for ALL or ALMOST ALL of lesson with skillful redirecting as necessary)		√	√	−	

B4. LESSON PACING/FOCUS

	Yes		NI		NtOb
a. T. uses REASONABLE pace (not rushed or dragging). (+ = During ALL or ALMOST ALL of lesson; √ = MOST of lesson)	+	√	√	−	
b. T. MAINTAINS FOCUS on objectives/purpose; stays "on track." (+ = During ALL or ALMOST ALL of lesson; √ = MOST of lesson)	+	√	√	−	
c. T. spends reasonable and appropriate AMOUNT OF TIME on all lesson parts (long enough for students to learn; short enough to keep up momentum given students' ages, skill and developmental levels). (+ = ALL or ALMOST ALL lesson parts; √ = MOST lesson parts of reasonable length)		√	√	−	

B5. GIVING DIRECTIONS

	Yes		NI		NtOb
a. T. skillfully GAINS STUDENTS' ATTENTION before giving directions. (+ = ALL or ALMOST ALL students attending; √ = MOST students attending)	+	√	√	−	
b. T. skillfully MAINTAINS STUDENTS' ATTENTION while giving directions. (+ = ALL or ALMOST ALL students' attention maintained; √ = MOST students' attention maintained).	+	√	√	−	
c. T. gives directions CLEARLY (appropriate difficulty/length to ages and skill levels) and COMPLETELY (essential parts of the directions given BEFORE task started).	+	√	√	−	
d. T. CHECKS FOR UNDERSTANDING before beginning task.		√	√	−	

B6. PRESENTING NEW INFORMATION/SKILL/STRATEGY; REVIEW, PRACTICE

	Yes		NI		NtOb
a. T. skillfully PRESENTS a sufficient amount of relevant and helpful EXAMPLES or EXPLANATIONS of new information such as concepts, rules, facts, principles, operations (appropriate to lesson objectives and student's ages, developmental and skill levels).	+	√	√	−	
b. T. MODELS or DEMONSTRATES as necessary new or unmastered skill/strategy (well-timed, well-paced, of reasonable duration to ensure learning).	+	√	√	−	
c. T. provides GUIDED PRACTICE as necessary to help students learn skill/strategy (well-timed, well-paced, of reasonable duration to ensure learning).		√	√	−	
d. T. MONITORS and PROVIDES FEEDBACK during independent practice.		√	√	−	
e. T. presents ACCURATE information (e.g., word definitions, statements of facts, explanations of concepts, etc.).		√	√	−	
f. T. uses a VARIETY of presentation and response modes and activities (appropriate to lesson objectives and students' ages, developmental and skill levels).	+	√	√	−	

B7. MONITORING LEARNING/RESPONSIVE LESSON ADJUSTMENT

	Yes		NI		NtOb
a. T. PROMPTLY CORRECTS or CLARIFIES errors with patience and encouragement.	+	√	√	−	
b. T. PROMPTLY and APPROPRIATELY ACKNOWLEDGES correct responses.	+	√	√	−	
c. T. encourages students to MONITOR accuracy and quality of their own work.		√	√	−	
d. T. ADJUSTS lesson based on student responses (provides extra practice or examples; slows or speeds pace; modifies task/lesson)		√	√	−	

B8. QUESTIONING TECHNIQUES

	Yes		NI	NtOb
a. T. uses questions that FOCUS on KEY ELEMENTS in lesson (appropriate to content [fact/recall or open-ended/interpretive] and to students).	**+** √	√ −		
b. T. allows appropriate WAIT TIME after asking a question (varying for type of question, student ability/skill level).	√	√ −		
c. T. "STAYS WITH" or RETURNS TO student when initial response incorrect (prompting/probing for correct response; providing correct fact then returning later to repeat question).	√	√ −		

B9. LESSON CLOSURE

	Yes	NI	NtOb
a. T. uses APPROPRIATE CLOSURE activities (may include SUMMARIZING/SYNTHESIZING key points; commenting on students' ACCOMPLISHMENTS; PREVIEWING upcoming learning; etc.).	√	√ −	
b. T. spends REASONABLE AMOUNT of TIME in closure.	√	√ −	
c. T. INVOLVES STUDENTS in closure activities when appropriate (given ages, skill levels, lesson subject, and time available).	√	√ −	

C. Classroom Management

C1. RULES: UNDERSTOOD; CONSISTENTLY AND FAIRLY APPLIED

	Yes		NI	NtOb
a. T. USES rules in teaching; REMINDS students of rules as necessary.	√	√ −		
b. T. ENFORCES rules APPROPRIATELY, CONSISTENTLY, and FAIRLY.	**+** √	√ −		

C2. MANAGEMENT ROUTINES/PROCEDURES

	Yes		NI	NtOb
a. T. uses PROACTIVE, PREVENTATIVE TECHNIQUES to minimize lesson interference (voice tones/volume; continual scanning of students; purposeful movement among students; effective use of proximity control; non-verbal signaling; changes in pacing; removing distractions).	**+** √	√ −		
b. T. has effective ROUTINES/PROCEDURES to MINIMIZE DISRUPTIONS TO LEARNING in place and USES them (handling student questions during work time; administrative tasks; tasks for those finishing work early; distributing/collecting papers/materials, etc.).	**+** √	√ −		
c. T. ensures SHORT, SMOOTH TRANSITIONS between tasks and lessons minimizing, confusion, off-task behaviors, and lost instructional time (students know what to do; function independently).	**+** √	√ −		
d. T. PHYSICALLY ARRANGES CLASSROOM to minimize distractions and focus on learning.	√	√ −		

C3. POSITIVE REINFORCEMENT/MOTIVATION

	Yes		NI	NtOb
a. T. is POSITIVE, ENCOURAGING (tries to "catch students in the act of being good").	**+** √	√ −		
b. T. uses SPECIFIC, DESCRIPTIVE age/developmentally appropriate praise; CONTINGENT on good/correct behavior.	**+** √	√ −		
c. T. demonstrates VALUE OF and/or SINCERE INTEREST in lesson content.	**+** √	√ −		
d. T. uses mostly SOCIAL REINFORCERS (smiles, pats/handshakes, encouraging remarks, non-verbal signals, etc.) appropriate to age/developmental levels of students; token/tangible reinforcements (stickers, candy, etc.) used appropriately and only as necessary.	√	√ −		

C4. OFF-TASK, NEGATIVE BEHAVIORS ADDRESSED

		Yes		NI		NtOb
a.	T. REDIRECTS OFF-TASK behavior to on-task focus.	+	√	√	–	
b.	T. effectively and appropriately IGNORES minor behaviors (paired with praise/appropriate attention).	+	√	√	–	
c.	T. PROMPTLY STOPS DISRUPTIVE BEHAVIOR with minimum interruption of lesson.		√	√	–	
d.	T. administers consequences FAIRLY, CONSISTENTLY, and NON-EMOTIONALLY.	+	√	√	–	

Scale for Coaching Instructional Effectiveness (SCIE)
Summary Form

Date: ____/____/____   Start Time: _____   Stop Time: _____

Teacher: _____   Observer/Rater: _____

Grade/Class: _____   Number of students in instructional group:_____

Lesson Content:

SCORING:

+ = 2   √ = 1   NI = 0   NTOB = NO SCORE

A. PLANNING & ORGANIZATION	SCORE	GOAL?
A1. Lesson Planning/Preparation *4 possible*		
A2. Quality/Match of Curriculum Materials/Media *3 possible*		
COMMENTS:		

B. INSTRUCTION	SCORE	GOAL?
B1. Starting Lesson *6 possible*		
B2. Communication *2 possible*		
B3. Active Learning *5 possible*		
B4. Lesson Pacing/Focus *5 possible*		
B5. Giving Directions *7 possible*		
B6. Presenting New Information/Skill/Strategy... *9 possible*		
B7. Monitoring Learning/ Responsive Lesson Adjustment *6 possible*		
B8. Questioning Techniques *4 possible*		
B9. Lesson Closure *3 possible*		
COMMENTS:		

C. CLASSROOM MANAGEMENT	SCORE	GOAL?
C1. Rules: Understood; Consistently & Fairly Applied *3 possible*		
C2. Management Routines/Procedures *7 possible*		
C3. Positive Reinforcement/Motivation *7 possible*		
C4. Off-Task, Negative Behaviors Addressed *7 possible*		
COMMENTS:		

Debriefing Checklist

Date/Time of observation: _____   Date/Time of debriefing: _____

GOAL(s) TARGETED FOR IMPROVEMENT (*list SCIE items by number*):

DID YOU AS A COACH ...	Improvement Needed	Adequate	Very Good	Comments
1. accurately CODE the lesson?				
2. USE SCIE DESCRIPTORS to interpret results during debriefing?				
3. help set and maintain a POSITIVE TONE?				
4. ENCOURAGE the observed teacher to EXPRESS ideas/opinions?				
5. EQUALLY SHARE talk time?				
6. use ACTIVE LISTENING procedures?				
7. help LOGICALLY PRIORITIZE a target area for setting improvement goal(s)?				
8. uncritically encourage BRAINSTORMING of IDEAS for improvement?				
9. fairly EVALUATE ideas for improvement and help the observed teacher make a SELECTION?				
10. help with LOGISTICS (scheduling next observation; assigning tasks, completing forms, etc.)?				

Lesson Reflection Form

Class _____ Date _____

What were my goals?	What happened in the lesson?
What should I change?	**What should stay the same?**

What's the plan?

STRATEGIC COACHING PROFESSIONAL DEVELOPMENT PLANNING GUIDE (SCPDP GUIDE)

Introduction

Ground Rules for Planning Professional Development

The Reading Coach: A How-to Manual for Success lists three "commandments" for planning professional development: Focus on student outcomes and plan accordingly; promote instructional practices that are based on the best available research; and plan all aspects of professional development in a purposeful, unified way. This *SCPDP Guide* is designed to assist the reading coach in addressing these three critical aspects of effective professional development. In particular, it is designed to provide a framework to help coaches plan purposeful, focused, integrated professional development for teachers with the goal of improving instruction to support student success in reading.

Step 1: Assess the Needs in the School

Just as effective reading instruction is guided by assessments of students' strengths and needs, effective professional development is based on an assessment of needs in a school. The most important evidence of needs in a school reading program is found in the outcomes of student assessments. Above all, the goal of the reading coach is to increase student achievement in reading, and the results of assessments are the ultimate barometer of success. The *SCPDP Guide* includes a form the coach can use to summarize the needs reflected in student assessments. It is also important that the reading coach directly address the needs of the teachers. The guide includes two forms for this purpose: a needs assessment that teachers can complete to communicate what they would like the coach to address, and a form to summarize the needs the coach has observed in teachers' classrooms.

Survey of Teacher Priorities

The *Survey of Teacher Priorities* is a needs assessment form included in the *SCPDP Guide*. It lists important aspects of effective research-based reading instruction. Each teacher completes the survey, indicating whether the topics are a high, medium, or low priority to help the teacher and students meet their goals. The teachers may also write in other topics they would like to see addressed in the row marked "Other." See Figure A.1 for a completed sample.

Summary of Teacher Needs Assessment

The *Summary of Teacher Needs Assessment* (Figure A.2) is a form the coach can use to compile the results of the *Survey of Teacher Priorities* for each grade level (or subject area) in the school. To complete this summary:

1. Fill in the grade level or subject area and the current date.

2. Enter the names of all teachers for that grade level on one form.

3. The topics from the *Survey of Teacher Priorities* are listed across the top of the form. Enter each teacher's ratings (1, 2, or 3) for each of the topics. There is also a space for "Other" topics the teachers may have written on their surveys. Note that "Teaching Phonemic Awareness" would be primarily appropriate for kindergarten and 1st grade teachers.

4. Add the scores for each topic and enter the totals in the row marked *Total Score*.

5. Divide these total scores by the number of teachers who responded to arrive at the *Average Score* for each topic for this group of teachers. The topics with the highest average scores are the highest priorities for professional development from the point of view of the teachers.

Figure A.1 *Survey of Teacher Priorities*

Name <u>Sally Jones</u>   Grade <u>3</u>   Date <u>9/13/05</u>

Survey of Teacher Priorities

Please help me plan the focus of coaching in our school by completing this form. As we determine the priorities for this school year, I will try to address them in several ways, including brief study group sessions, meetings with individual teachers or grade-level groups, and other activities.

Please circle the appropriate number to rate each of the following topics as *High Priority*, *Medium Priority*, or *Low Priority* to help you and your students meet your goals this year. Thank you!

Area of Reading	High Priority	Medium Priority	Low Priority
Teaching Phonemic Awareness	3	2	1
Effective Phonics Instruction	3	2	①
Teaching Spelling and Word Study	③	2	1
Teaching for Fluent Reading	3	②	1
Teaching Vocabulary	3	②	1
Teaching Comprehension Strategies	③	2	1
Effective Instruction for Struggling Readers	3	②	1
Selecting Appropriate Text for Reading Instruction	3	2	①
Organizing and Managing Small-Group Reading Instruction	③	2	1
Using the Results of Assessments to Plan Effective Instruction	3	②	1
Monitoring Student Progress in Reading	3	2	①
Getting the Most Out of the Core Reading Program	3	2	①
Other:	3	2	1

Figure A.2 *Summary of Teacher Needs Assessment*

Summary of Teacher Needs Assessment

Grade ___3___ Date ___9/13/05___

Enter the names of all teachers for one grade level. Enter each teacher's rating for each topic.

Teacher	Teaching Phonemic Awareness in Grades K–1	Effective Phonics Instruction	Teaching Spelling and Word Study	Teaching for Fluent Reading	Teaching Vocabulary	Teaching Comprehension Strategies	Effective Instruction for Struggling Readers	Selecting Appropriate Text for Reading Instruction	Organizing and Managing Small-Group Reading Instruction	Using the Results of Assessments to Plan Effective Instruction	Monitoring Student Progress in Reading	Getting the Most Out of the Core Reading Program	Other: Where to find supplemental materials
Sally Jones		1	3	2	2	3	2	1	3	2	1	1	
Rachel Miller		1	2	3	1	2	2	1	2	3	1	1	
Jack Day		2	3	2	1	3	3	2	2	2	2	2	3
Holly Harper		1	2	3	2	3	3	1	3	1	2	2	
TOTAL SCORE for This Grade Level		5	10	10	6	11	10	5	10	8	6	6	
AVERAGE SCORE for This Grade Level (Divide total score by number of teachers)		1.25	2.50	2.50	1.50	2.75	2.50	1.25	2.50	2	1.50	1.50	

Summary of Observations

The *Summary of Observations* (Figure A.3) is a tool that allows the coach to summarize the needs observed during reading instruction in individual teachers' classrooms. For example, results from classroom observations using the *LIFT Observation* tool included in the Appendix might indicate that some teachers do not provide explicit instruction that would be likely to be effective for struggling readers. This would indicate a need for professional development on the topic of "Effective Instruction for Struggling Readers." To complete the *Summary of Observations*:

1. Review the records of your observations during classroom reading instruction.

2. Based on these records, rate each topic according to the needs you have observed at each grade level.

3. Under "Notes," note specific observations you have made or specific aspects of the topic that should be addressed.

Summary of Needs Reflected in Student Assessments

As we stated earlier, the most important indicator of needs for a school's reading program is data from student assessments. The "bottom line" for the reading coach is supporting student reading growth. That's the true purpose of coaching. Use the *Summary of Needs Reflected in Student Assessments* (Figure A.4) to rate the needs reflected by student outcomes. To complete this form:

1. Enter the grade level (or subject area) and date at the top of the form.

2. Enter the names of each teacher in that grade level or area.

3. Review the results of assessments in the areas of phonemic awareness, phonics, spelling and word study, oral reading fluency, vocabulary, and comprehension. You may have assessment data for only some of these aspects of reading.

4. Using the guidelines at the top of the form, rate the needs students displayed in each aspect of reading.

5. Enter the total for each topic at the bottom of the form.

6. Divide these totals by the number of teachers to arrive at the average rating for each area. The highest average ratings indicate the greatest needs.

Step 2: Prioritizing the Needs

At this point, you have indicators of the teachers' priorities for topics that should be addressed in professional development, the needs you have observed in teachers' classrooms, and the needs reflected by the results of student assessments. This is a lot of information! The *Prioritizing Needs* form (Figure A.5) is designed to help you put it all together to determine the needs that should be addressed. This form is designed to be completed for teachers at one grade level or subject area. To complete this form:

1. For each domain of reading, enter the average scores from the *Summary of Teacher Needs Assessment*, the *Summary of Observations*, and the *Summary of Needs Reflected in Student Assessment*.

2. Compare the total scores for each topic to determine priorities for coaching efforts at this grade level.

3. If areas have similar total scores, *the needs reflected in student assessments should be given higher priority*.

You may also address different priorities with individual teachers according to their needs. Note that student assessment needs were rated only for Domain 1.

This form should be considered a tool to guide you as you prioritize needs in the school, but its results should not be taken as hard-and-fast rules. Your professional judgment is the most important tool for determining what aspects of reading should be targeted first. For example, simply learning how to monitor students' progress in key reading domains such as oral reading fluency or phonemic decoding may motivate teachers to adopt effective instructional strategies.

Figure A.3   *Summary of Observations*

Summary of Observations

Grade ___3___   Date ___9/14/05___

Using records from observations in classrooms, rate each topic according to the needs at each grade level. Note any specific areas that should be addressed.

Topic	High Need	Medium Need	Low Need	Notes
Teaching Phonemic Awareness (Grades K–1)	3	2	1	
Effective Phonics Instruction	3	2	(1)	
Teaching Spelling and Word Study	3	(2)	1	
Teaching for Fluent Reading	(3)	2	1	No fluency instruction observed
Teaching Vocabulary	3	(2)	1	
Teaching Comprehension Strategies	(3)	2	1	J, M, and H not teaching strategies
Effective Instruction for Struggling Readers (explicit instruction, active involvement, opportunities for practice, scaffolding, etc.)	(3)	2	1	
Selecting Appropriate Text for Reading Instruction	3	(2)	1	Struggling readers in hard text
Organizing and Managing Small-Group Reading Instruction	(3)	2	1	
Using the Results of Assessments to Plan Effective Instruction	(3)	2	1	
Monitoring Student Progress in Reading	(3)	2	1	Teachers are not regularly monitoring progress
Getting the Most Out of the Core Reading Program	3	(2)	1	

Figure A.4   *Summary of Needs Reflected in Student Assessments*

Summary of Needs Reflected in Student Assessment

Grade ___3___   Date ___9/14/05___

Use the results of assessments of students in each classroom to target areas of need. Rate the needs using this scale:

Score 3: Most students in the class display this need.
Score 2: Many students in the class display this need.
Score 1: Some students in the class display this need.
Score 0: No students in the class display this need, or the area was not assessed.

Teacher	Phonemic Awareness (Grades K–1)	Phonics/Decoding	Spelling and Word Study	Reading Fluency	Vocabulary	Comprehension	Other:
Sally Jones		1	2	3	0	2	
Rachel Miller		2	3	3	0	2	
Jack Day		1	2	2	0	3	
Holly Harper		1	2	3	0	3	
TOTAL SCORE for this grade level		5	9	11	0	10	
AVERAGE SCORE for this grade level (Divide total score by number of teachers)		1.25	2.25	2.75	0	2.50	

Figure A.5 *Prioritizing Needs*

Prioritizing Needs

Grade ___3___ Date ___9/14/05___

1. **Teacher Need Assessment:** Enter the *average score* at this grade level for each topic from the *Summary of Teacher Needs* form.

2. **Observations:** Enter your rating for this grade level from the *Summary of Observations* form.

3. **Student Assessments:** Enter the *average score* at this grade level for each topic from the *Summary of Student Assessments* form.

4. *Within each domain below:* Compare the total scores for each topic to determine priorities for coaching efforts at this grade level. If areas have similar total scores, *the needs reflected in student assessments should be given higher priority.* (You may also address different priorities with individual teachers according to their needs.) *Note that student assessment needs were rated only for Domain 1.*

TOPIC	Teacher Needs Assessments	Observations	Student Assessments	TOTAL	Priority
Domain 1: Student Knowledge and Skills					
Teaching Phonemic Awareness (Grades K–1)					
Effective Phonics Instruction	1.25	1	1.25	3.5	4
Teaching Spelling and Word Study	2.5	2	2.25	6.75	3
Teaching for Fluent Reading	2.5	3	2.75	8.25	1
Teaching Vocabulary	1.5	2	0	3.5	5
Teaching Comprehension Strategies	2.75	3	2.5	8.25	2
Domain 2: Instructional Strategies					
Effective Instruction for Struggling Readers	2.5	3		5.5	1
Selecting Appropriate Text for Reading Instruction	1.25	2		3.25	5
Organizing and Managing Small-Group Reading Instruction	2.5	3		5.5	2
Using the Results of Assessments to Plan Effective Instruction	2	3		5	3
Monitoring Student Progress in Reading	1.5	3		4.5	4
Getting the Most Out of the Core Reading Program	1.5	2		3.5	6

Step 3: Write Objectives

We believe that coaches should write objectives based on assessments of needs in their schools, just as we ask teachers to write objectives for their lessons. Focusing on particular objectives has two benefits. First, it helps the coach plan a unified program of professional development that targets specific needs, and, second, it keeps the coach from trying to teach too much at one time. If you simply go into each teacher's room and model effective instruction without asking teachers to focus on particular aspects of the lessons, teachers are likely to be overwhelmed. They would be likely to get a general sense of what you were trying to demonstrate but might not be able to integrate each component of effective instruction into their own lessons. Changing teaching practices is not easy, and people are unlikely to change many things at once. Teachers are more likely to be successful if you focus on one or two important aspects of effective instruction at one time. Once they are successful, they will be better able to incorporate other new strategies you teach them.

For example, let's say that the *Prioritizing Needs* form indicated that teachers in your school need to learn to use the results of assessment to plan instruction for struggling readers. Your objective might be, "By January, teachers in Grades 1 and 2 will routinely administer and use assessments of decoding and oral reading fluency to flexibly group students and plan instruction targeting student needs, measured by the coach's observations and teacher

lesson plans." You might address the objective through study groups, demonstrating the administration of assessments, and co-planning with teachers. Having specific, measurable objectives can help you plan your activities to move teachers along toward the overall goal of providing instruction that promotes success in all students.

Use the *Coaching Objectives* form (Figure A.6) to write an objective to address two or three priorities at each grade level. For each objective, state *who* (1st grade students; kindergarten teachers) will *do what* (read 50–60 words correct per minute on a cold read with no practice; demonstrate effective strategies for teaching phonics) by *when* (December 1), measured by (*DIBELS* assessments; *LIFT* observations). Here are some examples:

- The kindergarten teachers will demonstrate explicit instruction in phonemic awareness by November 15, measured by *LIFT* observations.

- The 3rd grade students will increase their oral reading fluency at a rate of at least one word correct per minute per week by October, measured by *DIBELS* oral reading fluency assessments administered every three weeks.

- By December 1, the 1st grade teachers will demonstrate explicit instruction in phonics based on the results of assessments of letter-sound knowledge, measured by the coach's observation of grade-level planning meetings and teachers' instruction.

Figure A.6 *Coaching Objectives*

Coaching Objectives

Write an objective to address each of the top two priorities at each grade level. For each objective, state:

- Who (e.g., 1st grade students; kindergarten teachers)
- Will do what (e.g., read 50–60 words correct per minute on a cold read; demonstrate effective strategies for teaching phonics)
- By when (e.g., December 1)
- Measured by what (e.g., *DIBELS* assessments; *LIFT* observations)

Grade Level 3   **Date** 9/15/05

Objective	Who?	Will Do What?	By When?	Measured by What?
Teaching for Fluency	3rd graders	Read orally at a minimum of 100 words correct per minute	January 15	*DIBELS* benchmarks
Effective Instruction for Struggling Readers	3rd grade teachers	Demonstrate explicit reading instruction	January 15	3 *LIFT* observations: Score of 3 or higher on all indicators

Grade Level 3   **Date** 9/15/05

Objective	Who?	Will Do what?	By When?	Measured by What?
Objective 1				
Objective 2				

Step 4: Plan Activities to Address the Objectives

The final step in the strategic coaching planning process is to complete a coaching plan based on the objectives. The *Coaching Plan* form provides space to write the objective you are addressing, along with information for each of the activities that will address the objective. These include the planned date(s), a list of the teachers (or groups of teachers) who will participate, the size of the group, a description of the activity, and a list of materials you will need. You may plan several activities to address each objective. Figure A.7 illustrates the kinds of activities that might address specific objectives. Having a unified plan that systematically focuses on specific aspects of effective reading instruction should help both teachers and students meet their goals.

Figure A.7 *Coaching Plan*

Coaching Plan

Grade __3__ Date __9/14/05__

Objective: _3rd graders will read orally at a minimum of 100 words correct per minute by January 15._

Plan the steps you will take to address the objectives for each grade level.

Date(s)	Time	Participant(s)	Group Size	Activity	Materials
9-21, 9-28, 10-4, 10-12	3:30-4:15	3rd grade team	4	Study groups on fluency instruction and monitoring	Stories, timers, handouts, student assessments (*DIBELS*)
9-28 to 10-12 and as needed	Reading Class	3rd grade team	1	Model fluency instruction for teachers during small-group reading lessons	Stories, timers, graphs
9-29, 10-5, 10-13	1:30-2:15 (Planning period)	3rd grade team	4	Co-plan fluency lessons with 3rd grade teachers	Stories
10-12 to 10-26	Reading class	3rd grade team	1	Cover portion of reading classes to allow teams of teachers to observe each other during fluency instruction	See teachers
11-2	3:30-4:15	3rd grade team	4	Team discussion of fluency instruction, evaluate student assessment data	Student assessments

Figure A.7 Coaching Plan (continued)

Objective: 3rd graders will read orally at a minimum of 100 words correct per minute by January 15.

Plan the steps you will take to address the objectives for each grade level.

Grade ___3___   Date ___9/14/05___

Date(s)	Time	Participant(s)	Group Size	Activity	Materials
10-26, 11-9, 11-16	3:30-4:15	3rd grade team	4	Study groups on explicit instruction, examine assessments for 2 target students in each classroom	Handouts, word study materials, PowerPoint presentation, student assessments
10-27 to 11-16 and as needed	Reading class	3rd grade team	1	Model explicit instruction for teachers during small-group reading lessons	Varies according to lessons
10-27, 11-10, 11-17	1:30-2:15 (Planning period)	3rd grade team	4	Co-plan explicit lessons with 3rd grade teachers	
11-18 to 12-6	Reading class	3rd grade team	1	Cover portion of reading classes to allow teams of teachers to observe each other delivering explicit instruction	See teachers
12-7	3:30-4:15	3rd grade team	4	Team discussion of explicit instruction, evaluate assessment data for the 2 target students from each classroom	Student assessments

APPENDIX

Master Forms for Strategic
Coaching Professional Development Planning

STEP 1: ASSESS THE NEEDS IN THE SCHOOL

- *Survey of Teacher Priorities*
- *Summary of Teacher Needs Assessment*
- *Summary of Observations*
- *Summary of Needs Reflected in Student Assessments*

STEP 2: PRIORITIZE THE NEEDS

- *Prioritizing Needs* form

STEP 3: WRITE OBJECTIVES

- *Coaching Objectives* form

STEP 4: PLAN ACTIVITIES TO ADDRESS THE OBJECTIVES

- *Coaching Plan* form

Name _____ Grade _____ Date _____

Survey of Teacher Priorities

Please help me plan the focus of coaching in our school by completing this form. As we determine the priorities for this school year, I will try to address them in several ways, including brief study group sessions, meetings with individual teachers or grade-level groups, and other activities.

Please circle the appropriate number to rate each of the following topics as *High Priority*, *Medium Priority*, or *Low Priority* to help you and your students meet your goals this year. Thank you!

Area of Reading	High Priority	Medium Priority	Low Priority
Teaching Phonemic Awareness	3	2	1
Effective Phonics Instruction	3	2	1
Teaching Spelling and Word Study	3	2	1
Teaching for Fluent Reading	3	2	1
Teaching Vocabulary	3	2	1
Teaching Comprehension Strategies	3	2	1
Effective Instruction for Struggling Readers	3	2	1
Selecting Appropriate Text for Reading Instruction	3	2	1
Organizing and Managing Small-Group Reading Instruction	3	2	1
Using the Results of Assessments to Plan Effective Instruction	3	2	1
Monitoring Student Progress in Reading	3	2	1
Getting the Most Out of the Core Reading Program	3	2	1
Other:	3	2	1

Summary of Teacher Needs Assessment

Grade _____ Date _____

Enter the names of all teachers for one grade level. Enter each teacher's rating for each topic.

Teacher	Teaching Phonemic Awareness in Grades K–1	Effective Phonics Instruction	Teaching Spelling and Word Study	Teaching for Fluent Reading	Teaching Vocabulary	Teaching Comprehension Strategies	Effective Instruction for Struggling Readers	Selecting Appropriate Text for Reading Instruction	Organizing and Managing Small-Group Reading Instruction	Using the Results of Assessments to Plan Effective Instruction	Monitoring Student Progress in Reading	Getting the Most Out of the Core Reading Program	Other: Where to find supplemental materials
TOTAL SCORE for This Grade Level													
AVERAGE SCORE for This Grade Level (Divide total score by number of teachers)													

Summary of Observations

Grade _____ Date _____

Using records from observations in classrooms, rate each topic according to the needs at each grade level. Note any specific areas that should be addressed.

Topic	High Need	Medium Need	Low Need	Notes
Teaching Phonemic Awareness (Grades K–1)	3	2	1	
Effective Phonics Instruction	3	2	1	
Teaching Spelling and Word Study	3	2	1	
Teaching for Fluent Reading	3	2	1	
Teaching Vocabulary	3	2	1	
Teaching Comprehension Strategies	3	2	1	
Effective Instruction for Struggling Readers (explicit instruction, active involvement, opportunities for practice, scaffolding, etc.)	3	2	1	
Selecting Appropriate Text for Reading Instruction	3	2	1	
Organizing and Managing Small-Group Reading Instruction	3	2	1	
Using the Results of Assessments to Plan Effective Instruction	3	2	1	
Monitoring Student Progress in Reading	3	2	1	
Getting the Most Out of the Core Reading Program	3	2	1	

Summary of Needs Reflected in Student Assessment

Grade _____ Date _____

Use the results of assessments of students in each classroom to target areas of need. Rate the needs using this scale:

Score 3: Most students in the class display this need.
Score 2: Many students in the class display this need.
Score 1: Some students in the class display this need.
Score 0: No students in the class display this need, or the area was not assessed.

Teacher	Phonemic Awareness (Grades K–1)	Phonics/Decoding	Spelling and Word Study	Reading Fluency	Vocabulary	Comprehension	Other:
TOTAL SCORE for this grade level							
AVERAGE SCORE for this grade level (Divide total score by number of teachers)							

Prioritizing Needs

Grade _____ Date _____

1. **Teacher Need Assessment:** Enter the *average score* at this grade level for each topic from the *Summary of Teacher Needs* form.

2. **Observations:** Enter your rating for this grade level from the *Summary of Observations* form.

3. **Student Assessments:** Enter the *average score* at this grade level for each topic from the *Summary of Student Assessments* form.

4. *Within* each domain below: Compare the total scores for each topic to determine priorities for coaching efforts at this grade level. If areas have similar total scores, *the needs reflected in student assessments should be given higher priority.* (You may also address different priorities with individual teachers according to their needs.) *Note that student assessment needs were rated only for Domain 1.*

TOPIC	Teacher Needs Assessments	Observations	Student Assessments	TOTAL	Priority
Domain 1: Student Knowledge and Skills					
Teaching Phonemic Awareness (Grades K–1)					
Effective Phonics Instruction					
Teaching Spelling and Word Study					
Teaching for Fluent Reading					
Teaching Vocabulary					
Teaching Comprehension Strategies					
Domain 2: Instructional Strategies					
Effective Instruction for Struggling Readers					
Selecting Appropriate Text for Reading Instruction					
Organizing and Managing Small-Group Reading Instruction					
Using the Results of Assessments to Plan Effective Instruction					
Monitoring Student Progress in Reading					
Getting the Most Out of the Core Reading Program					

Coaching Objectives

Grade _____ Date _____

Write an objective to address each of the top two priorities at each grade level. For each objective, state:

– Who (e.g., 1st grade students; kindergarten teachers)
– Will do what (e.g., read 50–60 words correct per minute on a cold read; demonstrate effective strategies for teaching phonics)
– By when (e.g., December 1)
– Measured by what (e.g., DIBELS assessments; LIFT observations)

Objective	Who?	Will Do What?	By When?	Measured by What?
Objective 1				
Objective 2				
Objective 3				

Coaching Plan

Grade _____ Date _____

Objective: _____

Plan the steps you will take to address the objectives for each grade level.

Date(s)	Time	Participant(s)	Group Size	Activity	Materials